MADAME BRUSSELS

MADAME BRUSSELS

THE LIFE AND TIMES OF MELBOURNE'S MOST NOTORIOUS WOMAN

BARBARA MINCHINTON

WITH PHILIP BENTLEY

LA TROBE UNIVERSITY PRESS

IN CONJUNCTION WITH BLACK INC.

Published by La Trobe University Press in conjunction with Black Inc.
Wurundjeri Country
22–24 Northumberland Street
Collingwood VIC 3066, Australia
enquiries@blackincbooks.com
www.blackincbooks.com
www.latrobeuniversitypress.com.au

La Trobe University plays an integral role in Australia's public intellectual life, and is recognised globally for its research excellence and commitment to ideas and debate. La Trobe University Press publishes books of high intellectual quality, aimed at general readers. Titles range across the humanities and sciences, and are written by distinguished and innovative scholars. La Trobe University Press books are produced in conjunction with Black Inc., an independent Australian publishing house. The members of the LTUP Editorial Board are Vice-Chancellor's Fellows Emeritus Professor Robert Manne and Dr Elizabeth Finkel, and Morry Schwartz and Chris Feik of Black Inc.

9781760644932 (paperback)
9781743823613 (ebook)

 A catalogue record for this book is available from the National Library of Australia

Cover design by Beau Lowenstern
Text design and typesetting by Tristan Main
Cover photo of Caroline Hodgson reproduced courtesy of State Library Victoria
Author photo by Viv Mellina
Index by Belinda Nemec

CONTENTS

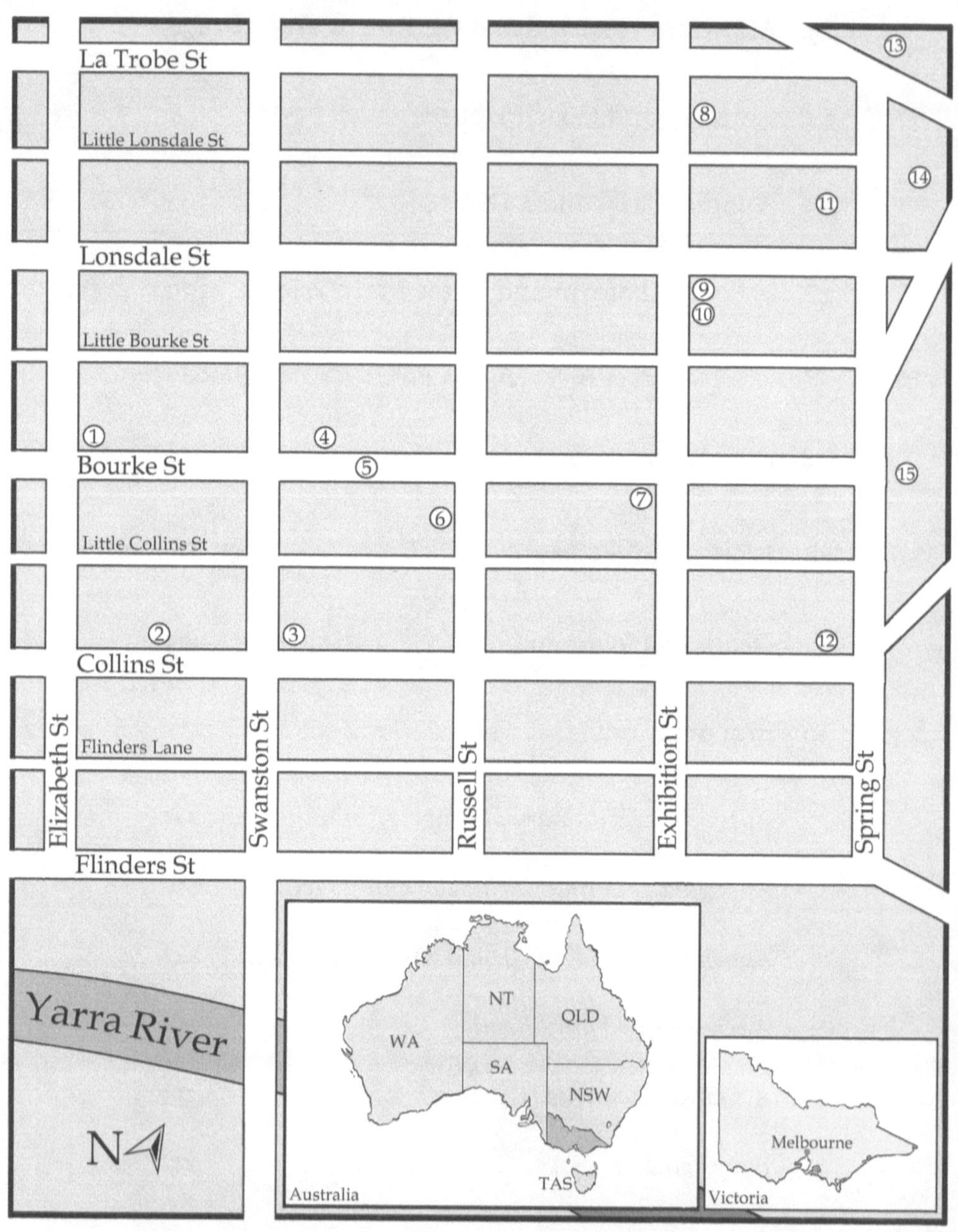

Eastern portion of the Melbourne central business district, showing locations mentioned in the text and sites of general significance

1. **GENERAL POST OFFICE (GPO):** One of the most important services for a far-flung colony.

2. **'THE BLOCK':** The portion of Collins Street from Elizabeth to Swanston streets was known as 'the Block' and was the prime location for fashionable society in the nineteenth and early twentieth century to shop and be seen.

3. **MELBOURNE TOWN HALL:** Principal site for concerts and other large public events in the nineteenth century.

4. **THEATRE ROYAL, 236 BOURKE STREET:** Renowned as much for its adjacent bar frequented by the *demi-monde* as for its theatre, and consequently nicknamed 'the Saddling Paddock'. This was undoubtedly why Henry Varley chose the theatre as the site of his Sunday afternoon lectures in the late 1880s. Site of Kmart as of this writing.

5. **ENTERTAINMENT PRECINCT:** The block of Bourke Street between Swanston and Russell streets was the epicentre of the entertainment precinct. Occupying both sides of the road, it was full of theatres, cafés and hotels, which were a source of custom both for street sex workers and brothels in 'Little Lon'.

6. **YMCA, 131 RUSSELL STREET:** In 1889, this was the site of Mrs Clarke Wells' lecture in the street outside.

7. **THE EASTERN MARKET:** The principal fruit and vegetable market of the late nineteenth century, also renowned for its sideshow amusements on a Saturday night. From 1962 to the early 2000s, the Southern Cross Hotel occupied the site.

8. **SARAH FRASER'S BROTHEL:** The principal 'flash brothel' prior to Madame Brussels'. At its height in the late 1870s, it occupied five houses, then at 190–198 Stephen Street.

9. **ROSALIND HOUSE:** Brothel initially operated by Kitty West (as 124 Stephen Street), later taken over by Charlotte Adams (as 218 Exhibition Street). In the late 1870s, it was known as Rosalind House. Martha Burrell worked here before becoming housekeeper to Madame Brussels.

10. **ANOTHER OF MRS WEST'S BROTHELS (FORMERLY 122 STEPHEN STREET):** Adjacent to Rosalind House – the two houses were bought by Samuel Nathan after Mrs West's death.

11. **'LITTLE LON' PRECINCT:** See detailed map of the eastern portion.

12. **THE MELBOURNE CLUB (36 COLLINS STREET):** This men's only establishment was (and remains) a home away from home for the elite of the day.

13. **CARLTON GARDENS AND ROYAL EXHIBITION BUILDINGS:** Stretches out beyond the confines of the map to encompass a 26-hectare site. Location of the Great Exhibitions of 1880 and 1888.

14. **THE MODEL SCHOOL:** For a time, the location of the Board (and later Department) of Education, as well as containing regular schools and facilities for teacher training. Its location adjacent to the brothels of Little Lon caused some negative comment at times.

15. **PARLIAMENT HOUSE:** Seat of the Victorian government.

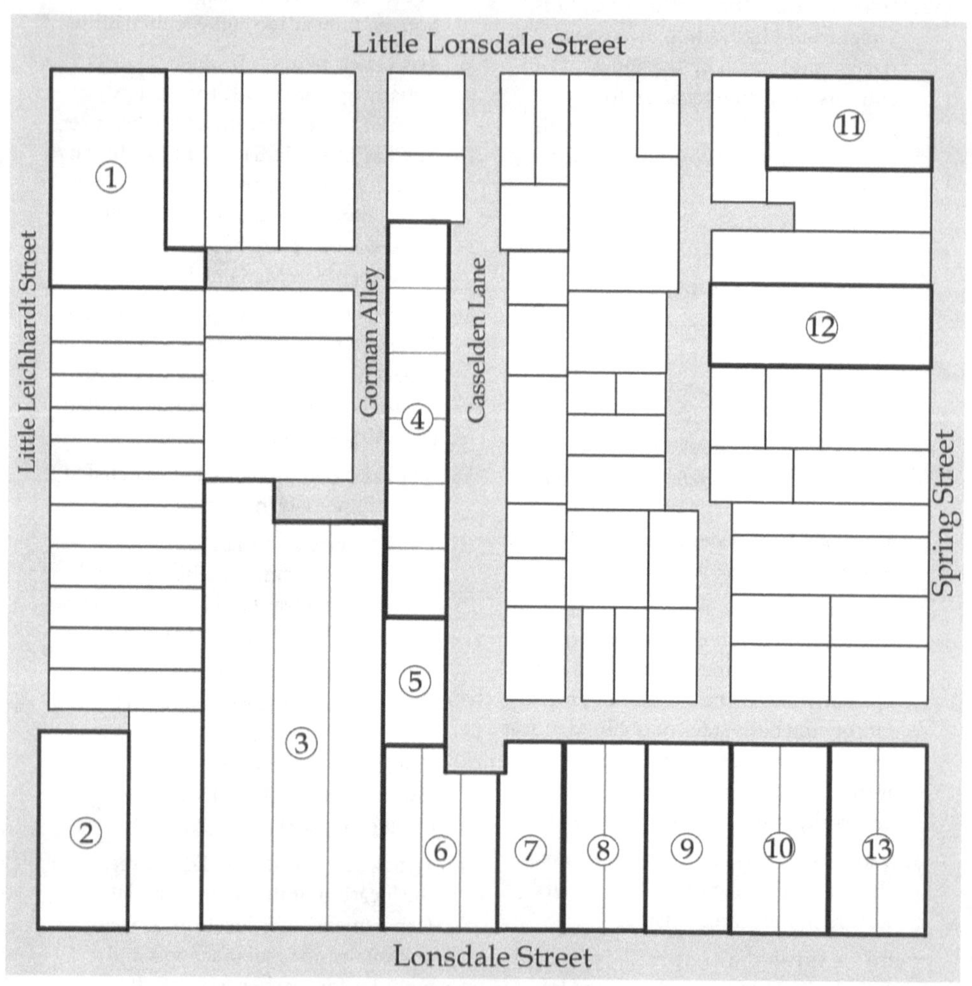

Madame Brussels' environs: part of the 'Little Lon' district in 1886

1. **ODDFELLOWS HOTEL, 39 LITTLE LONSDALE STREET:** The saying that Melbourne had a pub on every corner is borne out in this precinct. This 1854 building, with its distinctive corner entry, still remains.

2. **BLACK EAGLE HOTEL, 42–44 LONSDALE STREET:** Dating from 1848, it is one of the earliest surviving commercial buildings in the city. Despite having two doors, it was one business from the beginning.

3. **MADAME BRUSSELS' DWELLING AND BROTHEL:** Three properties progressively acquired from 1876. Despite being three, the whole was known after 1888 as 32–34 Lonsdale Street. The middle property, with cottage (no. 32), was occupied first as her home and brothel. She added the property on the right (nominally no. 30), with its garden and outbuildings, before purchasing the house on the left (no. 34) for her private residence (Studholme Villa). The adjacent cottage on Casselden Lane (see 5 below) was first rented and operated as a separate brothel before being purchased. The properties were demolished in the early twentieth century and the factories that replaced them have now also been replaced and the street numbering altered. Madame Brussels' establishment occupied the space between the existing building numbered 38–40 and the start of the Casselden Place tower, incorporating the newly created Madame Brussels Lane and the low-rise office building and shop numbered 36.

4. **CASSELDEN LANE COTTAGES:** A line of six two-roomed cottages from the 1870s, the northernmost of which (no. 17) has been preserved and as of this writing is a gin distillery.

5. **COTTAGE, CASSELDEN LANE:** Rented by Madame Brussels c.1886–1906 (see 3, above), although c.1889–92 Annie Wilson (see 6, below) ran a brothel here. Purchased by Caroline Hodgson in 1906.

6. **BROTHEL, 22–26 LONSDALE STREET:** Traded under various proprietors, most notably Annie Wilson's Boccaccio House c.1893–94. All buildings from here to the corner of Spring Street were rebuilt as factories in the early twentieth century and have now been replaced with the Casselden Place tower.

7. **BROTHEL, 18–20 LONSDALE STREET:** Only seems to have operated c.1894–1907.

8. **BROTHEL, 14–16 LONSDALE STREET:** Had various proprietors, including Catherine 'Kitty' West c.1866–79 and 'Scotch Maud' Miller c.1893–99.

9. **BROTHEL AND DWELLING, 10 LONSDALE STREET:** Used intermittently as a brothel c.1878–1908, including by Madame Brussels, 1879.

10. **BELLEVUE HOUSE, 6–8 LONSDALE STREET:** Madame Brussels' main rented brothel c.1879–91 and c.1903–07.

11. **THE ELMS FAMILY HOTEL, 269 SPRING STREET:** Built in 1924, replacing another hotel on the site. Closed early twenty-first century. The modified building remains as part of the 271 Spring Street complex.

12. **261 SPRING STREET:** A site with mixed use over the years. Initially Best's New Royal Dancing Academy (1876–c.1886), then Victor's Athletic Hall, then a cigar factory until it was taken over by the Church of England in 1895 and subsequently rebuilt. As St George's Mission Hall it was part of the church's mission to help the poor and the 'fallen' until the late 1950s. Now a part of the 271 Spring Street complex.

13. **HOTEL, 2–4 LONSDALE STREET:** Shop and hotel, later combined as hotel alone (Star of the East 1874–78, South Australian Club 1879–1908). It, along with the Oddfellows and Black Eagle, had its licence revoked in the early twentieth century, during a push to reduce hotel numbers throughout Victoria.

1.

TELLING CAROLINE HODGSON'S STORY

FOR MANY MELBURNIANS, MADAME BRUSSELS is a cult figure of sorts. Since 2006, her name has been emblazoned on a popular rooftop bar in Melbourne's central business district, and Madame Brussels Lane now occupies the land where one of her brothels stood.[1] Curious visitors can gaze at photographs of her as they sip their cocktails at the Little Lon Distilling Co., or take walking tours with guides describing events that took place in her time. In that context Madame Brussels is often presented as an amusing caricature from colourful days gone by, but Caroline Hodgson – the woman who so successfully created and marketed Madame Brussels and her establishments – actually represents much of what Melbourne was in the nineteenth century and what it became in the twentieth. She rode the wave of Melbourne's boom in the 1880s, weathered the storm of the depression years in the 1890s and suffered as a result of the outburst of moral panic in the 1900s. Her death in 1908 signified the end of one kind of Melbourne and the beginning of another: in terms of sex work the city went from uneasy tolerance to complete prohibition in the space of her working life, and she was a central figure in much of the politics surrounding the change. But despite the public's enduring fascination with her, our understanding of Melbourne's most famous brothel keeper and her business has been relatively superficial.

From the arrival of Europeans in 1835 and through the gold rushes of the 1850s, Melbourne was a rough and not-at-all-ready frontier, populated to the greatest extent by single men motivated by an ambition to be rich. The skewed demographic combined with the crude morality of greed led to a burgeoning trade in sex. Brothels and sex workers were in demand, and remained so for the rest of the century as Melbourne grew to nearly half a million people. At the same time, those who regarded themselves as the cream of the pre-gold-rush settlement were being challenged for supremacy by those with suddenly acquired wealth minus genteel breeding. Melbourne's social world was in turmoil, and compared with Sydney and other major Australian cities of that era Melbourne's sex industry developed an unusual character. It had all the usual street walkers and poor back-lane cribs – and, like other big cities, it boasted plenty of middling-class brothels and hotels with barely disguised sex workers behind the bar – but in Melbourne the 'flash brothels' at the top of the industry were run by female brothel keepers across many decades. Other cities had top-of-the-range establishments too, but in Melbourne the names and locations of the 'flash madams' who ran them were familiar to readers of the local newspapers.[2]

Sarah Fraser, whose house in 1867 entertained Prince Alfred the Duke of Edinburgh, Queen Victoria's second son, was the first of these 'flash madams' to develop a public profile, but after her death in 1880 Madame Brussels gradually became the most eminent among them.[3] Both women appear in Melbourne's public memory today as brothel keepers at the bawdy margins of the city's history, but in their time neither of them was marginal, standing as they did at the centre of a substantial economic network and catering to the tastes of Melbourne's social and political elite.

Yet no matter how important Caroline Hodgson's clients may have been, they were never identified alongside her in public discourse, and since she left behind no visitors' books or reminiscences of her own, her influence over her clients has not been the subject of any historical inquiry. Along with the laneway in the CBD, her reputation has brought her a short biography and an entry in the *Australian Dictionary of Biography*, but despite all the public contempt, moral disapproval and ridicule she received during her lifetime, the real Caroline Hodgson remained in the shadows.[4]

This began to change in 2018, when Denis James, a descendant of her first husband's brother, read an article in *The Conversation* co-written by one of this book's authors about Melbourne's nineteenth-century sex workers.[5] He subsequently made contact with Barbara, asking whether she was interested in his family's collection of memorabilia relating to Caroline Hodgson. She immediately asked whether there were any photographs. 'No,' he replied. 'There was a pretty little album of photos, but there were no names on any of them, so I gave it to my niece for her children to play with.' Fortunately he was able to retrieve it.

Following the clues in the images themselves, Barbara was able to identify most of the subjects, and Denis, along with his brother Greg, subsequently donated the collection to the State Library Victoria.[6] As a result of the identification of those images, an exhibition at Melbourne's Old Treasury Building was able to feature at least some of her story.[7] *Madame Brussels* builds on this work, setting out what has been learnt about her since the photographs came to light, and exploring the moral and political context of her venture into commercial sex.

The book begins in 'the old world', piecing together the circumstances of Caroline's early life in Prussia. A German genealogist found few details, but enough to set the scene for us before Caroline met her first husband, Studholme Hodgson (known as 'Stud'). She married him in London in 1871. Using details from their marriage certificate we can speculate on how she came to be there, and despite their limited time together Stud's aristocratic English family provides an important backdrop to Caroline's brothel-keeping.

The second section – 'early days in Melbourne' – describes Caroline's first few years in the town with Stud, and traces how she came to be running a brothel. When they arrived in 1871 Melbourne was a distant outpost of the

British Empire but its social values and institutions were by no means isolated or out of touch with those of Europe and America. It was not long before Stud joined the police force, and Caroline's choice of the nom de guerre 'Madame Brussels' prompts an examination of the European sex trade and how she set up and ran her own houses.

British ideas about both moral purity and the 'necessary evil' of prostitution were largely accepted in nineteenth-century Victoria, but the moral politics of sex work became increasingly complex. In 'the halcyon days' – Madame Brussels' heyday during Melbourne's boom years of the 1880s – the legal restrictions placed on sex work are explained along with how the police interpreted and implemented the laws. The issues relating to sex work in England, in particular the scandals associated with flagellation, pornography and the sale of virgins, come into consideration, and the section ends with the moralists gaining some changes to the laws relating to sex work in Victoria.

Every Australian city negotiated the challenge of shifting moral certainties in its own way, and Caroline Hodgson's creation of Madame Brussels was one of the unique aspects of Melbourne's sex industry. Her story contains many of the usual elements of drama, with 'the complicated years' encompassing a supposed lover, Alfred Plumpton, an adopted daughter (the abandoned baby Irene) and Stud's death, as well as a second marriage, to Jacob Pohl. But there were also some elements that were less common in the nineteenth century: she was a poor Prussian orphan girl who had married a well-to-do Englishman and made a dash for the colonies, and her English husband may have been gay. Their time together was brief but his return to her at the end of his life came at an important moment for her and entangled them both in Victoria's economic woes of the 1890s.

By following her property investments, this story of Caroline Hodgson's life teases out her accumulation of wealth and property in an unusual social setting, but it is also about the ordinary intersections of sex and power, the law and women's rights in Victoria. In particular, by examining police records and newspaper reports of the court cases she was involved in, it tackles the question of whether she was likely to have wielded influence over members of the various benches of magistrates who heard cases against her.

Caroline Hodgson's creation of Madame Brussels occurred at a formative time for the city of Melbourne and left a substantial mark on its history, but she left very few written words of her own. Thanks to Denis James, and Rosalie Savage, whose grandmother, Irene, was adopted and raised by Caroline Hodgson, we have been able to learn a little about Caroline as a person. Divorce records also provide some insight into the failure of her second marriage.

When the owner of *Truth* newspaper enters the fray in 'the new century', providing the images and calumnies that have populated stories about Madame Brussels ever since, we read between the lines of social history to reassess Caroline Hodgson's side of the story. We reconsider the political scandal she was drawn into involving the resignation of a member of parliament, and take a look at detailed newspaper reports about the forced closure of her brothels. In 'the end', despite the lack of extensive personal material, we reach some conclusions about the kind of people providing and using the services in Caroline's houses and about the accusations of corruption against her.

Tracing Caroline Hodgson's life has been a labour of curiosity, fascination and frustration for us. Despite our best efforts there are still some unanswered questions, including the important one: was she ever a sex worker herself? And her death certificate notes that she died in her house in Lonsdale Street, despite having been ordered to leave by a magistrate the year before. How and why did she stay? We don't know. But still her story matters to Melburnians, because it opens our eyes to how our city was made.

As a woman moving between Europe and Australia, London and Melbourne, German and English, Caroline Hodgson shows us how difficult women's lives could be. The rise and fall of her business also reflects changing ideas about women and sexuality within the Western world's increasingly influential middle-class population, which was wedded to the twin notions of domesticity for women and respectability for all. In the way that Caroline provided a challenge to Melbourne's moralists regarding prostitution, her story encourages us to think about the rights and wrongs of sex work today. We might judge sex workers favourably when their lives are circumscribed by poverty or the threat of it, but should we judge Caroline Hodgson, as a wealthy madam, in the way that Madame Brussels' detractors did, calling her 'a moral monster' who grew rich 'by the ruin of her own sex'?[8] Or should we accept that the women who worked in her boarding houses were making their own choices and had a right to do so?

After the closure of Madame Brussels' brothels in 1907, Victoria criminalised sex work, making it illegal for anyone – including landlords – to benefit from prostitution. Over a century passed before that law was undone, but the hostile beliefs about sex work that created it were still very much in evidence during the parliamentary debates in 2021 which eventually decriminalised the trade.[9] Caroline Hodgson's story not only presents us with some understanding of the world in which she lived and worked, it also tells us about a world that is still deeply embedded in Melbourne's culture today.

A note about names

Throughout the book we have reluctantly chosen to refer to Caroline Hodgson as 'Caroline' and her first husband as 'Stud'. It suggests a familiarity that we are uncomfortable with, but the traditional alternative 'Hodgson' would be confusing applied to both people and inaccurate applied to Caroline over her lifetime. We have matched the names of other characters to this convention where appropriate.

PART I:
THE OLD WORLD

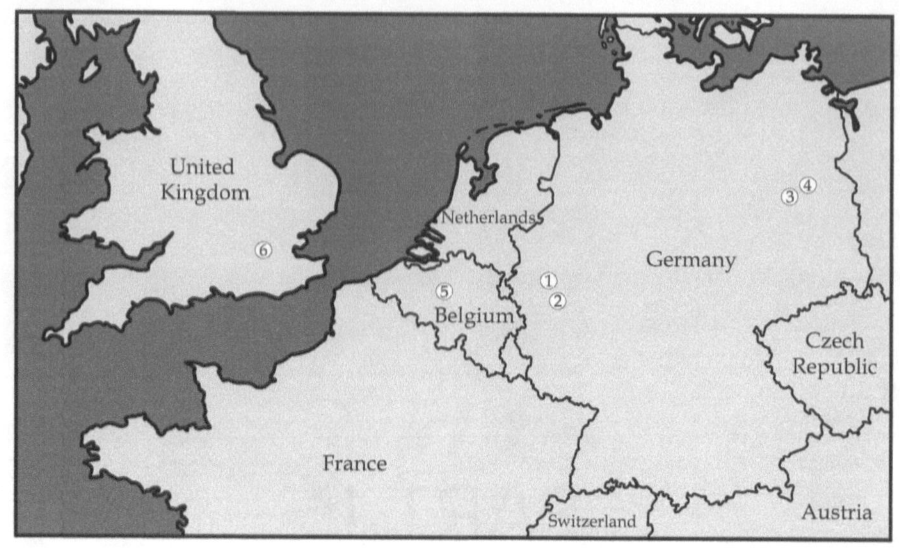

Caroline Lohmar's early life in Europe (national borders as in 2024)

KEY

1. COLOGNE
2. BONN
3. POTSDAM / BEELITZ
4. BERLIN
5. BRUSSELS
6. LONDON

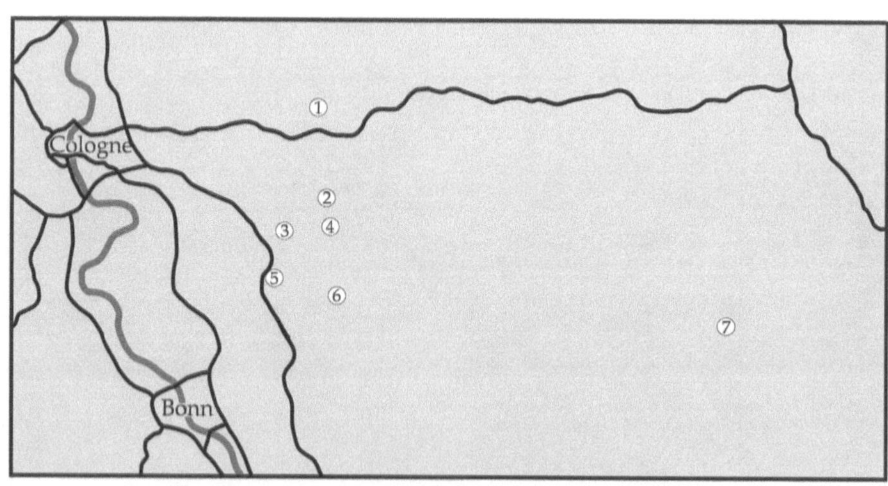

Caroline Lohmar's childhood homes in Prussia

KEY

1. KLEFHAUS
2. NEUHONRATH
3. SCHEIDERHÖHE
4. ROTHERHÖHE
5. LOHMAR
6. BRASCHOSS
7. KATZWINKEL

2.

A WEDDING IN LONDON

Madame Brussels, Melbourne's most infamous flash madam of the nineteenth century, first appears in official records in 1871, when she married Studholme George Hodgson at St George Hanover Square – *the* venue for society weddings in London at that time. She gave her name on the marriage registration as Caroline Lohmar and her father as John Lohmar, gentleman.[1] But the wedding of Lohmar, age twenty-two years (she said), and Hodgson, age thirty-three (he said), was not a romantic upmarket wedding, despite the location and the Hodgson family background. It took place in the registry office rather than the church, and theirs was a marriage by licence, not by banns.

A marriage by banns – the usual route – involved couples announcing their intention to marry over three successive Sundays in their parish church. It meant that couples had to belong to the church's congregation and placed a halter on those wishing to marry in a hurry. It also provided an opportunity for families or others to object to the proposed union. A marriage by licence, on the other hand, meant that couples could marry away from their home churches, including in private locations, without waiting and without making any public announcement that might lead to objections being raised. Marriage by licence was often the choice of wealthy or famous people wishing to avoid publicity, marry somewhere special or marry without the usual three-Sunday delay.[2] The same reasons, of course, which might apply to more ordinary mortals.

Why did Caroline Lohmar and Studholme Hodgson opt for a marriage by licence? Neither one of them would have had a parish church of their own to go to in London. Caroline Lohmar came from Prussia, and Studholme Hodgson from Appleshaw in Hampshire. But even if they had each had their own church, they were of different persuasions: he was Church of England and she was Roman Catholic.[3] Without sharing a Church of England heritage, the church of St George's, Hanover Square, may not have been willing to publish their banns.

No one from either family was present, so it may have been a hasty wedding, with no time to waste on gathering families from abroad. The marriage was conducted by the Registrar of Births, Deaths and Marriages, and the two necessary witnesses were drawn from the household of the Superintendent Registrar, whose wife and servant, or 'nurse domestic', were of similar age to the bride.[4] In different circumstances these young women might have been friends of the bride attending the wedding, but their signatures in the place where we normally find the bride and groom's family members probably means their presence was functional rather than friendly.

Or the wedding might have been arranged in such a way as to avoid gathering families who were unlikely to approve of it. If Studholme Hodgson was from a family with higher status than Caroline Lohmar, then marrying 'down' would have been an embarrassment best kept from his family's notice, and Caroline most certainly came from a much lower rung on the ladder of nineteenth-century British society than her husband. Her background was unlikely to have been genteel, despite claiming her father was a 'gentleman'.

In later years she gave her birthplace as Potsdam in Germany, but Caroline was most likely born at Beelitz, a small town outside Potsdam, where her mother, Friederica Schulze, was born.[5] Friederica's father was a manual worker or a musician, according to different sources, and Beelitz was a garrison town. By the time she was sixteen Friederica had had an illegitimate child there – Caroline's older sister, Maria, born in 1844.[6] Caroline (pronounced 'Caroleena' in German) was probably illegitimate too, and born in Beelitz a few years later, but her birth was not recorded; we know from the flyleaf of a book she was given by a friend that she was born on 8 August, which – from the births of her siblings – makes the year most likely to have been 1846 or 1847.[7]

Were Maria and Caroline born out of wedlock because their mother was a sex worker? It is possible – garrison towns were notorious for their legions of sex workers – but when their mother moved east with the itinerant miner Johann Baptist Lohmar, both Maria and Caroline took his name, so perhaps Caroline's parents were committed to each other but unable to marry.[8] Johann Lohmar was Roman Catholic and Friederica was 'evangelisch', or Lutheran, which would have meant a 'mixed marriage' at a time when the Roman Catholic church was strongly against such unions.[9]

As a child Caroline would have been aware of the death of at least one sibling in 1852, before the loss of her mother in 1855 threw her world into turmoil.[10] She was about seven, old enough to grieve heavily. Her father's second marriage a year later, another baby's death and then the loss of her stepmother in 1859 would surely have been devastating enough without the increased responsibility for Caroline and Maria as they became the women of the house. When their father also died three years later, leaving Maria and Caroline with three younger siblings to care for (ages eleven, eight and four), the weight of their loss must have been extreme. If Caroline had not completed her eight years of compulsory schooling by then, this surely would have ended it. She was barely into her teens and had probably moved schools from Scheiderhöhe to Katzwinkel to Neuhonrath to Klefhaus to Rothehöhe in that time. They were all in the area immediately east of Cologne, but far enough apart to mean changing schools. Nevertheless, she did learn to read and write.

In 1874 Maria married at Rothehöhe, where their father had died; by that time the younger siblings were old enough to be making their own way in the world. She was thirty, and went on to have seven children of her own, but

Caroline would not meet any of them in those early years, despite keeping in contact, because she was in Melbourne.[11] It is not known when Caroline left Prussia or where she went at first, because from the time of her father's death (just before Christmas in 1862) Caroline does not appear in the records again until 1871.

The Englishman Caroline married had an entirely different family background from her own. It is sometimes said that the sun never set on the British Empire in the nineteenth century, and there was probably one of Studholme Hodgson's relatives drenched in sunlight the whole time, either governing a far-flung territory or making war on it. Britain's empire was controlled by its army, and since Caroline's husband came from illustrious British army stock, both on his father's side and his mother's, they were part and parcel of the ruling elite in many British colonies. Some of these men became very wealthy as a result, while others became notorious. It began three generations back.[12]

Studholme Hodgson's great-grandfather, Field Marshal Studholme Hodgson (c.1708–98),[13] married the daughter of a lieutenant-general and spent seventy years in the army, becoming a governor, although this role went no further than Inverness in Scotland.[14] However, one of the field marshal's sons – Stud's grandfather, General John Studholme Hodgson (1759–1846) – went as far as Bermuda to serve as governor. That is where Stud's father, Robert Brownrigg Studholme John Hodgson (1810–84), was born, the third of three boys.

The eldest son, General Studholme John Hodgson (c.1803–90), commanded what was then Ceylon, while the second, Major-General John Studholme Hodgson (1805–70), served in India during the Sikh wars.[15] Robert Hodgson, however, did not join the army but gained access to some serious money by marrying into another family of British army careerists. Stud's mother, Selena Duke, came into a small fortune not long after she married, which included freehold land at Appleshaw in Hampshire and two substantial annuities: one for her and another for her husband.[16]

3.

A PHOTOGRAPH
IN BRUSSELS

AROUND THE TIME OF THEIR WEDDING, Caroline and Studholme had their photograph taken in Brussels by Ghémar Frères, 'Photographes du Roi' (Ghémar Brothers, 'Photographers to the King'). We cannot be sure whether the photograph was taken before or after they were officially married in London, but in the years around 1871 we can see the props used in their photograph in other images by Ghémar Frères.[1] The chair, in particular, is distinctive, and it appears in many of their pictures of this period.

The placement of Caroline's hand on Stud's shoulder, though, is a clue to the occasion which prompted their visit to a photographer. It is an indication of intimacy which is rarely seen in photographs of this era, and was inclined to be viewed as risqué in buttoned-up England. Ghémar Frères discovered this when they issued a series of carte-de-visite images in 1862, on the occasion of Queen Victoria's son's engagement.[2] Ghémar Frères might have styled themselves 'the King's photographers' but when they depicted the future King Edward VII and Queen Alexandra in a similar pose it caused a minor furore in England. The *London Review* was horrified enough to question the authenticity of the image.

Caroline Lohmar and Studholme Hodgson
at the time of their wedding in 1871

The future King Edward VII and Queen Alexandra,
also by Ghémar Frères

His Royal Highness sits in a chair, while the Princess stands over the back of the chair, with her two hands resting on his shoulders. Pretty, is it not? – sentimental, sweet, and lover-like? Very – only not quite probable, or in the best taste. That a young lady may have stood, in that attitude of tender watching, at the chair of her future husband, is likely enough – but she would never think of being photographed at so confiding a moment. The lover would certainly object to the artist 'posing' his intended in any such way, and the lady herself would object to it with still greater vehemence. Can Paterfamilias possibly believe that the Prince and Princess allowed themselves to be shown after this fashion to the general gaze?[3]

In 1871 things were not much different from 1862 in terms of English moral judgment, so we can reliably assume that the positioning of Caroline's right hand on Stud's shoulder means that the photograph was taken either shortly before or after their marriage. And that Stud's family might have recoiled from the intimacy it revealed, and from the woman depicted in such a way.

Looking closer at the young Hodgson couple, neither of them is dressed in what would be considered 'finery' in that era but there are some indications in Caroline's outfit that she was aware of fashion without having the means to indulge it. In some ways her dress is very 1870s: there is no crinoline, and no dropped shoulders as there would have been in the 1860s, and the high neck was common in the 1870s. At the same time, the tightly fitted bodice with a higher-than-natural waist was prominent in fashions of the late 1860s, along with the tablier, or apron, at the front and the mid-length overlay, or peplum, at the back. The looseness of the way the rear peplum hangs, though, suggests that it was taken off a crinoline dress and recycled. And while the decorative ruffles are indicative of a 'special' outfit, the above-floor length of the skirt raises the suspicion that it was borrowed from a shorter woman or began as a working-class girl's more practical outfit. Altogether it is a melange of styles and pieces reused from earlier costumes, which was typical of everyday wear for all but the wealthiest of women but unusual in a wedding image. People who could afford to have their photograph taken could usually have a dress made for the occasion. Unless, of course, the wedding was arranged in a hurry or there was a mismatch between the person paying for the bride's clothing (a single woman with few resources) and the groom (an independent comfortably-off gentleman). In any case, Caroline's clothing does not project the kind of social standing that Stud's family would have recognised as their own; Caroline would have been seen for what she was: an outsider in the Hodgsons' world.

In this context Caroline's jewellery is intriguing; the Albert chain at her midriff is very similar to the one that Stud is wearing in an earlier photograph with his brother John, and he is not wearing one at all in this image. Did he lend his new wife some silver for the photograph, or did he gift it to her? The somewhat awkward hold of her left hand – as though she is deliberately posing it to show off her ring finger – draws attention to the faintest outline of a wedding ring, suggesting that the photograph was taken post-wedding. That would make sense of her displaying his watch chain, and the fact that the ring appears on her left hand (the English tradition) rather than her right (the German tradition).

Stud's clothing is harder to read, but his beard is decidedly untrimmed and even through the discolouration on the image his jacket and pants seem tired rather than new. Another indication, perhaps, of a hastily arranged occasion, or else a man not accustomed to gentlemanly attire. And despite his family background in the English gentry, between leaving school and marrying Caroline Lohmar Stud had indeed been out of the habit of wearing anything but outdoor working clothes. Australian ones at that.

Stud was born at Appleshaw in Hampshire in 1835, and two more siblings followed him there, but by the time he was five years old his parents were living 'on the Continent'. He had an older sister, and another was born at Constance in 1840, and a brother at Frankfurt in 1842.

Stud's education probably began with an English-speaking governess or tutor during his years in Constance and Frankfurt, but he would doubtless have picked up some German too, providing a means to bond with his future wife. As teenagers, though, he and his younger brother, John, attended

Lancing College, an English boarding school in the south of England.[4] Lancing College was one of a new variety of school, set up by the Reverend Nathaniel Woodard for children of the upper middle classes; the education they offered was particularly suitable for the children of British Army officers, with a view to preparing them for similar careers.

Neither Stud nor John was seemingly impressed with the idea, or perhaps they did not prove to be suitable army material, because after a short time Stud moved to a day school and John joined the merchant navy.[5] Both of the boys were off to see the world at a relatively young age, and although they took different routes they both eventually found themselves in Australia.

While John was sailing the high seas, Stud left England at the age of twenty with letters of introduction to family friends in New England, New South Wales.[6] Whether it was his choice or his parents' solution to the problem of a wayward son is unknown, but it took him away from his family for over a decade, first living and working with sheep and cattle in New South Wales, and then in outback Queensland. It was to be the late 1860s before Stud met his brother again, this time in Sydney before he went home.[7]

When Stud sailed back to England in a cabin, he took with him a vast experience of isolation and outback living.[8] He had spent his youth working hard and long under trying conditions, and he had become a practical man; one who didn't waste time, money or energy on fashion. Or, it would seem, on the social expectations of his class.

PART II: EARLY DAYS IN MELBOURNE

4.

ARRIVING IN MELBOURNE

WHEN CAROLINE AND STUDHOLME HODGSON arrived at Railway Pier in
June 1871, Melbourne had just been favoured with a performance of
Donizetti's *La favorite* at the Princess's Opera House, and was looking for-
ward to Mozart's *Don Giovanni* the following week.[1] Combining these
cultural attainments with advertisements for the Old Colonists' Anniversary
Festival – headlined by 'Reminiscences of Port Phillip, by G.W. Rusden,
Esq.' – the Hodgsons could have been forgiven for thinking they had arrived
in a place that had left its rough frontier ways behind.[2]

Yet Melbourne was a city struggling to define itself after the heady days
of the 1850s gold rushes. It had grand buildings and men with grand fortunes, but it was still a binge centre where working men from around the
colony came to knock down their cheques. It was not backward in import-
ing whatever material goods money could buy and was at the forefront of
adopting all sorts of new technology, but it still had no sewerage.

If Caroline and Stud had read the current newspapers after their journey
of 113 days under sail on the *Melmerby*, they might have been impressed by
advertisements for a return journey of 'under 60 days' on the steamship
Somersetshire.[3] At the same time, reports of the inquiry into the wreck of the
S.S. *Auckland* off the Victorian coast might have given them a sense of relief
at having arrived safely, while accounts of the floods in Gipps Land [*sic*],

where the river at Bairnsdale had risen 10 feet above the ordinary level and the inhabitants of low-lying land 'had to beat a precipitate retreat', might have been less comforting.[4] So, too, the lengthy lists of criminal offences reported in the newspapers and being dealt with by Melbourne's courts; their new home had many of the hallmarks of old England, but it also had hazards of its own.

Politically and economically the 1870s were a tumultuous time in Victoria. At the beginning of the decade when the Hodgsons arrived, Melbourne was still the centre of vast pastoral holdings and goldmining ventures, but it was no longer relishing the miners' easily gotten gains from the goldfields of the early 1850s. The alluvial gold had run out, leaving hard times for the miners through the 1860s; the big deep-lead quartz crushing batteries took some time to take over.

Melbourne was on its way to developing a strong local manufacturing sector, too, but the boost of government protection policies was still to come, and while the cry of 'unlock the lands!' that started in the 1850s had finally been met by a workable land act in 1869, the rush of labouring men to buy a plot and settle on it was only just beginning.[5]

There were also other signs of increasing demands for social equality, with parliament putting legislation in place to enable men without wealth to represent their fellows in parliament; initially it only allowed for reimbursement of the expenses of office rather than a full salary, but it was a step away from the stranglehold money had had on legislative power in Victoria.[6]

The Hodgsons were probably oblivious to everything except their own personal affairs on the day they arrived. To begin with there was the issue of finding a roof to put over their heads. And doubtless that began with a hunt for Stud's brother John and his family, who were already living in Melbourne.

John Hodgson had been at sea for most of his life, having gained his certificate of competency as a second mate in Dublin at twenty-three. That was in 1861.[7] He had married a young Irishwoman in Sydney in 1866, but by the end of the following year John and Lizzie Jane Hodgson had made their home at Sandridge (now Port Melbourne), the seafarers' suburb of Melbourne, and

John was working on the coastal steamer S.S. *Penola,* plying back and forth between Victoria and South Australia in the years when their first two babies made their appearance.[8] When Caroline and Stud Hodgson disembarked from the *Melmerby* in June 1871, therefore, John and Lizzie Jane were well settled in Melbourne, less than two blocks from the bay and a short walk from Railway Pier. They had been there long enough to have sent their address to family in England, so the newly arrived couple may have been able to walk off the ship, make arrangements for their luggage and head straight to Stokes Street, Sandridge.

A quick glance at the rate books shows Sandridge as a small distinct part of the overall city at that time, largely defined to the west by the railway line and to the east by the lagoon, but street upon street, block upon block were made up of small workers' cottages, filled with all that the tradesmen and sailors needed to serve a thriving port. John and Lizzie Jane were renting a house with a relatively long garden at the back and three rooms rather than the usual two.[9] As the first tenants in a new brick cottage they were doing well, but with two little ones to look after, not to mention a husband away at sea for whole weeks and longer, the arrival of more sets of hands may have been welcome.

Caroline was probably slightly younger than Lizzie Jane, but their shared life in 1870s Melbourne forged a lifelong friendship.[10] Married to brothers, too, there was a particular part of their experience that would have been difficult for both of them in those heavily sectarian days: they had each been raised as Roman Catholics, but their husbands belonged to the Church of England. It was not a comfortable state of affairs in other places in the world, but it was especially difficult in Victoria. A Roman Catholic Provincial Council had assembled in Melbourne early in 1869 and the question of how to stamp out 'irreligious connexions' with Protestants had taken up a goodly number of local newspaper columns.

John Hodgson spent his entire life as a sailor, and although it was a precarious existence – both physically and financially – he and his family can be readily traced in the 1870s through the movement of his ships. His brother

Stud had no such calling, and his experience as a drover and a station manager in Queensland was not readily transferable to urban Melbourne. He found employment for a time with the Melbourne Omnibus Company, but whether he was using his newly claimed occupation of 'clerk' (listed on the shipping list) or his skills with the horses is unknown.[11] But at the end of 1872 Studholm [*sic*] Hodgson committed himself to a role that involved both horses and clerical work: he joined Victoria Police.

Caroline Hodgson's sister-in-law, Lizzie Jane Hodgson, 1870s

5.

A SINGLE WOMAN'S BUSINESS

STUD HODGSON BEGAN HIS CAREER in the Victorian police force with a lie. The rules said recruits had to be under thirty years of age, because:

> the great wear and tear of a policeman's life, the exposure to wet and cold, to parching winds and fierce heat, at all seasons, night and day, render it indispensable that none but vigorous men in the prime of life should be employed in the service.[1]

Stud had to alter his date of birth by a full eight years when he applied. The untruth put his age conveniently at twenty-nine on 13 November 1872, when he was actually thirty-seven.[2]

Stud's experience droving sheep had given him skills in handling horses that were to prove invaluable when it came to working as a mounted constable over Victoria's rugged terrain, but having the skills to do the physical work was probably less important than having the mental toughness to deal with the horrors of human behaviour. A few months after he joined the police Stud was transferred to the Upper Goulburn Depot at Mansfield in Victoria's high country, and his police record shows that country Victoria could be

Stud Hodgson in Melbourne, 1870s

a violent place. Over the next two decades his careful work produced convictions for crimes as varied as cruelty to animals, rape and murder.[3]

Caroline did not move to the country with her husband; she stayed in Melbourne. It is possible that since their arrival in 1871 Caroline had been helping her sister-in-law Lizzie Jane with her children, and she may have stayed with them for a time after Stud left. She would no doubt have had domestic and child-raising experience to draw on from her own motherless and orphaned years, and Lizzie Jane would have had plenty of need for assistance while her husband was away at sea – her third child was born not long before Stud went to Mansfield, giving her three children under four years of age.[4] But John Hodgson was declared bankrupt in August that year, through 'sickness in the family, and want of remunerative employment', so the pressure for Caroline to earn her own living would have been acute.[5] An entry in the Hotham (now North Melbourne) rate book at the end of the year reveals her solution.

In this era both owners and tenants were recorded in the council rate books but it was the tenants who paid the rates, and the rules of social propriety dictated that a woman who had a husband – even if he was not living with her – listed her husband as the rate payer. Caroline Hodgson, tenant, conformed to that expectation by listing Stud as the occupant of a two-storey house in Peel Street, in December 1873.[6] The 1874 post office directory also shows 'Studholme Hodgson' at '1 Central-ter., Peel St, Hotham', despite his police record showing that he was stationed at Mansfield.[7] But the terrace was no town residence for a country policeman; it was Caroline's business venture.

At this time, it seems Caroline Hodgson was not yet running a brothel. She was running a boarding house.

Caroline Hodgson's boarding house in 'Central-terrace',
Peel Street, North Melbourne; number 1 is first on the left

Nineteenth-century Melbourne was full of people coming and going. It was a city of immigrants and emigrants, some with money, many without, but mostly with a middling sort of income. Men earned their livelihoods from various pursuits relating to trade, goldmining and land settlement, but women who wanted or needed to live a respectable life without a supporting husband were largely confined to dressmaking, domestic or factory work. Some were able to set up their own schools, teaching young ladies the refinements needed for married life in Melbourne's middle or upper classes, but they were rare. Some, especially if they were the widows of publicans, were also able to take out hotel licences, and others with a little capital were able to set up shops. More commonly, women with a little education and greater expectations than life as a servant could fulfil, turned their domestic skills to account by setting up a boarding house.

The extreme shortage of accommodation which had prevailed in the early gold-rush years of the 1850s had eased by the 1870s when Caroline Hodgson was looking for an independent income, but men still outnumbered women, and single men, especially, were often in need of short- or long-term accommodation.[8] Melbourne catered for this passing parade of temporary residents in a great variety of ways, but mainly through hotels, licensed lodging houses and private boarding houses. Hotels were regulated through the licensing laws, and came in all shapes, sizes and qualities, but it required capital to set them up. Lodging houses were regulated by the *Common Lodging Houses' Act* of 1854, and required a licence. Boarding houses also came in a variety of guises, but they were most often domestic houses renting spare bedrooms. They might offer full or partial board, together with other comforts such as a sitting room, but they were not regarded as lodging houses.[9] An aspiring boarding house keeper need not submit a registration form or pay a licence fee of 10s. (ten shillings) for registration, but merely set up rooms for occupation and find boarders to fill them. This is how Caroline Hodgson started her career.

The parapet decoration of Central Terrace, Peel Street, shows that it was constructed in 1872, the year before Caroline Hodgson took up residence. It is a block of four terrace houses, with classic Victorian iron lacework balconies and verandahs. Boarding houses might have been common in the nineteenth century, but public transport was not, which made location an important consideration for prospective tenants. At that time Caroline's house – as one of her advertisements indicated – was only '10 minutes walk' from the post office, although she was probably referring to the one at North Melbourne rather than Melbourne's General Post Office in Elizabeth Street.[10] The convenience meant there were already several boarding houses in Peel Street.

Boarding houses – like brothels – could range from very poor to moderately reasonable to the most exquisitely decorated accommodation, even in the same street, and reading the class of boarding houses from their advertisements was one of the challenges of life for nineteenth-century travellers. The clues could be subtle, especially when the cost of a week's accommodation was not often stated. For instance, Henry Kelly, one of Caroline's neighbours at Central Terrace, advertised his boarding house as follows:

> **FURNISHED** and unfurnished **ROOMS**
> to **LET**, gas, bath, private. Terms moderate.
> 2 Central-terrace, Peel-street, Hotham.[11]

The quality of Henry Kelly's boarding house can perhaps better be gauged by the following advertisement placed in *The Argus* by one of his boarders:

> **LOW COMEDIAN** (to dance), Singing Chamber-maid,
> and Hi-ti-ti-ty Ladies and Gentlemen **REQUIRED** for
> tour. Apply, by letter, **X. Y. Z**, 2 Central-terrace, Peel
> street, Hotham.[12]

Kelly was there when Caroline Hodgson first set up her business, but after a short time his place was taken by Mrs Wickham, a widow who was obviously aiming for a higher class of customer:[13]

> **SUPERIOR BOARD** and **RESIDENCE**, gas, bath,
> 2 Central-terrace, Peel-street, Hotham. Terms moderate.[14]

Caroline, however, was aiming for a more sophisticated clientele again. Her advertisements mentioned not only a bath, but also a piano:

> **PRIVATE BOARD** and **RESIDENCE,** or furnished
> Rooms. Bath, balcony, piano. Moderate. 1 Central-
> terrace, Peel-street, Hotham.[15]

Despite Mrs Wickham having furnished her boarding house in some considerable style, her business did not last long. In October 1874 she sold all of her 'superior and nearly new household furniture and effects' by auction, the inventory included the following:

> Walnut suite in maroon rep, walnut centre table, rosewood Canterbury whatnot, Brussels carpet and rug, fender and irons, ornaments, pictures, timepiece, splendid trichord rosewood **COTTAGE PIANO,** by **CARL RONISCH, DRESDEN.** Handsome Arabian and other bedsteads, mattresses of best hair, bedding, chest drawers, mirrors, washstands, toilet table, carpets, oilcloths, &c., kitchen furniture, and usual culinary requisites.[16]

Mrs Wickham remarried the following year.[17]

Caroline's advertisements in the 'Board and Lodging' columns of *The Argus* early in 1874 offered accommodation with a strong resemblance to Mrs Wickham's 'superior board and residence', possibly emulating her furnishings, but towards the end of August she advertised a few times, minus the piano, for gentlemen only:

> AT 1 Central terrace, Peel street, Hotham, superior
> **BOARD** and **RESIDENCE** for gentlemen, bath.[18]

After this, Caroline's notices for boarders ceased as abruptly as her neighbour's. An advertisement at the end of September underlines how

Caroline's world had changed to something that needed disguising from public view:

> **WILLIAM COOK,** of Collingwood, is requested to call on Mr Hodson, Peel street, Hotham, Immediately. Urgent.[19]

There was no 'Mr Hodson [*sic*]' residing in Peel Street, Hotham, so presumably Caroline had some private reason for wanting a man to call on her without telling the world why or giving anyone reason to suspect her of less than respectable behaviour.[20] Which of course leaves us suspecting her of less than respectable behaviour. There was no more pretence about Stud paying the rates.

How did Caroline come by the idea of switching from one kind of boarding house to another? After a fruitful late-night offer from one of her boarders, perhaps? Or after a broken promise from a lover such as Mr William Cook of Collingwood? In the years between her father's death in Prussia in 1862 and her marriage in London in 1871, Caroline would have seen quite a lot of the world, including women turning to brothels for a living. She could have seen and heard quite a lot about it in Melbourne, too.

In 1869, when her brother-in-law John Hodgson was working on the *Penola* between Melbourne and Adelaide, for instance, one of his passengers was Austin Saqui, brother of the courtesan Sarah Saqui.[21] Sarah worked in Sarah Fraser's house, and entertained the Duke of Edinburgh when he visited Melbourne in 1867. The *Penola* had also been drawn into the duke's orbit when he left 'a valuable snuff box' at Government House in Adelaide and asked the ship's captain to retrieve it for him. Such tales bore frequent repetition for the entertainment of passengers.[22] Perhaps John Hodgson the sailor might have heard the story of Sarah and the duke one night at sea and repeated it for his family's amusement, planting the idea in Caroline's mind.

But no matter how it came about, from 1874 onwards Caroline's husband was a country policeman and she was an independent woman who earned a far greater income than his by running a brothel.

By December 1874, the rate books note that 'Caroline Hodson [*sic*], Boarding House Keeper' had moved her business into a newly constructed house next door to 1 Central Terrace; she had begun her new life as a brothel madam.[23]

The house had been built during her time in the terrace, and appears to have been redesigned to fit her needs. Before she moved in, it was listed as two brick dwellings 'in course of construction', but during Caroline's occupancy it became first a single brick dwelling of six rooms with one chimney, and then two brick dwellings of three rooms each, with only one having access to the chimney.[24] The two front doors visible today suggest that even at this early stage in her career she separated her private space from her business.

Caroline Hodgson's first brothel, next to 1 Central-terrace,
Peel Street, North Melbourne

Stud returned to Melbourne for about eight months from early August 1875 until the beginning of March 1876 while he was in between country assignments, but there is no indication that he took up residence with Caroline again, or even visited her, although he might have done; he was simply reported as an 'intelligent steady Constable' when he was transferred out to Sandhurst (Bendigo). During his time at the Sandhurst depot he was also considered 'steady and well conducted', and he was then sent to Swan Hill as 'keeper of the gaol'.[25] He was doing well, but his financial rewards were nothing like those achieved by his wife in her flourishing business.

6.

THE MOVE TO LONSDALE STREET

Six Bendigo bank clerks and I came down to Melbourne to see Briseis win the Melbourne Cup, and we spent the night before sight-seeing. Melbourne was a roughish sort of town in those days, wide open and frankly immoral. Hotel bars did not close till 11.30, and as 'wowsers' had not been invented then, and the police force was below strength, there was no repression of drink or of gaiety. During our evening stroll we country greenhorns called in wherever there was an open house. The Exchange Hotel in Swanston Street, with bars upstairs and down, was filled with well-dressed hetirae, gay, laughing and chatty. All were drinking 'bubbly' and nobody was tipsy. Diagonally across the road at the Blue Posts Hotel … there were about six bars filled with filles de joie, to the number of one hundred. The kerosene lamps shone brightly … and everybody was jolly. The next port of call was the Earl of Zetland where more Cyprians, descendants of Thais, Lais and Phryne, were gathered in a crowd of fifty.[1] Then we sallied up to Cleal's and found the 'pub' packed with the frail sisterhood, pleasant and charming, and not a vulgar troll nor trollop amongst them. It was an easy tack to the 'Saddling Paddock' of the Theatre Royal, then a vast vestibule with a quarter of a mile of bars enclosing a coulisse crowded with well-dressed men and a few diggers in red shirts and cabbage tree hats, bookmakers, jockeys, club men and the omnium gatherum of a superior village, with more and more women.[2] Here there were literally hundreds more ladies of pleasant manners and easy virtue, who had never even heard of a cocotte or a wanton. Right up Bourke Street to the top we called at all the places where fermented and spirituous liquors were retailed; also at Ned Bitton's for oysters and Jack Heard's for a dressed crab. The demi-monde were everywhere in crowds.

—George Meudell, *The Pleasant Career of a Spendthrift,* ~1929[3]

IN 1876, WHEN BRISEIS WON THE MELBOURNE CUP, George Meudell was a few months shy of seventeen.[4] He and his six mates were working at the time for his father, who was the manager of the Bank of Victoria in Bendigo.[5]

While his memoir tends towards nostalgia and self-interest, much of its description of Melbourne in 1876 can be verified by a glance through *Sands & McDougall's Melbourne and Suburban Directory*. The hotels are all there, Edward Bitton is selling fish and oysters at 170 Bourke Street East, and the Heard brothers are at 50 Swanston Street.

Other sources confirm the existence of the 'Saddling Paddock' at the Theatre Royal, but they are far less complimentary about the women in the streets and bars. Journalists such as Marcus Clarke and the Vagabond (Julian Thomas), writing about the same period, would not argue with Meudell's assessment of the number of sex workers offering their services, but they were far less enamoured with the women's behaviour, abhorring 'their lack of grammar and utter vulgarity of speech and soul'.[6]

The number of 'drunk and disorderly' cases heard every week by the City Court makes nonsense of Meudell's claim that 'nobody was tipsy', but he was probably right about the reduced number of diggers in their 'red shirts and cabbage tree hats' compared with the well-dressed men. After the gold rush of the 1850s and the doldrums that followed it, in 1876

Melbourne was on the cusp of its land boom years. There was still plenty of poverty and old-world problems relating to drink and gambling and violence, not to mention all the widowhood and wife-desertion exacerbated by the gold-digging frenzies, but there was also a sense that Victoria was no longer an outpost of civilisation. It had been visited by royalty, and it was taking advantage of the advances in technology to build railways and tramways and enormous steam-driven ore-crushers that were working the gold mines at a profit again.

But Melbourne was also a place – as Meudell depicts – where morality was lax and a good time could be had, as long as a person's pockets were not empty. And for many women, keeping some gold (or silver or copper) in their pockets meant doing sex work.

From the point of view of respectable people (a fluid category), stepping outside the norms of respectability to join the sex industry was no small matter in 1870s Melbourne, even though many women did. Single working-class women might expect to do the work for a few weeks or a few years to get them through periods of poverty, and then leave the industry behind by marrying, but for middle-class women there was rarely any prospect of turning back.

As a young, attractive, married-but-separated woman, Caroline might have seen flirting as fun and a way to assuage the loneliness of her emigrant's life, before it gradually dawned on her that there was money to be made from her charms. But it is also possible that the decision was made with reason and in cold blood; she had nothing to lose, no family to object and the sex industry allowed Caroline to earn a lot of money, very quickly.[7]

In September 1876, after a period of about two years as a brothel keeper, she paid £850 for her first house, at 169 Lonsdale Street East (later 32 Lonsdale Street). She put down a substantial deposit in cash, which her husband Stud declared was 'her own sole absolute and separate money'.[8] He also declared that he had 'no interest claim or demand whatsoever' on the property, and that his wife was purchasing the said property 'for her own separate use and benefit'.

The wording tells us nothing about his attitude towards Caroline's business, because it simply reflects the legal provisions relating to married women's ownership of property at that time. Under Victorian law, women who married after 1 January 1871 – as Caroline had done – had the right to hold property in their own name, 'free from the debts and obligations of her husband and from his control and disposition in all respects', but her husband could challenge that ownership at any time.[9]

She signed the contract on 19 September 1876, and he – in Swan Hill – signed the declaration prepared by her solicitors a mere four days later. Given that they were no longer living as a married couple, the speed with which Stud signed and returned the statutory declaration to her solicitors suggests they were in easy contact with each other and he was not at all antagonistic towards her.

Although the declaration tells us little more about Stud's feelings, it does tell us something about Caroline's caution and financial acumen. Stud's declaration confirmed in writing that he would not challenge Caroline's claim to the ownership of 169 Lonsdale Street East. Under Victoria's *Married Women's Property Act* 1870 the declaration was not legally necessary, so either she didn't trust her husband or she and her solicitor, Samuel Gillott, were being extra careful to protect her interests. Stud's behaviour suggests that she had nothing to fear from him, but history and events with her second husband were to show that their caution was wise.

In the 1870s the imbalance of the sexes left over from the influx of single men during the gold rushes combined with the double standard about sexual experience that allowed men to carouse outside marriage gave strength to the idea that women were either saints or sinners, damned whores or God's police. Women were increasingly idealised as the Angel in the House, but the double standard and the lack of remunerative work for women meant that there was still a lively market for sex work, and Caroline Hodgson was riding the wave.

For an attractive woman with a demure middle-class exterior and the confidence to appear in theatres and bars – Caroline was described in later years as 'a magnificent pink white and golden-maned animal' – it could be an easy market to exploit, though how much sex work she did herself is unknown.[10] Her longer-term financial success seems to have come mainly from her ability to choose the right location for her houses, to establish the right environs and ambience, and to offer the best forms of entertainment – that is, to manage the market. It began with her decision to buy a house in Lonsdale Street East.

She paid a £50 deposit in cash for 169 Lonsdale Street East on 19 September, and a month later paid a further £200 deposit in cash. She borrowed the other £600 for the settlement from Samuel Gillott but had no trouble paying off the loan; three years later she owned the house outright, and set about saving for her next house.[11]

In 1876 Melbourne's flashest brothel was Mrs Sarah Fraser's in Stephen Street, soon to be renamed Exhibition Street in honour of the Exhibition Buildings being built in the Carlton Gardens. But by the mid-1870s she was ageing, and Stephen Street had developed a low reputation because of the less salubrious houses to the south of hers.[12] By purchasing at the top end of Lonsdale Street, closer to the government offices and parliament house in Spring Street, the fresh, classy young Mrs Hodgson changed the scene.

Her first house was set back from the street behind a picket fence, and she kept it relatively discreet; within a few years her business outgrew her premises.

In 1878 the future Madame Brussels made her intentions clear: she would set aside the moral earnestness of her Prussian education[13] and play the world by Melbourne's rules. She followed the lead of Sarah Fraser and Kitty West, leasing more houses in the same area and expanding her business, but she outdid them both.

Mrs West, referred to by newspapers in Sydney as 'the well-known [or celebrated or notorious] Kitty Wright', had come to New South Wales as a convict in 1828 and was convicted numerous times for running disorderly houses and committing associated criminal offences.[14] When Sydney began cracking down on women in the sex industry, like many others (including

Sarah Fraser) she moved to Melbourne. When Mrs West (aka Mother West) arrived in 1857, she found it more lucrative to lease houses throughout the city and sublet them to sex workers rather than set up her own brothels.[15] She could charge the women exorbitant rates.

It is probable that Caroline was having some building work done on her house at 169 Lonsdale Street East when she arranged to move out for six weeks in 1878. She rented a house in Stephen Street from Mrs West, where she could continue her brothel business as usual.[16] At £3 per week the rent was considerable, but with seven rooms it was bigger than her own and perhaps gave her an opportunity to try expanding her home business.[17] She paid the agent the first week's rent, but each time he called to collect it after that she refused to pay.[18] After six weeks she moved back to her own place and resumed business there, leaving Mrs West £15 short of the agreed amount. Mrs West took her to court to obtain redress (and her money). Caroline Hodgson employed Dr Madden (later Sir John Madden, Victoria's chief justice) to defend her. He argued that Mrs West could not claim the debt, because the contract was illegal. She had – he argued – known when she rented it to Mrs Hodgson that 'it was intended to be used for immoral purposes', and under the law 'it was illegal to let houses for such purposes, being contrary to public morality'.[19]

It was not explicitly illegal at this time to rent a house to a sex worker. That was not the issue. Mrs West's problem was that it was a basic principle of British law – and remains so today – that a debt contracted for illegal purposes cannot be recovered in the courts. She could not recover a debt over a contract that was 'tainted with illegality in its inception', and the illegality in this case was that the house was to be used in a way that was 'contrary to public morality'.[20] The question of whether or not a brothel was 'contrary to public morality' was not canvassed in the court that day – it seems there was instant agreement on that score between the barristers and the judge – but there was some argument over correct process. 'Illegality' was a 'special defence' in debt recovery that could only be used after notifying the plaintiff in advance, and Mrs West's barrister argued that he and his client had not been notified.[21] The judge offered an adjournment so the paperwork could be rectified, at which point Mrs West's barrister threw in the towel and agreed that the case could go on as it was, and it was then promptly 'non-suited'. Caroline got away with not paying her rent, but the compromise was that she had to pay her own costs, because she hadn't given Mrs West notice of her use of a 'special defence'.

Caroline Hodgson [c.1875–80]

It is doubtful that Caroline knew about the particular legal principle her barrister would pull out in her favour when she refused to pay the agreed rent – it is more likely that she simply did not have the money (or the will) to pay the bill at the time. But the outcome would certainly have given her confidence in using legal processes to defend her interests, confidence she would draw on throughout her life. It probably also produced (or perhaps confirmed) some bad blood in Lonsdale Street for a time, with Mrs West owning two houses in Lonsdale Street East and Caroline owning one and renting several others close by.[22]

But Caroline's star was on the rise, and when Mrs West died in 1879 Caroline was beginning to expand her business on that side of the street.[23] With her move into houses beyond her own she adopted the title which gave her an edge over both of her rivals and many others: 'Madame Brussels'.

After Mrs Fraser's death in 1880 Caroline became the flashest of the flash madams in the area.[24] She raked in a small fortune over the next decade, but unlike her predecessor she poured her earnings into property. She had grand plans from the beginning, and with her head for business, and the capacity to find the people she needed to make the world work to her advantage, she capitalised on the conditions of the time.

7.

WHAT'S IN A NAME?

THE FIRST RECORDED USE OF THE NAME 'Madame Brussels' was in 1879, as the 'occupant' listed in the rate books of the houses Caroline Hodgson was renting in Lonsdale Street East. 'Mrs Hodgson' is recorded at number 169, but 'Madame Brussells [*sic*]' is the occupier of 183/5, 187 and 189 Lonsdale Street East – that is, she was 'Madame Brussels' in the houses she was renting and 'Mrs Hodgson' in her own. The new name seems to have been an immediate success in terms of marketing her profile, with a police report noting later the same year that a woman from a brothel in Little La Trobe Street had 'gone to Madame Brussels in Lonsdale st'.[1]

It was not uncommon for sex workers in Melbourne to use multiple names and aliases in the nineteenth century, just as it happens now. Some names were a result of serial marriages or de facto relationships (as with Catherine Fern's aliases 'Kitty Wright' and 'Kitty West'), while others were deliberately chosen by sex workers to suit their profession (Cecilia Scarlet and May Blanch, for example).[2] Others were named by their clients, usually by prefacing their name with the title 'Mother' (as in 'Mother Fraser' and 'Mother West'), but also sometimes because of a distinctive feature: 'Big Jane', for example, was a large woman, and it is probable that 'Scotch Maude' came from Scotland, although it is also possibly a pun on a 'shepherd's maud' shawl worn by the Scots to keep them cosy.[3]

'Madame Brussels' was deliberately chosen by Caroline Hodgson; it was not her single or married name, and she was Prussian rather than Belgian. However, Brussels was somewhere she had visited – her 'wedding' photograph was taken there – and it was a place with a reputation for prostitution and licentiousness. Is that why she chose the name? And if so, was she ever a sex worker in Brussels herself?

It was the French, under Napoleon, rather than the Belgians who started the formal regulation of sex work in Europe, which is why it became known as 'the French system'.[4] It was adopted by a number of European countries.

Beginning in 1844 Brussels required all sex workers to register on a 'list of public women'.[5] A personal file was created under their name, recording their age, their birth certificate, the social status of their parents and their sanitary condition (that is, whether doctors thought they were clear of disease) together with 'subsequent observations on their behaviour, change of address and health'.

By the late 1860s, when Caroline Lohmar could have been in Brussels, the women were divided into two classes: those who worked in the higher-class licensed brothels (the *maisons de tolérance*) and those who worked the streets and took clients back to shared houses (the *maisons de passe*). The control over registered women's lives was invasive; women needed to undergo a medical examination by a municipally appointed doctor twice a week, and if there was no evidence of a sexually transmitted infection they were given a card they could show to the police or clients.[6] Any sign of an infection led to forced treatment, and infringements of various rules including 'indecent' dress, drunkenness and missing medical checks were punished with short stays in a special prison. Not surprisingly, many women avoided registration despite the apparently strict regulations, and worked instead in the 'clandestine brothels disguised as hotels, restaurants, and tobacco or liquor shops [that] continued to pop up'.[7]

Given her subsequent career and her choice of a nom de guerre, it is reasonable to ask whether Caroline Lohmar had worked in the sex industry in Brussels, and whether that might have been how she met Stud Hodgson.

Research on the nineteenth century from other countries has shown that economic need was the most common circumstance pushing young women into the industry, so it is certainly possible that an orphan such as Caroline Lohmar might have taken that path.[8] Many of the sex workers in Brussels – especially in the higher-class houses – came from outside the city, and the higher the class of the brothel the further they were likely to have come. The age of consent in Belgium at this time was also no barrier: girls over the age of twelve could legally consent to sex, and Caroline was presumably with her family until she was in her teens (when her father died). It was therefore not impossible for a German-speaking teenager to be found on the streets of Brussels working in a *maison de passe* or an illegal brothel, or even in one of the Belgian *maisons de tolérance*, but proving it is not possible, because all the registers of 'public women' have been destroyed. We know Caroline and Stud Hodgson were in Brussels in 1871 because of the 'wedding' photograph, and we know her dress is unusual – so could it be that of a young sex worker?

If Caroline had been working in the sex industry in Brussels it could explain the photograph taken there, and the decision to marry in London, where her background would be less likely to be known or investigated, but is it likely that she would have met her husband that way? Stud Hodgson certainly came from a family of men who – by reputation and class – were familiar with brothels and mixing socially with less respectable women. His class background would also have meant he was familiar with working-class servant girls. But would Stud have taken up with a woman he met on the streets and dallied with in a *maison de passe* or an illegal clandestine brothel? And if he had found Caroline in a *maison de tolérance*, how easy would it have been for her to leave the establishment? Women working in the more expensive closed brothels in Belgium were required to purchase their clothing and goods from the madam in charge, and the debts they incurred made it almost impossible for the women to leave unless they found someone able and willing to pay the money owed.[9] Stud could possibly have afforded to do that. However, he was not in a position to have a woman's entry removed from the register of public women. Céleste de Chabrillan was a courtesan whose husband became Melbourne's first French consul.[10] They married for love but he was a count of the French aristocracy and she had been a sex worker, famously known as Mogador. The countess's memoirs show how difficult it was for women to have their names removed from the register of sex workers in France; it was only after Prince Napoleon (a nephew of Napoleon Bonaparte and cousin of Emperor Napoleon III) interceded on her behalf that she was able to have her name erased.[11] If the wife of a French count, with connections in very high places indeed, found it difficult to have her name removed from the register of public women, it was probably impossible for a young Prussian woman with an unknown English suitor to do so in Belgium.[12] And if Caroline Hodgson's name had been placed on such a register, is it likely she would have wished to draw attention to her servitude in such a system by adopting a name that reminded her of it?

There is no clear answer to the question of whether Stud Hodgson found Caroline Lohmar doing sex work in a brothel in Brussels, but if she had been present in a *maison de tolérance* as a domestic servant rather than as a sex worker it would explain many things about her subsequent career: she would have been familiar with the fashions of the day without having the means to fully emulate them, she would have gained invaluable insights into how such a place was run, and she would have had no trouble leaving whenever she chose. She might also have come away from the place with a sense of upper-class manners and luxury, and hence without a wish to escape its reputation. From Stud's point of view, he might well have been seduced by the quiet charms of a 'perfect little lady' he met in a *maison de tolérance*, but whose skills appeared domestic rather than sexual.[13]

Given her background as an orphan, it is highly probable that Caroline's qualifications and employment experience were limited to the domestic sphere. Her education would have been basic and the deaths of her mother and then stepmother, combined with her family's frequent house moves, would have given her little opportunity to learn the art of dressmaking or any other cottage industry. She gave no formal occupation when she married Stud at St George's, Hanover Square, but under the circumstances – marrying a man of higher social standing than her own – she would not be expected to do so. Of more interest is the fact that both husband and wife gave their address as 'No 26 South Molton Street'.

The address Stud and Caroline gave as their 'residence at the time of marriage' was a boarding house in upmarket Mayfair, run by a widow named Maria Meredith. At the time of the 1871 England census,[14] Mrs Meredith's lodgers included a 'colliery proprietor' and his wife, a student of the Royal Academy, an assistant at the British Museum and a 'gentleman' lodger. Mrs Meredith's ten-year-old granddaughter was also living with her, along with a twenty-year-old female servant from Durham. Ten years later, her granddaughter and a domestic servant were still in residence, with four boarders.[15] These 1881 lodgers were listed as two 'commercial clerks', one 'accountant', and a middle-aged man with 'income from dividends'. Mrs Meredith was seemingly running a boarding house for middle-class people, mainly young single men working in sub-professional roles. Since she did not take single women as lodgers, there are two possible ways in which Stud and Caroline might both have been living there at the time of their marriage: as a couple (in the way that the colliery proprietor and his wife were doing), or as individuals, with Stud as one of the working men (he gave the occupation 'clerk' on the shipping list) and Caroline as the domestic servant.

Living there as a married couple would have required them to deceive Mrs Meredith, because there is every indication that she was running a respectable boarding house and would not have accepted a de facto couple. Living there as a lodger and a servant is far more likely; Stud was the kind of lodger she took in, and Caroline was the right age and background for the servants she employed – working class, and the same age as the two servants in subsequent census records. The young servant girl recorded at 26 South Molton Street a few months after Caroline left also married a young man who had been a lodger; he was not a member of an elite English family, but by the time he was twenty-five he was employing two apprentices and his wife had a servant of her own.[16] Their marriage certificate also shows them residing at the same address at the time of their marriage.[17] Given her background Caroline would most likely have had the domestic skills for such work, but if she was living at 26 South Molton Street as a servant, how did she come to be in London? The answer might be found in Mrs Meredith's connections with the German-speaking community.

Mrs Maria Meredith's husband, Charles, was a plumber and glazier, and his business had obviously been a good one; when he died at South Molton Street in 1868 his wife was left relatively well provided for.[18] The property was hers, and she had a successful boarding house business to provide an income. As a couple they had raised four children, and the eldest was named Maria after her mother. This younger Maria Meredith married Andreas Furtwängler, a German watchmaker who had moved to London in 1849.[19] Alice Furtwängler, daughter of Andreas and Maria, was the ten-year-old granddaughter living with the elderly Mrs Meredith at South Molton Street in 1871.[20] The Furtwänglers were part of a community of German jewellers and watchmakers in London. They came from Baden near Bremen in Prussia, and the census records show a pattern of chain migration, with the young men starting out as lodgers, then marrying and bringing in family members and others to work in their businesses.[21] Andreas Furtwängler had followed his older brother, Ferdinand, and after Ferdinand died John took his place;[22] their business was in Drury Lane in central London, but life was not all work. Andreas joined the Euphrates Lodge of Freemasons in 1860, which meant he was mixing regularly with many of London's German and European businessmen. Along with most of the other married members of the Lodge, Andreas and Maria always had a young servant girl of Caroline's age to help with the domestic chores. Some of the masons would doubtless have brought lady's maids and children's nurses with them from home, and helped each other out by providing recommendations and references for servants. Andreas and Ferdinand had both travelled to London from Baden through Belgium, so Caroline could well have found her way from Prussia to Belgium to London in the company of one of these families.[23]

So why did Caroline Hodgson, brothel madam, choose to be called 'Madame Brussels'? It seems most likely that she chose the name simply for the effect it would have on its hearers. When England's *Obscene Publications Act* 1857 clamped down on publishers of erotic material, other European cities took up the industry with glee, but through the 1860s Brussels took the lead and became the 'epicentre of erotic publishing in Europe'.[24] By the end of the 1870s in Melbourne the mention of 'Brussels' would have invoked its reputation for both brothels and bawdy books among a certain class of men, and the use of the title 'Madame' would have signalled the nature of her business. The combination would have promised the elite version of the trade, simply because in Melbourne that is what being European meant: clients could expect culture, sophistication, a salon-like atmosphere, perhaps, or a mastery of the arts of arousal, and the mention of Brussels in particular implied regularly checked, disease-free women.[25]

In the end, Caroline's choice of the name 'Madame Brussels' was a clever advertising ploy, designed to turn her 'foreignness' – her accent and her language – into a commercial advantage. Melbourne's cultural cringe towards Europe provided her with an opportunity, and she took it. By choosing to call herself 'Madame Brussels' rather than 'Madame Paris' – after a place she had probably never been – Caroline stuck to what she knew, and avoided being linked with Melbourne's somewhat seedier 'Café de Paris' in Bourke Street. Caroline was a woman who forged her own path, but that is not to say she did not have models to follow.

8.

THE SHAPE OF A 'FLASH BROTHEL'

'A cottage with a double coachhouse, a cottage of gentility' for select guests, and a couple of terrace houses higher up for rough work.[1]
—'Memories of Brussels', *Truth* (Melbourne), 31 March 1906, p. 6

WHEN SARAH FRASER, KITTY WEST and Lewis Allen (Mrs Fraser's landlord) died, Melbourne lost the top tier of its brothel madams, owners and landlords in a short few years around 1880. The police attitude was changing too; they wanted to clear the brothels away from the approaches to Melbourne's international exhibition at the newly built (now Royal) Exhibition Buildings that year, but Mrs Fraser's influence was such that they waited until after her death before clearing Stephen (now Exhibition) Street. Captain Standish (the Chief Commissioner of Police who introduced the Duke to Mrs Fraser's house) retired soon after, completing the shift to a new generation. The 1880 clearance did not put the sex workers out of business, and in fact they basked in all the work coming from the exhibition patrons, but it moved Melbourne's better class brothels and put Caroline Hodgson's house at the epicentre.

Caroline flourished through the 1880s; she was top of the tree in Lonsdale Street East, but that does not mean life was easy. The sale of alcohol was a big

50

part of her profits, and she had to learn how to manage drunken customers. When two men took exception to her methods they assaulted her, as a policeman reported later:

> they went in here and got a bottle of beer, and had a glass each out of it, and paid 5s for it, and there was some portion remaining in the bottle, and Madame Bussel [*sic*] took away the remaining portion that was in the bottle and wanted them to shout another bottle; and they got a little 'riled' at that, and she was pushing them out, and they pulled her out as they were going.[2]

He added that he 'had very little doubt that the woman had been ill-treated by someone, but whether she brought that on herself or not I did not know'.

It was a tough business, but Caroline was ambitious; in terms of price she covered the whole trade – apart from the cheapest back-lane cribs – by making her own house exclusive and renting other houses for lower-class custom. Her fancy establishment, though, had some close competition from Mrs Kemp in Drummond Street.

Mary Jane Kemp was a married woman who took her children and moved to Melbourne without her husband not long after their second child was born in 1860.[3] She built her business first in Fitzroy, before buying her own place in the very best area of Drummond Street, Carlton.[4] Mrs Kemp kept her business extremely quiet, but by 1882 it was known as 'a very flash place', with one policeman describing it as 'more select' than Mrs Fraser's: 'the cab drove by, and the place was always shut up'.[5] The police would not interfere unless there was some kind of disturbance providing an excuse, and Mrs Kemp, better than Caroline, made sure there was none. The only report involving police at her house was through the theft of 'a pair of gold earrings, star-shape, set with a single diamond in each. Value, £50'.[6] But it was theft *from* her, not theft *by* her. Mrs Kemp was a few years ahead of Caroline Hodgson, and she, too, invested in property.

Mrs Kemp's brothel and residence (1872–95)
in Drummond Street, Carlton

When she died in 1895 she was able to leave her daughters five houses, including her two-storey brothel in Drummond Street.[7]

There are no known photographs, etchings or sketches that show what Caroline Hodgson's house looked like, but streetscapes include the location of her rented houses. It is possible to pinpoint on them where she lived and worked, but her home is not visible because it was set back from the street, even though most of the surrounding buildings fronted directly onto the footpath. She (and no doubt her clients) kept a deliberately low profile for her most exclusive establishment. The clearest photograph was taken a year or two before Caroline bought 169 Lonsdale Street East in 1876, and all that can be seen is a series of fences beneath a sign indicating the presence of a 'Wood Yard'.[8] Number 169 is behind the second of the four fences from the left.

Lonsdale Street, 1870–75, looking west from Spring Street

The photograph also shows the houses Caroline began renting around 1879 when she greatly expanded her business and adopted the name Madame Brussels. She took over Henry Seyfarth's shop next to the Star of the East Hotel (where she obtained after-hours champagne), and she also rented the next building, part of which was previously occupied by W.H. Dorsey, clothes cleaner. As one of Madame Brussels' establishments it was known as Bellevue House.[9] All of these rented properties were owned by the same man, Robert King, who had built them in the gold-rush years of the early 1850s; they were her less expensive venues.[10]

Caroline's main house, 169 Lonsdale Street East, was built before the gold rushes took off in mid-1851. It began as a brick house with four rooms, one of which was designated as a kitchen, but another brick room was added in 1860.[11] Caroline herself extended the house by another two rooms before 1880, although there is no record of a builder having submitted the required 'Intention to Build' notice to the city surveyor.[12] Nor is there any record of the city surveyor checking up on the omission. Rules did not necessarily apply to everyone in nineteenth-century Melbourne, at least not if you knew the right people, but perhaps Caroline and her builder were simply ignorant of the requirement.

Two years after extending 169, she purchased 171 Lonsdale Street East, next door on the east (in front of the bushes beneath the 'Wood Yard' sign).[13] She paid £665 in cash for it, giving her two adjoining properties in Lonsdale Street, but the majority of women boarding with Madame Brussels were still located in the houses she rented closer to Spring Street (and to parliament house and the government offices filled with male clerks). Her purchase of 171 was about buying garden space rather than additional rooms; she appears to have been trying to recreate or emulate the kind of outdoor space the wealthy men she was attracting (or hoped to attract) were used to, both at home and at their city club. At least as early as 1860 the Melbourne Club, for instance, had an enclosed area where members might disport themselves on balmy evenings.

While the block of 171 was mainly garden and offered Caroline the opportunity to develop a similar environment, there was also a small wooden house on it. At least in the beginning the cottage was let separately; the carpenter who was in residence when she bought it remained there, and doubtless made himself useful at times.[14]

The location of Madame Brussels' brothels in the 1880s: 32–34 Lonsdale Street in oval, rented brothels in circle

Caroline's next purchase was a house outside the city, in St Kilda; it was only two and a half years since her last purchase, but again she paid cash and did not need a mortgage.[15]

The house was a substantial free-standing Victorian villa with a bay window and a side drive. It was only a few years old, and appears to have been purely an investment; St Kilda was a long way from Lonsdale Street, and through the decade and more that she owned it Caroline never lived there, instead renting it to several long-staying commercial salesmen. For many of the years that Caroline owned number 76 Loch Street, David Gaunson and his family occupied a very similar house next door at number 78. Gaunson was a solicitor and a parliamentarian, and he was well known for his spirited behaviour, occasionally in defence of women in the sex industry. Like Samuel Gillott, Gaunson was an intelligent lawyer who smarted over the treatment of sex workers, and of women in general. He was a champion of the underdog – he had in previous years defended Ned Kelly.

Historian Geoffrey Serle has said that Gaunson was Caroline Hodgson's 'legal adviser', but Gillott's firm had that role until at least 1906, when Gaunson first defended Caroline in court.[16] Nevertheless it is reasonable to think that Caroline Hodgson knew David Gaunson from early in her career, whether through his business or hers, or through the proximity of their houses in St Kilda.

Since Caroline bought at the beginning of the land boom, this first St Kilda house probably rose considerably in value over the following decade, as did her Lonsdale Street properties.

Caroline's earnings from her business in Lonsdale Street seem extraordinary, because after four more months she added another property to her portfolio: 167 Lonsdale Street, to the west of 169, directly beneath the 'Wood Yard' sign.[17] That gave her three adjoining properties fronting onto the main street.

167 Lonsdale Street East was to become Caroline Hodgson's private residence.[18] Curiously, she called it 'Studholme Villa', and she christened it with a formal party on 8 August that year.[19] It was her birthday.

By the mid-1880s Caroline had successfully built up a different kind of business to the usual house-brothel, turning her three adjoining properties into an exclusive entertainment venue – 'Dancing at 9 o'clock' – while her rented houses continued with the more traditional sex trade.

Invitation to Caroline Hodgson's birthday party at her residence,
34 Lonsdale Street

9.

A DAY IN THE LIFE
OF A 'FLASH MADAM'

CAROLINE HODGSON LEFT BEHIND NO DIARIES that recorded her doings, or letters that described the shape of her days. But from court reports and newspaper stories we can put together a rough picture of her everyday life. We know that her business kept her up every night until 3 or 4 a.m., and in her early days she took a glass of wine (or champagne) with her clients, so she probably rose late in the morning and started each day quietly, taking breakfast, perhaps, and consulting with her housekeeper about the practical details of running the houses.[1] There were the stocks of alcohol to be checked, the cleaning and laundry to be seen to, the supplies of bacon, eggs, bread and milk to be replenished along with the caviar and pâté de foie gras, and doubtless at times there was the question of settling menus with the cook. Meals were served to both the women and their clients, though the produce from local oyster saloons was a favourite late-night snack at all of Melbourne's brothels.[2]

During an ordinary day there would perhaps have been accounts to be settled with the tradespeople the houses relied on, and banking to be done, with cash coming in from both boarders and clients, and of course in that era there were cheques as well. Sometimes payments went direct to the women, but mostly clients paid the house.

There was also gardening and maintenance to be arranged and pianos to be tuned. And while some dressmakers and milliners may have visited for fittings and the like, choosing fabrics and styles would have meant attending shops. Doctors might have been called for home visits at any time, but dental treatment and legal advice also meant going out during business hours.

After supper the women in Caroline's houses would have done what sex workers in brothels did everywhere: sat around talking, smoking, doing their hair, singing, generally amusing themselves until a client appeared. Caroline would have spent her evenings monitoring them all, moving between the houses, facilitating a good time, encouraging the men to drink and spend and the women to flirt and relieve the men of their cash. There was usually a pianist in attendance at her main house for singing and dancing, with the dance card issued for Caroline's birthday party in 1885 listing both waltzes and polkas for couples, and quadrilles for four couples forming a square.

On nights when she went to the theatre Caroline still checked in on her houses. One night in 1882 she was about to set off for the theatre when two men arrived and called for a glass of wine.[3] She stayed. A bottle of champagne was opened in the front parlour, the men drank it with the women of the house, put a half sovereign down on the table and then Caroline went off to the theatre. The two men, it transpired, were customs officers, and thought they had caught her red-handed; they charged her with selling liquor without a licence. That caused Caroline to sail off to her solicitor, Samuel Gillott, and ask him to defend her. Gillott argued in court that when one of the men put the half sovereign down on the table it was one of the other women who picked it up, not Caroline. He said the wine was in fact 'given to the Custom officers out of good fellowship' and the money could equally have been 'given to defray an outstanding debt'. The Police Magistrate, Joseph Panton, deliberated with his brother magistrates and agreed that 'there was some doubt about the sale of the liquor' and struck the case out. Caroline sailed home again, doubtless pleased to have escaped conviction.

Managing multiple brothels meant that Caroline's days were full of people; the work of maintaining full bedrooms was as much about minimising the high turnover of boarders as it was about maximising the knocks on the door from clients, and that meant developing relationships with the women inside her house as well as the men outside it. Advancing the business also meant building up the trust of her clients until 'there was a tradition pretty well established … that unless a man was an utter damn fool he was as safe at Brussels' as at Scott's or Menzies'. Safe in reputation as in pocket, for "Madame" knew too much to blab.'[4]

Caroline provided a haven for her clients, but it was a tenuous security for many of the women. In 1884 a man called John O'Brien, who had been living in the cottage at no. 171, wrote to *The Herald* effectively accusing Caroline of abducting his wife and children; he demanded that the police 'move on the matter' or else he would 'create a disturbance at Madame Brussels' house'.[5] She responded with her own description of events that day:

Sir,— I absolutely deny the charges made against me by a bootmaker named O'Brien which appeared in last evening's HERALD viz: that of harboring [*sic*] and enticing his wife and children. Mrs O'Brien has worked for me for from fifteen to eighteen months but has left my service some time. She was always well paid for what work she did. I allowed her husband, self and children to live in one of my cottages rent free. On Saturday night, between 8 and 9 o'clock, Mrs O'Brien came to me crying, and severely injured by her husband, and asked me for a night's lodging, being afraid to return home. I gave her money for herself and children, as they had no food in the house, her husband being out of work and drinking for weeks. I then sent her to the hospital, where her wounds were dressed. She stayed that night at my house, and left next day. This is all I know of the matter.[6]

Such disturbances may not have been a common occurrence, but violent men were certainly part of her experience.

PART III:
THE HALCYON DAYS

10.

THE LEGAL SETTING

IN THE ROILING, GOLD-CHASING 1850S the women working in the sex industry in Victoria had little difficulty fitting in and being accepted as part of the frontier environment. They lived anywhere they could afford in the towns and goldfield settlements and they were highly visible: part of the general hustle and grasping atmosphere created by the influx of miners. Victoria's first homegrown attempt to regulate the industry came in an act 'for the better prevention of vagrancy' in 1852; women doing sex work could be deemed 'idle and disorderly persons' under crimes relating to drunkenness, 'riotous or indecent behaviour', or 'having no visible lawful means or insufficient lawful means of support'.[1] Then in 1854 it became illegal for owners of refreshment houses to 'suffer prostitutes or persons of notoriously bad character to be assembled therein'.[2] Women could be excluded from places of ordinary social interaction on the basis of their reputation as sex workers, allowing police to direct where the women congregated and whom they associated with. From 1864 police could also take the women's children away.[3] Any child whose mother had a reputation as a sex worker could be brought before two magistrates and sent to an industrial school for between one and seven years.

There were also penalties for procuring girls under the age of twenty-one 'to have illicit carnal connexion with any man'.[4] 'Procuring' was an accusation that generally arose when journalists sniffed a good story about a colourful brothel madam and took the opportunity to whip up a fine case of moral panic, but formal charges of procuring were rarely brought to court and even more rarely prosecuted successfully. The case of Madame Diana de Beaumont is a good example. Billed as 'a notorious procuress' who 'enticed, by false advertisements, young girls into her house for the purposes of prostitution',[5] the prosecution was unable to prove she had placed the advertisements for shop girls produced as evidence, or that they were concocted 'with the object of decoying innocent girls to a life of infamy'.[6] So she was charged with being the keeper of a disorderly house rather than procuring, and after giving her word that she would vacate her brothel within a week – and then having done so – she was discharged without conviction.

The policing of prostitution before Caroline entered the business was therefore not intended to shut down the industry but to keep it, along with other disreputable activities, well-behaved and out of sight. Charges of 'disorderly behaviour' against individuals were laid to keep raucous, rough men and especially riotous women off the streets – a second offence relating to 'disorderly behaviour' could result in gaol for *two* years – and charges against the 'keepers of disorderly houses' were used to close down any rowdy anti-social venues that were disturbing the peace.

This relatively tolerant gold-rush period was ending just as Caroline arrived in Melbourne. As the alluvial gold ran out and the miners either decamped to the newest strike elsewhere or settled into more traditional labouring lives, Victoria developed a more respectable veneer. The wealth that had flowed into the community as a result of the gold, combined with the social changes brought about by the growth of the middle classes, produced a self-consciousness in the community about respectability. There was pride among those who had risen in the world, with money providing the means to assert and display their new status; the rules of respectable behaviour provided another means of measuring their success.[7]

About the time when Caroline moved to Lonsdale Street, wealthy people in Melbourne began moving their residences away from the central business district and into the leafy surrounding suburbs, cloistering their women in large houses on even larger gardened blocks behind hedges and fences. Caroline's inner-city pleasure garden, set close to the businessmen's workplaces, emulated that ideal; she played to this wealthy end of town by providing services in the kind of environment that matched their experience and their aspirations. She supplied champagne and quadrilles rather than beer and skittles, and for entertainment she provided women who could play the dual role of nice in public and naughty in private.[8] But in parallel with middle-class women's move to the suburbs, society demanded a less visible public presence from women generally, and sex workers in particular.[9] When a quiet, controlled and demure woman was the social ideal, a loud, flamboyant and expressive sex worker was liable to be seen as offensive, but the law did not change. Instead 'vagrancy' became a weapon to prevent the business activities of sex workers offending the sensibility of respectable people.

Charges that were laid against sex workers were heard in the Police Courts (now the Magistrates' Court). The men who sat on the bench – they were all men – were usually justices of the peace: respectable men appointed for their fine, upstanding reputation who donated their time for the good of the community. But the fact that they were rarely legally trained meant their decisions were often based on what they considered to be justice rather than the letter of the law. When it came to dispensing justice to sex workers, their decisions often had more to do with their personal beliefs about the morality or otherwise of prostitution than with any considered interpretation of the legislation or the evidence. It often happened that a man sitting on a police court bench hearing a case of disorderly behaviour against an attractive young woman dismissed the charges with a shrug, but at the same time on the same day a man sitting on a police court bench elsewhere in the city might send a similar young woman to gaol because he believed that commercial sex was a blight upon respectable Melbourne.

In Caroline's early years as a brothel owner, when Captain Standish was chief commissioner, and again at the beginning of Hussey Chomley's reign, the police often voiced their frustration over the refusal of magistrates to convict women they brought up for disorderly behaviour.[10] As a result their standard line to people complaining about sex workers became 'these women have to live somewhere', and their preferred responses were to charge the more difficult women with disorderly behaviour, to warn the nuisances to move on, and to leave the quiet houses alone.[11] Another standard line in response to complainants was that 'as long as these people conduct themselves in an orderly manner the police have no legal power to eject them', despite commonly threatening to charge the women with disorderly behaviour in order to force them to move.[12] But in the early 1880s the police decided to try a different tack.

Samuel Nathan was a furniture dealer in Bourke Street, and – as the evidence would show – his business involved renting houses from owners, furnishing them from his shop's stock, and then subletting the furnished houses to sex workers for highly inflated amounts.[13] It was a lucrative business model because sex workers paid higher than usual rents, and as his profits accumulated he leased and bought more properties to use the same way. In 1883 the police set out to make an example of him. They charged one of his tenants in South Melbourne – 'a rather well-looking young woman named Minnie Fitzgerald' – and two other women from her house under the vagrancy provisions. The intention of the police was that once they had obtained convictions against the women, they could then charge their landlord, Samuel Nathan, under section 50 of *The Justices of the Peace Statute 1865* with 'aiding and abetting' unlawful practices – that is, aiding and abetting the women in their crime of being idle and disorderly persons. The major difficulty for the police (they thought) lay in the timing, because it was critical to their case against Nathan that Minnie Fitzgerald be available to give evidence. They therefore needed her to be convicted before Nathan's charges were heard, but she could not be out on bail because she could easily forfeit the money and leave Melbourne, in which case the prosecution of Nathan would fall apart.

The case was first heard at the South Melbourne Police Court; Minnie was actually arrested in the city and should have been brought before the

Melbourne Police Court, but that would have meant the case being heard by a sympathetic police magistrate.[14] Instead the case was heard in front of volunteer justices of the peace. After hearing evidence about the 'disgraceful scenes [that] were nightly enacted at the place' they promptly convicted all three of the women, but remanded them for sentence and agreed to the police request to refuse them bail. As it turned out the court's paperwork was faulty and Minnie Fitzgerald's lawyer managed to free her on bail despite the magistrates' refusal. The police promptly rearrested her 'as a witness unwilling and unlikely to attend unless compelled to do so' and gaoled her again, before justifying their action by inventing a story about her hiding under the counter of the shop man who provided her surety.

When the women came up for sentencing the following week the police asked for the hearing to be put off until the day of Nathan's trial (which had been delayed). They also asked for Fitzgerald's bail to be refused again. The women's lawyer, Mr Daly, pointed out the unfairness and illegality of the police request:

MR DALY: I never heard of such a course of proceedings. Bail can't be refused.

THE CHAIRMAN: I am quite aware that bail can't be refused, legally speaking, unless it is shown that the accused party is endeavouring to evade justice by getting out of the colony.

MR DALY: This is a charge under the Vagrancy section of the Police Offences Statute … They are innocent until they are found guilty, and they have a right to appeal against your decision. I don't think they should be kept in gaol merely for the convenience of the Inspector …

INSPECTOR TOOHEY: I wish the Bench to understand that we don't do this to persecute the girl, but simply—

MR DALY: You can't refuse bail … All we ask you is to fix it and not deny the women justice.

THE CHAIRMAN: We are not in the habit of denying anyone justice.

MR DALY: I ask you to read the information. There is not the slightest evidence in the document that the women are about to leave the colony.

To get over the difficulty, the magistrates finally did set bail for Minnie Fitzgerald – but in the impossible amount of two sureties of £300 each. *The Herald* reported that 'As Mr Daly said, this would indicate that the girl was the most valuable of her class in the city.' It kept the women in gaol.

When the case against Samuel Nathan eventually came up for hearing, the three women, convicted as idle and disorderly persons, were first brought from gaol to receive their sentences. David Gaunson appeared for two of them. He said the police had 'most unwarrantably interfered with the process of the law', and he 'regarded it as … grossly outrageous, and as … an arbitrary stretch and abuse of power'. He was clearly incensed at the underlying moral judgment and mistreatment of the women on the charge of disorderly behaviour, and to make his point he went on:

With very few exceptions – and he did not pretend to be one – there was not a man in the community including the gentleman who was prosecuting (the inspector of police) who would not have to take his stand upon the floor of a police court and run the risk of an irate justice sending him to prison for a period of 12 months (Laughter.)

Minnie Fitzgerald's barrister agreed:

Mr. Purves. – Including the Bench. (Laughter).

The magistrates rejected the lawyers' arguments and committed Minnie Fitzgerald to another week's gaol to await Samuel Nathan's adjourned case on the same extravagant bail conditions. When Nathan's case was finally heard it became a contest between the prosecutor, Sir Bryan O'Loghlen, who was well known and popular with the magistrates, and Nathan's defending solicitor, Samuel Gillott, who was a stickler for the letter of the law. The clash came to a head with the chairman of the bench making the following statement of intent:

> Mr Gillott should not forget that it was the desire of the general public to put down such places. There were a number of marriageable young women who were deprived of husbands through these houses of ill fame. Young men who were capable of marrying were induced by those women to put off marriage. If those places are allowed to go on it will not only effect this generation, but generation after generation will be affected with diseases contracted through the toleration of these houses for the practice of immorality. It is the duty of the police and magistrates to help to put down these places, and we are determined to do justice to the community.

Doing justice to the community, according to this bench of magistrates, involved stretching the evidence and misusing the law to suit their moral judgments. As it happened, one of the women they had convicted of having no visible lawful means of support was actually the servant in the house, not a sex worker. Working as a servant meant that she did, in fact, have lawful means of support, but by the time her conviction was quashed the poor woman had spent several weeks in gaol as a direct result of the magistrates' error. In Nathan's case, the magistrates convicted him and sentenced him to hard labour for twelve months in accordance with their beliefs about what was good for the community.

With that decision made, Mr Gillott immediately gave notice of appeal. It was heard by the Court of General Sessions (now the County Court) the following February, in front of a judge assisted by a police magistrate with negligible legal training.[15] At one point His Honour remarked, 'I must say I never saw a conviction like this in my life,' and later he added, 'a prostitute must live. She has a perfect right to be a prostitute, and there is nothing illegal about it so long as she conducts her house quietly, and is not a nuisance to the neighborhood [*sic*].' He believed the conviction should be quashed, but the police magistrate disagreed on similar grounds to the South Melbourne magistrates'. Rather than fighting about the law the divided bench decided to pass the matter on to the next General Sessions. By that time, despite the best efforts of the police, Minnie Fitzgerald had managed to catch the train to Sydney and disappear, supposedly with a tidy £50 to set her up in a new life in America. Samuel Nathan's conviction was quashed, and the police made no further attempts to prosecute landlords by this means. It had been an expensive failure. Nathan told *The Herald* that he had 'decided not to, in any way, do business with improper houses or people in the future, and that his houses are now being let to respectable tenants. The Salvation Army has taken some of them.' The houses he owned around Caroline Hodgson in Lonsdale Street, however, continued as brothels, except for 167 Lonsdale Street. He sold that to Caroline early in 1885 to become part of Madame Brussels' infamous empire.[16]

Late that year Victoria's Legislative Council passed a Protection of Women Bill aimed at punishing procurers and brothel madams and raising the age of consent for girls to sixteen, but it also made it a crime for landlords to rent premises to be used as brothels.[17] Somehow the Legislative Assembly, with its seats filled with men of property, was not interested in placing the bill on the order of business. It was delayed for six months and then, despite a deputation to the government from the Salvation Army and the Society for the Promotion of Morality, it fell off the list altogether; it was not revived for another half decade.[18]

Throughout her career Caroline Hodgson styled herself as a 'boarding house keeper' and collected weekly rent from her 'boarders', providing services for them and their visitors in a discreet setting. The women dressed in the best silks and satins (sometimes at her expense) and sometimes went to the theatre, but in the 1880s they did not solicit in public. As Constable Stokes reported in 1889, her women were 'well conducted and seldom come out on the streets at night', an observation which was confirmed by some young women at her house who said she advised them 'not to go out as the people might see us', and 'if anyone came for us we could be down at the cottage and say we were servants'.[19] That advice was designed both to protect the women and to ensure that Caroline was not susceptible to charges of 'running a disorderly house'. If it could have been shown that her house was frequented by 'thieves or persons who have no visible lawful means of support' she could have ended up in gaol for a year, but Madame Brussels' clientele knew to seek her attentions past the white picket fence and through the front door of 169 (later 32) Lonsdale Street East, where the façade of quiet propriety gave way to hedonistic delights if their wallets were full enough.

So while sex workers in the 1850s were occupying houses all over Melbourne, by the 1880s many were finding it more convenient to locate their business in the north-east corner of the city's old street grid where the landlords accepted them, the government offices and entertainment precincts (from the Exhibition Buildings to Bourke Street) provided custom, and the neighbours – 'the poor, the destitute, the non-British immigrants ... and larrikins' – were less likely to complain.[20] Police hastened the influx through the 1880s by using the vagrancy laws to remove women from other areas. Senior Constable McHugh reported in April 1887, for instance, that 'since last July fully 100 prostitutes have been locked up out of Collins Street alone on a charge of insulting behaviour. The P[lain] C[lothes] Police are there nightly and give more attention to that street than to any other place in the City.'[21] That kind of police activity dealt with women soliciting in areas where they were not wanted, but for those living near respectable people who complained, the police simply threatened them with charges of disorderliness if they stayed where they were, giving the women an incentive to move of their own accord.[22] And move they did – often to the area around Caroline Hodgson's brothels, if not into them. She had chosen her location well, which is why she had Samuel Nathan for a neighbour.

11.

A CURIOUS GENTLEMEN'S CLUB

MELBOURNE WAS A BRITISH CITY in the nineteenth century, albeit a colonial one. It was also a global marketplace, and although most of its outward goods – gold and wool – went to Britain, its inward goods (which in the early years meant almost everything *except* gold and wool) came from anywhere and everywhere. In the early 1850s, when the mad influx of gold-seekers caused traders in Melbourne to bring in whatever they could find from the closest possible source, that mainly meant goods from ports in neighbouring colonies, especially Sydney, Launceston and Adelaide. But ships were like street hawkers in those days, trading whatever might be profitable from one place to another – so as soon as news about Melbourne's gold spread abroad, vessels appeared in Port Phillip Bay bringing furniture from China, prunes from Mauritius, nutmegs from Singapore and even tea from Belfast, in the hopes of turning a profit. There was also a strong reciprocal trade with New Zealand, and Hong Kong was supplying straw hats, dried fish and tea as well as opium; ships from Boston were bringing dried apples and cornmeal, and traders from Chile were providing essential grains and flour as well as walnuts.

With the goods, too, came ideas, especially from other English-speaking places, such as New York and San Francisco, and from the centres of

European culture, such as Paris. Melbourne, however, only tended to listen eagerly to ideas from Home – the United Kingdom. Despite being a global city in terms of trade, in its attitudes and style Melbourne was British to its bootstraps, with a gold-rush flavour of brashness and wealth, and the men who ruled Melbourne had an apparently unswerving confidence in the ideas peddled by Britain to its Empire, as opposed to those from 'French', 'American' or 'Oriental' sources. So, while Melbourne women closely followed French fashions, when it came to social and sexual relations they followed British customs. London's habit of structuring social connections through the use of calling cards continued among the upper class, despite its unsuitability in Melbourne's climate and sprawling suburbs, and Government House set the standards and tone for acceptable behaviour despite the lack of an aristocracy.[1]

With regard to sex work, there were no *maisons de tolérance* or *maisons de passe* in Melbourne – they were spoken of derisively as 'the French system' – but nor were there any forced medical examinations or lock hospitals such as Britain introduced through the contagious diseases acts of the 1860s.[2] Instead the sex industry in Melbourne was left to run itself through most of the nineteenth century, on condition that the women didn't make a nuisance of themselves. Sex workers could readily be seen on the streets and in the theatres, but respectable women pretended not to see them. Young middle-class women from respectable families were expected to remain virgins until marriage, but their brothers were 'sowing their wild oats' with impunity, and their fathers were doing whatever they regarded as 'necessary' for their own sexual wellbeing. Whom, exactly, the young men were sowing their wild oats with, or where their fathers were being entertained, were questions that were studiously avoided, and such pre- or extra-marital activities continued as long as families were not forced to confront the reality of sex workers and brothels. At the same time the women who reaped the wild oats of these young men and served their fathers' desires were widely and soundly condemned in public discourse.

The Victorian era – that part of the British nineteenth century encompassing the birth and explosive growth of the city of Melbourne – bears a reputation for such double-standards and prudishness, but in Britain at least there was a lot going on beneath the surface. The idea of respectability might have meant modesty, domesticity and ignorance of sexual matters for women, but for men there was also a great deal of questioning and exploration going on, and at least some of it was taking place through the dissemination of what came to be known as pornography.[3]

In 1857, England introduced legislation to control obscene publications, to rid itself of 'the Holywell Street literature' – Holywell being a street of 'unprincipled vendors of demoralizing books and pictures', whose 'old temples of infamy' were inclined to 'outrage decency by the display of vile obscenities in their windows'.[4] Making the trade illegal, of course, did not stop it, especially for men of means, but the bulk of the publishing moved to Paris, Amsterdam and Brussels, and the purchase price then had to include the cost of smuggling it back to Britain.[5] In the same period Melbourne appears to have had no substantial trade of its own, either in publishing or selling such material, and Victoria was slow to follow England's lead in terms of legislation. From 1852 the colony used its customs act to prevent 'indecent or obscene' materials crossing its borders, and added 'blasphemous' materials to the list in 1857.[6] There is no doubt that smuggling occurred, but there was little concern about such materials in Melbourne until 1875, when Richard Egan Lee, the editor and proprietor of a risqué broadsheet called the *Police News*, was charged with the publication of an indecent picture entitled 'The St. Kilda Beauty and the Young Squatter'.[7] It apparently depicted 'one of the most obscene pictures – if such a smudge as it was can be called a picture – and filthy description of a sinful intercourse between a young man and woman that could possibly be imagined'.[8]

Mr Lee pleaded innocence on the grounds that he was unaware of the obscenity before publication, and the jury (all men) pronounced him 'not guilty'.[9] A subsequent publication from Mr Lee, however, was 'so outrageously offensive and scurrilous' that there were objections from the public, but the existing decades-old legislation made it difficult to success-fully prosecute the publisher.[10] The government responded quickly by passing new legislation against such material, largely copying the English act of 1857.[11] But England had moved on; it was about to launch its old *Obscene Publications Act* against a different class of literature entirely: in 1877 Charles Bradlaugh and Annie Besant were charged with publishing a pamphlet which described male and female genitals and reproductive organs in great detail, and provided extensive advice and information about contra-ception.[12] It was neither scurrilous nor blasphemous, but Bradlaugh and Besant were convicted of publishing obscene material and were sentenced to gaol. Their conviction was overturned on appeal, and sales of the pam-phlet soared. At least one copy got past Victoria's customs clerk undamaged, because there was a Sunday lecture on it in Melbourne soon after the con-viction but before the appeal.[13]

While Bradlaugh and Besant were openly challenging the meaning of obscenity in England, Bradlaugh was also part of a more clandestine group of British men who were exploring the minutiae of different genitalia and cultural expressions of sexual behaviour, and contributing to the under-ground current of sexual discourse and experimentation that was trickling through English society. The group he belonged to was known as the Cannibal Club, and it has become the subject of significant academic research around the development of pornography in England.[14] The identity of several members of the group raises the question of whether the interests of the club were in any way represented or duplicated in Melbourne.

The Cannibal Club began in 1863 as an offshoot of the Anthropological Society of London, which in turn was an offshoot of the Ethnological Society. The Ethnological Society, which was interested in the scientific study of humankind, had made the apparently outrageous decision to admit women to its ranks, and since a number of its male members found 'their presence in meetings inhibited frank discussion of all facets of human behaviour, including sexuality', they decided to set up an alternative – female-free – society of their own.[15] Hence the Anthropological Society of

London.[16] But even having their very own society free of the restraining influence of women was not enough for some of the men; they also wanted to be able to explore subjects that the rest of British society regarded as deviant or beyond the pale of ordinary discussion, no matter how scientific, in more convivial surroundings (again without women present). The subjects of interest often involved detailed descriptions of different sexual anatomies and behaviours, and since such discussions were seemingly best accompanied by hearty meals and lusty consumption of alcoholic beverages, the men set up a dining club that met at a restaurant near Leicester Square – the Cannibal Club. There they indulged in pseudo-scientific conversation on topics that ranged from cannibalism to clitoridectomy, and from fetishes to flagellation.[17] These men were generally well-heeled members of Britain's elite, and they included several Oxford dons, the poet Swinburne, and the Lords Houghton and Penzance. George Augustus Sala, the journalist who christened 'Marvellous Melbourne' during his lengthy visit in 1885, was also a member, as was Stud Hodgson's uncle, General Studholme Hodgson.

The word 'pornography' was not coined until 1864, but according to scholars today these men of the Cannibal Club wrote and published most of the pornography that was produced in England from the 1860s to the 1880s, which includes the period when Stud Hodgson was back in England before marrying Caroline and sailing to Melbourne in 1871.[18] The generally moneyed and influential position in society of these men of the Cannibal Club allowed them to evade the *Obscene Publications Act* by publishing anonymously or under pseudonyms; General (then Colonel) Hodgson, for example, was 'one of the authors of the notorious *An Experimental Lecture on Flagellation* by 'Colonel Spanker', issued … in 1878–79'.[19] He is also credited by most scholars as having authored *The Pleasures of Cruelty: Being a Sequel to the Reading of Justine and Juliette by the Marquis de Sade* in 1886, though his name does not appear on it.[20] These men also invented at least one publishing company and utilised printers that were able to move their businesses quickly when they needed to evade police attention.[21] And since one of their number, Frederick Hankey, had been in residence in

Paris since the 1840s, and another (Henry Spencer Ashbee) regularly visited Brussels, Paris and other European centres for his business, they were also able to import materials relatively freely, including, reputedly, in diplomatic bags.[22]

The meetings of the Anthropological Society of London may have been quasi-scientific, but the meetings of the Cannibal Club seem to have been more social, and much of the bonhomie related to their shared interest in sadomasochistic practices such as flagellation.[23] Whipping as a path to sexual ecstasy was known as *le vice anglais* ('the English vice') in the nineteenth century, and current research in psychology links it with the British cultural phenomenon of sending children away to boarding school from a very early age. Boys were brought up in a system where corporal punishment in the form of caning or birching was meted out in a power pyramid from the headmaster down through the senior boys to the youngest ones (who often started boarding at age five).[24]

The boys were meant to be learning the kind of discipline and resilience that men needed in order to become leaders and rulers throughout the Empire, but for many of them the abandonment, cruelty and physical abuse of the system led to deficits in their capacity for both empathy and intimacy; they also led to a sexual association between pain and pleasure.[25] General Hodgson and his confrères at the Cannibal Club fitted this pattern of boarding school trauma, and works such as *The Pleasures of Cruelty* explored the links between flagellation, control and sexual pleasure (the subtitle of the 'Experimental Lecture' by Colonel Spanker is '*on the exciting and voluptuous pleasures to be derived from crushing and humiliating the spirit of a beautiful and modest young lady*'). Members of the Cannibal Club were especially intrigued by the scientific aspects of the connection between pain inflicted on the buttocks and genital stimulation.

Whipping was not just an 'English vice'; it was part of the upbringing and cultural milieu of Australia's gentlemen too; Melbourne's very own *Cole's Funny Picture Book* series shows a similar fascination with 'flogging'. Contrast the teacher's pleasure with the students' pain.

Cole's Patent Whipping Machine for Flogging Naughty Boys in School

So what did Caroline Hodgson know of this particular sexual proclivity? Her husband and his brother appear to have been educated on the Continent before being placed in an English boarding school at a later age than was usual, and they only stayed a very short time. Stud's time in the police force included some dogged work obtaining convictions in cases that suggest he had an abhorrence for cruelty, and perhaps his early exit from the English boarding school system is an indication of his rejection of those values.[26] But would he have discussed any of that with his wife? And given that his uncle was an active member of this band of sexual adventurers, was Stud aware of the activities and interests of the Cannibal Club, and did he pass that awareness on? Did Madame Brussels cater to such tastes in her Lonsdale Street business?

In the 1880s a woman known as Mrs Jeffries held a similar position in London's sex-work industry to that of Caroline Hodgson in Melbourne. Her brothels were quietly if not secretly run, they were expensive and exclusive, and they catered for gentlemen rather than tradesmen or manual workers. Mrs Jeffries had quite an empire of brothels, and two of them offered specialised sadomasochistic services. One was a 'flagellation house', and another (off Gray's Inn Road) was described as being 'like a torture chamber' with 'rings in the ceiling for hanging women and children up by the wrists' as well as 'the ordinary birch, whips' and so on.[27] At least one of these specialist brothels 'catered exclusively to many of the city's elite' businessmen, politicians and members of the nobility, including, it has been claimed, Belgium's King Leopold II.[28] Mrs Jeffries also reputedly had a hand in child prostitution and the 'white slave trade' of poor English girls sold to brothels in Europe, but there is little or no evidence to support these claims.[29] In 1885 she was charged with 'keeping disorderly houses' and brought to trial, but the case was settled in unusual legal circumstances – behind closed doors. The judge imposed a fine of £200, no client was named and Mrs Jeffries quietly went back to work, though she was successfully prosecuted again in 1887.[30] None of this appeared as front-page news in either London or Melbourne, but the editor of *The Pall Mall Gazette*, W.T. Stead, was not happy with the outcome in 1885. Nor was he happy with the fact that English legislators had neglected over a period of years – in the face of constant criticism – to pass a bill aimed at protecting young girls by raising the age of consent from thirteen.[31] In response he set out on a campaign to expose the underbelly of London's sex trade. First, he arranged the purchase of a young girl himself, had her examined (by a midwife/abortionist) to establish her virginity, and then made out that he had had sex with her to prove to his readers that it could be done.[32] He then wrote and published a series of hair-raising articles in *The Pall Mall Gazette* called 'The Maiden Tribute of Modern Babylon', describing and exposing the industry as he saw it in all its gory stench.[33] Public outcry was so intense that Stead was successful in getting the age of consent for girls raised to sixteen in a surprisingly short time, but he was also sentenced to three months' gaol for abducting the girl.[34]

The report of Stead's conviction gained more traction with Melbourne's newspapers than Mrs Jeffries' case or the activities of her brothels, but there was no follow-up investigation of Melbourne's sex trade or scrutiny of its brothels as a result. However, one historian has claimed that there was a trade in virgins between Melbourne and Tasmania in this period, run by ex-convicts.[35] The main source for the story appears to be the minutes of evidence from a parliamentary committee that met in 1878 to consider whether Victoria should introduce contagious diseases legislation such as England had done.[36] Two men said they knew of men trying to cure their syphilis by having sex with virgins, but out of twenty-seven witnesses who gave evidence to the committee only one man made the claim of trafficking, and it was based on hearsay and gossip rather than firsthand experience.[37] It seems that the story of the Tasmanian convicts trafficking girls is akin to that of the 'Belgian Traffic' in Europe.

Recent research has suggested that although a lot of women working in the sex industry moved around England and the Continent in the nineteenth century there was nothing like an orchestrated 'white slave trade' in operation there at all.[38] Women were led into sex work under false pretences at times, and there were certainly young girls working in the trade, but the movement of women had more to do with foreign women being seen as 'exotic', so French women, for instance, found a market in England, and English women were popular in Europe. In Melbourne new faces found a ready market too, no matter where they came from, and sex workers tended to follow the big events or entertainments from city to city and town to town, both locally and between the colonies. The police records we have examined reveal some appalling situations involving young girls in Melbourne (including mothers prostituting their daughters), and the newspapers provide plenty of stories of dysfunctional families and people doing unkind, unpleasant and ugly things to unfortunate young girls, but not even the tip-offs from the public mention any kind of regular 'trade' or trafficking in virgins.[39] And despite the flurry of concern in 1885, the age of consent for girls remained at twelve years.[40]

It was then that a member of the Cannibal Club was staying at the Menzies Hotel and writing long letters for London's *Daily Telegraph* about his thoughts and doings in Melbourne.[41] George Augustus Sala, the journalist flâneur, was producing articles that appealed to the taste of an enormous number of middle-class Victorian readers both in England and abroad. His writings have been described as 'the prose equivalent of flamboyant High Victorian design in domestic architecture and interior furnishing' – that is, 'rich and allusive, cluttered and eclectic' – but unbeknown to most of his readers, and not mentioned by the editor of his Melbourne writings, he was also the author of a substantial amount of flagellation pornography, including the first volume of *The Mysteries of Verbena House; or, Miss Bellasis Birched for Thieving*.[42] In his writings about Melbourne streets, however, Sala confined his interests to ''Twixt Bourke and Collins', 'the two leading thoroughfares of the metropolis'.[43] He does not compare the upper class (Collins) with the lower class (Bourke) streets, instead calling them 'equally enjoyable' and claiming that 'among all the streets of the world that I have wandered in I do not know any that … are more interesting or more amusing than the two'. Lonsdale Street, the centre of Melbourne's sex trade, parallel to both 'leading thoroughfares' and a mere block to the north, does not warrant a mention. Yet Sala was intensely aware of the social politics of sexuality in Melbourne, and derided what he called the 'fanatical devotees of "goody-goodyism" and "grandmotherly government"' – he was scathing about 'all the well-meant but generally imbecile attempts to make people pious, moral, social and pure by act of Parliament'.[44] Presumably these views were expressed in reaction to the public discourse about barmaids and the age of consent during the time he was in Melbourne. The question of barmaids should have been about improving working conditions for women, but Sala (like Victoria's parliamentarians) saw it as a moral question about the presence of women in male spaces; unlike the parliamentarians, though, Sala was effusive in his certainty that barmaids should continue working in pubs because it was better … for the men. Sala was a stirrer – he admitted after he left Australia that he knew nothing about Australian barmaids because 'I never go to bars' – but he was also expressing himself as a Cannibal Club member: he 'rejected the strictures of conventionality altogether, and particularly bourgeois calls to respectability'.[45] Like most of the Cannibal Club members, Sala walked the tightrope between the eccentric insider and the outcast; he could tease and stir while still dining at the

Melbourne Club and staying at Melbourne's best hotel and having his wife travelling alongside him, but his sexual interests had to remain secret.[46] If he had wanted to enjoy the pleasures available in a brothel, Sala would have had no trouble obtaining an introduction or a guide, but given his high international profile it would probably have led to some unwelcome gossip in Melbourne, in the way that the Duke of Edinburgh's visits to Mrs Fraser's house did in 1867.[47] And since Melbourne in 1885 was connected to Europe by the telegraph, how much more damaging would the gossip have been if any of Caroline Hodgson's houses were known to be providing flagellation services?

In all the records and writings and newspaper reports examined to date there is no suggestion that Caroline's establishments offered anything other than ordinary common-or-garden variety male–female sex. There are no wild rumours, no snide passing remarks from journalists or parliamentarians under privilege, in fact no hints at all of anything along the lines of the 'fladge brothels' in London. That does not mean it was not happening, of course; it means that if it was, we simply can't see it. Nor can we know what Madame Brussels' husband Stud knew about his uncle's membership of the Cannibal Club. When Stud arrived back in London in August 1868, his uncle Studholme Hodgson the pornographer was commanding the troops in Ceylon and about to become a lieutenant general, but by the time Stud and Caroline sailed for Melbourne he was back in England.[48] There is every chance that Stud and the lieutenant general crossed paths in those years when Stud was visiting his parents on the Continent and travelling to and from Brussels with Caroline. Stud would not have been carrying diplomatic bags, of course, but might he have done his uncle a favour and delivered or collected parcels for him in Brussels or Paris? And if he did, what might he have told his wife on that long sea journey to Melbourne? Caroline had built a substantial empire by the mid-1880s and Sala may well have visited her. But nothing suggests that her houses provided the kind of services that would have fully satisfied his lust.

12.

AN ADOPTION

WHILE W.T. STEAD WAS SERVING his gaol sentence in England, Caroline Hodgson was expanding her property portfolio and settling into her third adjoining property in Lonsdale Street. She was also still renting two houses further up the street (the easternmost one had been incorporated into the hotel). By 1886 Caroline's business was thriving, and so was her contribution to the after-hours sale of alcohol in the area. When she commenced business at her house in Lonsdale Street in 1876, Victoria's licensing act had allowed a boarding house keeper in the city of Melbourne to hold a 'colonial wine license', and there were no restrictions on trading hours if she occupied a house or premises paying rates of more than £10 a year. By the end of the year the legislation had been updated to restrict such licences to houses of the value of £50 a year.[1] This would not have prohibited Caroline from obtaining a colonial wine licence, since her house paid annual rates of £55, but the legislation also introduced restrictions such that she would only have been allowed to sell between the hours of six in the morning and twelve at night. Hardly useful for a brothel. She would probably also have found that the goods she was able to sell under such a licence – 'any wine cider or perry' produced from fruit grown in the colony – were not much to her customers' taste. Champagne and French spirits would have been more their style.[2] The problem was how to maintain a sufficient supply of such refreshments for clients without becoming vulnerable to charges of selling liquor without a licence. Especially since publicans were not allowed to trade on Sundays, which was often a busy day for the sex industry. The usual system was explained during a case against a publican early in 1886, when Caroline was called as a witness.

A policeman was on duty outside the South Australian Club Hotel on the corner of Lonsdale and Spring streets when he 'saw a little girl go to the window of the hotel and, after waiting there sometime, receive two bottles containing liquor'.[3] 'Caroline Brussell, residing in Lonsdale Street' then gave evidence that she had sent her servant for two bottles of champagne, and that she had brought it back, having paid a sovereign for it.[4] It was night time, and the publican said in his defence that he did not sell it – he was in bed, and it was 'the nurse girl' who sold it, and she had no right to go into the bar at all. A labourer who was standing outside the hotel, however, defended the girl. He was standing near the hotel that night, he said, and he heard the girl reply 'no' when Madame Brussels' servant asked for something. 'The nurse girl' then went away and when she came back he heard her say that the publican said she could have it tonight, and handed out two bottles. The publican was convicted of selling liquor on a Sunday, and fined £2. It might have put him off selling to Caroline Hodgson for a while, but it did not dent her business at all. After a decade in the trade, and with three properties in her ownership and another two rented further up the street she was in her heyday and there were plenty of other local pubs to supply her with alcohol.

But on 8 August 1887, exactly two years after the birthday party at Studholme Villa, a police constable heard 'very bad language and noise' coming from the house at twenty past one in the morning.[5] He dealt with the problem by attending the house and requesting that someone 'keep the girls quiet', before going on his way.

> After he had gone about 20 yards 'Madam' Brussels came rushing after
> him in a very excited manner, demanding to know if he was the con-
> stable 'who had dared to say he would report her house'. She used

obscene language to him and pushed him nearly into the gutter, upon which he ordered her away. She continued to abuse him, and attempted to strike him with her clenched fist. He then apprehended her. He had great trouble in getting her to the watchhouse, where more than once she spat in his face. Her conduct was disorderly and violent, and she called him a disgusting name.[6]

In all the numerous incidents involving Caroline Hodgson that were reported in the nineteenth-century newspapers this is the only one to report her indulging in this kind of unseemly behaviour. When the newspaper *Truth* began paying attention to her in 1903, it reported that 'she was clean of speech and angelically demure. She had none of the loudness and vulgarity associated with the common, fleshly, boozing, boisterous woman who follows illicit pleasure as a profession … Madame Brussells [*sic*] was a perfect little lady.'[7] But, just this once, she was behaving badly. Was it a special birthday, perhaps? Her fortieth? It is possible, and might explain her celebrating with more than her usual amount of alcohol, and thus some out-of-character behaviour. It might also explain her response to an event the following year.

On 22 September 1888, Caroline placed an advertisement in *The Age* in Melbourne:

> **EMILIE ZWEIKOUSKI** [*sic*],— Should this meet your eye, come to me at once, or else write. Am very anxious about you.
> CAROLINE HODGSON, LONSDALE-STREET.
> IF ANY FRIENDS SHOULD KNOW HER
> WHEREABOUTS PLEASE LET ME KNOW.[8]

Caroline was looking for the mother of an abandoned child. At the beginning of 1885 Emilie Zweikowsky had arrived in Melbourne on a boat from Hamburg with a baby (Amandus), and a 'single man' called Adolphe Grelcke, aged thirty-eight.[9] Emilie was eighteen. Five months later she gave birth to Adolphe's daughter, Alice, in Richmond.[10] Like many other babies in Melbourne in those awful years before sewerage, Alice died of diarrhoea and vomiting at the age of nineteen months; Adolphe registered her death on 17 January 1887.[11] Nine months later another daughter, Lily, was born to Emilie and Adolphe in Carlton, but she was born at the Women's Hospital, where destitute but respectable married women were offered care during a confinement.[12] Adolphe was not the informant for Lily's birth, suggesting that by then Emilie was fending for herself, Amandus, and the new baby. A year later Emilie disappeared, leaving baby Lily behind.[13]

By the time Lily was abandoned in September 1888, Caroline Hodgson had not only purchased three adjoining properties on Lonsdale Street, she had also bought a house in Park Road and two more adjoining houses in Carter Street, all in South Melbourne (today they are in St Kilda and Middle Park respectively).[14] Lily could have been abandoned at any of the Lonsdale Street establishments or the houses in South Melbourne; we have no way of knowing which. But tracing the occupant of one of Caroline's Carter Street houses provides a clue as to how it might have happened.

In April 1887 Caroline purchased the first of her two houses in Carter Street, number 95. At the time she bought it the house was let to a woman called Charlotte Niemann.[15] Charlotte was a widow with two children to care for, but she did have some support: her older sister Martha Burrell, who had landed herself a steady job and a generous employer in Caroline Hodgson.[16]

Charlotte and Martha were born in Tasmania, but their parents brought the family to Victoria with the gold rush of 1851.[17] The girls both married young and lost their first babies, but the family of Charlotte's German husband were very supportive.[18] The Niemanns had been active in the German community in Victoria since the 1850s, but when Charlotte and her husband decided to try their luck in New Zealand Martha went with them. She married (bigamously, since her first husband was still alive) and had three more children there, but, once again, she lost a child and then the marriage.[19]

Returning to Victoria in the mid-1870s without either of her husbands, Martha Burrell needed a job. She found it at Rosalind House, a brothel in

Stephen (which became Exhibition) Street.[20] In 1879 she was working as a servant there, next door to the place Caroline Hodgson had rented from Mrs West the year before. Martha was 'not a prostitute', she told the court when giving evidence about an assault that took place in the street after some men visited the brothel, 'I served the beer … [and] … I let them out the front door.' The following year, at the age of thirty-eight, she gave birth to twins, 'father unknown', at 187 Lonsdale Street – one of Madame Brussels' rented houses.[21] The twins' births were duly registered, but there are no later records of their lives or deaths; from that time on Martha Burrell worked for Caroline Hodgson as her housekeeper or cook, progressing to become her trusted confidant and business manager. Her sister Charlotte extended Caroline's connection with the German community in Melbourne and in turn the Niemanns seem to have been drawn into Caroline's orbit. When Charlotte's daughter Sarah had a child in January 1883, she named her 'Carrie', a name Caroline was known by, as though in tribute.[22] So, when Charlotte's husband died in 1885 and she moved to Carter Street, Martha would have known about it, and when Carter Street came up for sale she must have let Caroline know. Charlotte stayed on as the tenant of 95 Carter Street for several years after Caroline Hodgson bought it, and the connection with Emilie may well have come through Charlotte's relationships in the German community. Both Emilie and Charlotte may have worked for Madame Brussels as domestic servants, or even as sex workers. In April 1888, at the age of forty-two, Charlotte gave birth to a baby 'father unknown', though it only lived for two days.[23]

Charlotte was living at Carter Street when Emilie abandoned her baby. Did Emilie initially leave the baby with Charlotte? Is that how Caroline came to know about it? And did Charlotte then look after Emilie's baby for Caroline until she was ready to become a live-in mother? Despite her appeal in the newspaper for Emilie's whereabouts there is no evidence that Caroline and Lily ever saw Emilie again. Lily became Caroline's adopted daughter, renamed 'Irene Hodgson'.[24]

13.

WHAT KIND OF BROTHEL?

IN THE LATE 1880S A JOURNALIST attacked Madame Brussels under the heading of W.T. Stead's catchy phrase 'The Maiden Tribute of Modern Babylon', but the objections raised were about prostitution generally rather than the defilement of virgins.[1] Nevertheless, the question nags. Was she following Mrs Jeffries' business model, supplying different services to different clientele in different houses? It appears that the Carter Street properties, at least, were not being used as 'flagellation houses', but what about the different houses in Lonsdale Street East? Could they have offered a variety of services as well as a variety of prices?

In 1889, Melbourne's streets were renumbered such that Madame Brussels' business went from 167, 169 and 171 Lonsdale Street East, going away from Elizabeth Street, to street numbers beginning at Spring Street. Recognising that number 30 was just a garden-adjunct to the others, the three properties Caroline Hodgson owned were simply noted in the rate records and post office directories as '32–34 Lonsdale Street'. Caroline herself used '32 Lonsdale Street' as her personal address, even though her private house was at 34, and 32 became notorious as the location of Madame Brussels' brothel.[2]

Not long after the streets were renumbered, work began on planning Melbourne's long-awaited sewerage system. In preparation, the entire city was surveyed so the engineers and plumbers would know where the sinks and privies were located, and how best to connect the drains.[3] The sewerage survey books provide us with some detailed information about Caroline's properties as they were in the mid-1890s, but since the rate books indicate that there had been little change since 1886, the surveys represent her houses as they were in her heyday.[4] While the surveys cannot tell us what went on behind the walls, they can give us some idea about how the various properties were organised and used.

Under the new numbering, Madame Brussels' rented houses became 6 and 8 Lonsdale Street, and the survey shows two similar layouts, both fronting directly onto the footpath; one had an asphalt yard and the other was bricked. The houses were quite separate, with a brick wall between the

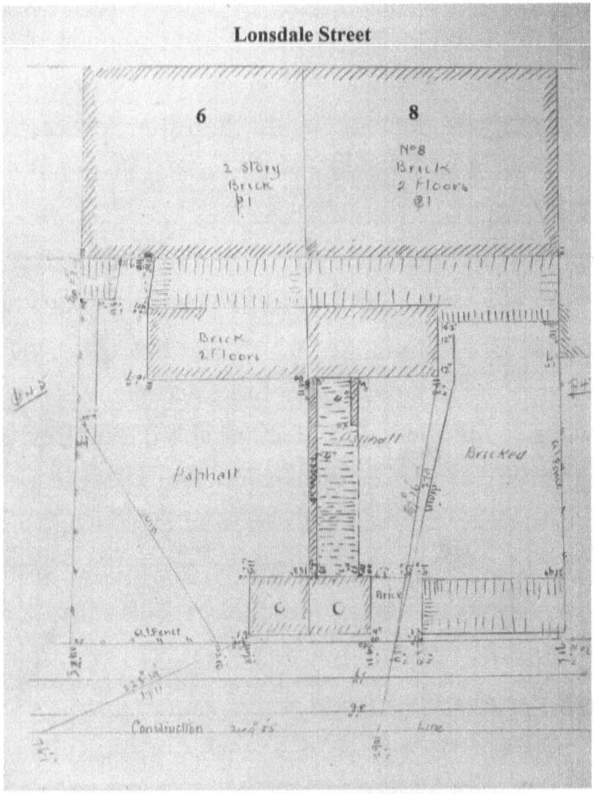

Madame Brussels' rented brothels at 6 and 8 Lonsdale Street

gardens at the rear, leading down to the privies on the back fences (marked 'C' for 'cesspit', although they were above-ground pans by this time).

With this kind of separation supplying privacy between the houses it might have been possible to provide different services in the two houses, but the plans show picket fences between both of the brothels and their adjoining properties – the hotel to the east and a shop to the west. There is no sign of a dungeon, and the see-through fence would hardly prevent gossip if there were unusual activities at either place. No hints of anything uncommon have turned up in the records, not even a piano.

With asphalt or brick yards and no garden space, the services on offer were most likely to have been restricted to the reception room at the front and bedrooms upstairs. The front room was often referred to as a parlour and it was a typical arrangement for the brothels of the period, as evidence at the Police Commission of 1882 attests. When two policemen were called to a disturbance at one of Madame Brussels' rented houses, one of them 'went in and sat in the parlour' while the other 'proceeded upstairs'.[5] It appears that rather than supplying virgins or flagellation the houses stuck to snacks, drinks and male–female sex.

The survey of Caroline's own property, however, indicates a different kind of business. There was an iron fence (20 feet, or about 6 metres) across the street boundary of number 30 (which had been 171) enclosing a yard which was 'not built on'. A single picket fence across the front of both number 32 (20 feet) and number 34 (26 feet, or about 8 metres) enclosed two separate front yards with a brick fence in between; a flagged path up the centre of a small garden led to a verandah in front of 32, while a tiled path led through the centre of the garden next door, providing Caroline with her own separate front entrance to 34 (Studholme Villa). The surveyor represented the brick front of the two houses ('No 32, 34') as one, indicating that he was aware of the joint ownership.

The entrance paths appear to lead to a door at the centre of each house, but number 32 was only 6 metres wide; that is, it was not wide enough for two rooms and a hallway, suggesting that in the beginning the front door led

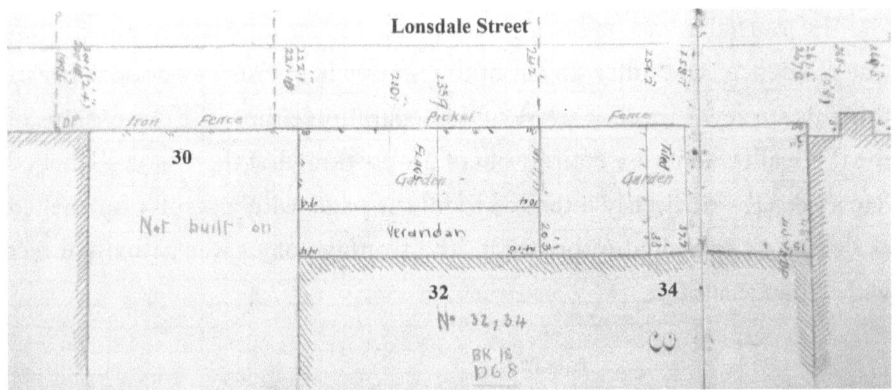

Frontage of Caroline Hodgson's properties
at 30, 32 and 34 Lonsdale Street

directly into a room which was used as a reception area. We learn a bit about
this room in the reports about the excise officers' visit to Caroline's house in
1882 mentioned previously (before she bought number 34); when they
arrived she 'was on the point of leaving for the theatre' but consented to
joining them 'in a glass of wine'.[6] Champagne was retrieved from a chiffo-
nier by one of the women of the house, and the money was placed on a table,
where the customs men sat with Caroline to enjoy it.[7] The front room was
therefore not the traditionally arranged middle-class sitting room of easy
chairs for guests, but instead was set up for drinking and playing card games.
It was a place where alcohol could be served and consumed before clients
retired to a bedroom. Once Caroline's three allotments were combined, the
room facing Lonsdale Street at number 32 became 'the front parlour', where
clients could find a pen and ink to sign their cheques.[8]

Beyond the parlour, according to the *Truth* in 1903, the houses had

> at great expense ... been connected interiorally forming
> a labyrinth of elegantly furnished rooms, sumptuous marble
> bathrooms and comfortable cosy nooks. The showpiece of
> the gigantic establishment is Madame Brussels own bed-
> room, the furnishing of which alone cost £2,000.[9]

The journalist was obviously not aware that Caroline had her own separate residence. The fuller sketch of the houses in the survey book suggests that this surveyor was not aware of the separation either. The dimensions of the three allotments are entirely out of proportion; first there is 32 – labelled 'No 32 & 34' – obviously intended to fill the page, with a scruffy unlabelled sketch of 34 squashed in beside it. The frontage of 34 was actually 6 feet wider than that of 32.

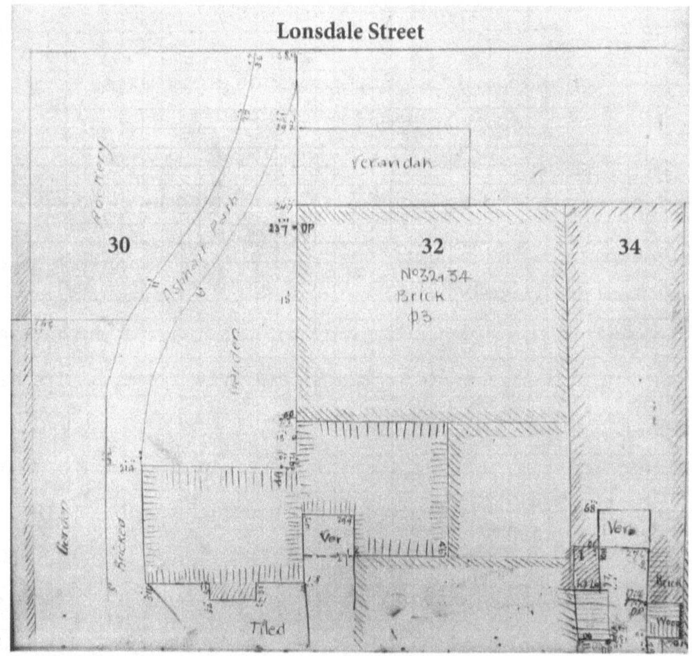

Street-facing portion of Caroline Hodgson's properties
in Lonsdale Street

Then there is the messy and out of proportion section at the rear of 34, as though the surveyor was given a quick guided tour and had to draw it later from memory. It is presumably in this section that one of the 'sumptuous marble bathrooms' and Caroline's £2000 bedroom might have been found, but there is no indication of any plumbing being installed apart from the 'DP' (drainpipes) to take water from the roof.

Overall the sketch shows no labyrinth of 'interiorally connected' rooms, but it does show a patchwork of brick and wooden inner rooms where there could have been no windows at all. Layouts like this were common before lightwells and internal courtyards were required by law to provide daylight and ventilation to every room, but privacy and seductive lighting were presumably part of the ambience.

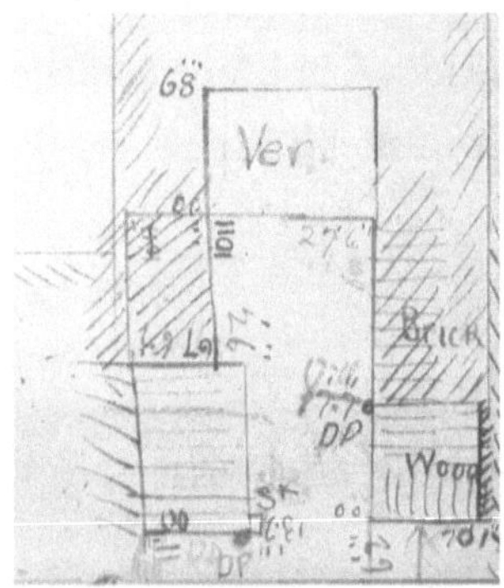

The back section of Caroline Hodgson's private house, Studholme Villa

This survey provides other clues about the way the houses were used. Behind the iron fence the land that was 'not built on' was actually a rockery at the front, with the wooden cottage that accommodated John O'Brien and his family set well back from the street in a garden setting. Behind that cottage, beside a garden which appears to have been landscaped in formal Victorian-era style and walled-in for privacy, there was a wooden 'Summer House' about four and a half metres square – perfect for dancing the lancers or a quadrille. Perfect also for music and singing, card parties (including fortune-telling) and all sorts of entertainments and hijinks for groups of people in various stages of dress and undress. There is a story told by Curtis Candler (one of Victoria's coroners from 1857 until his retirement in 1908) about a dinner party at the Melbourne Club that gives some idea of the possibilities.[10] It regards Frederick Standish, the chief commissioner of police until his resignation in 1881. Candler was a friend of Standish's who also lived at the Melbourne Club; his diary reported that

> One of the charges against Capt. Standish … was that he had given a select dinner party to some ladies who dined in a perfectly nude state, and the whiteness of whose fair forms was contrasted with black velvet chairs![11]

The story, Candler noted, was expunged from the committee's report.

Opposite the summer house and behind the formal garden the survey shows another detached wooden building (labelled 'cottage') with a verandah reaching towards the summer house.

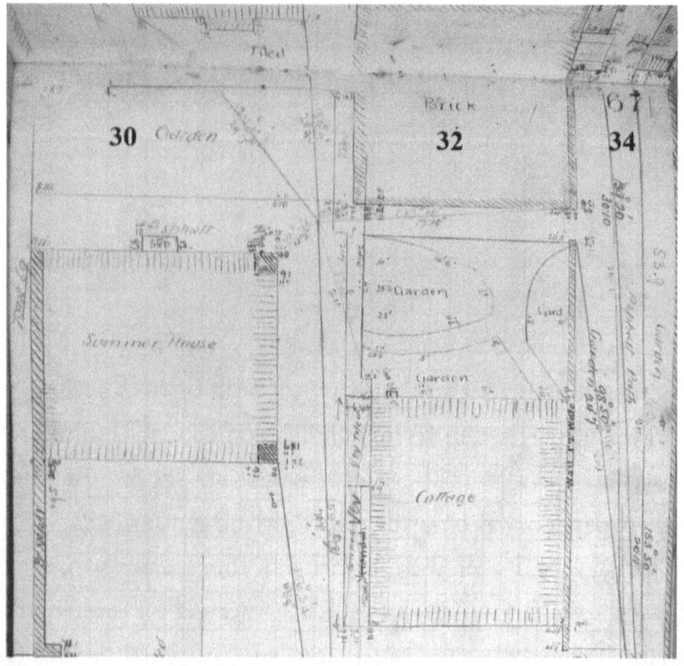

Midsection survey of Caroline Hodgson's properties in Lonsdale Street

Inside this building, on the wall next to the garden, the plans show the one and only kitchen sink ('KS') recorded on all three sites. Kitchens in nineteenth-century Victoria were often in a separate building at the rear of the main house because of the risk of fire, but the size of this building and its location between the houses suggest that Caroline Hodgson employed and housed a cook to prepare meals for those living and working on all of her sites.[12] It was probably built in September 1886, and may well be the building referred to as 'the cottage' where girls reported staying as servants before graduating to 'the big house' where they 'slept with gentlemen'.[13] 'The big house' being 32 Lonsdale Street. In later years Martha Burrell described herself as 'cook', doubtless preparing meals here for numerous women and overnight visitors.

From the kitchen there is a convenient path between number 32 and the garden adjoining the kitchen, which would have allowed for deliveries to Caroline Hodgson's private residence. The path leads through a break in a substantial dividing wall between the back gardens; the wall is made of stone or brick about 35 centimetres thick, but there would still have been limited privacy in the garden. There were numerous windows overlooking 34, and only a paling fence at the back of all three properties. Nevertheless, the brick walls, together with the large trees in her garden, suggest a comparison with that other famous walled garden: that of the Melbourne Club, where doubtless some of her clients were members. Those same clients probably enjoyed some of the kitchen produce too, since 'caviare [*sic*], *pàté de foie gras* and champagne were available in the evening, though in the morning, the more functional combination of bacon and eggs and coffee was popular'.[14]

Returning to the question of activities in Caroline Hodgson's brothels, it is certainly possible for bacon and eggs to follow sadomasochistic services, but given the freedom with which the women appear to have moved between all of the houses, where could they have been offered?[15]

There was only one part of Caroline's Lonsdale Street empire that was kept separate. It had no frontage to Lonsdale Street, instead fronting onto Casselden Lane, adjoining 32 to the east.[16] A man had left it to his widow for her lifetime, so when the widow moved out to live with her daughters Caroline rented it.[17] None of the Melbourne Metropolitan Board of Works plans of the early 1890s show a connection between the houses, and this four-roomed cottage on Casselden Lane was rented separately to Annie Wilson from about 1888 until she appears as the tenant of 'Boccaccio House' at 22–26 Lonsdale Street in the early 1890s.

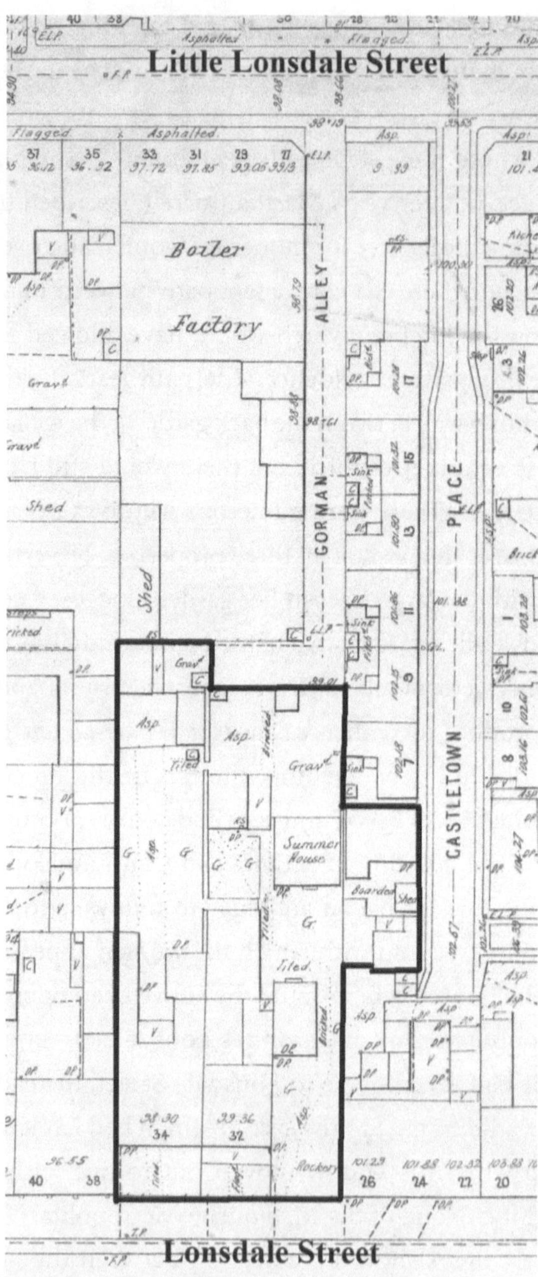

Boundary of Caroline Hodgson's establishment in Lonsdale Street
after renting the adjoining property on Casselden Lane
[misnamed as 'Castletown Place' by the surveyors] in 1887

Annie Wilson was a central character in the case of Victoria's missing parliamentary mace, which was stolen in December 1891.[18] *The Bulletin* in Sydney started a scandal by reporting the mace 'at a bagnio in Lonsdale Street' in November 1892, and then 'Boccaccio House' was implicated indirectly by *The Ballarat Courier* in January 1893; at about the same time Annie Wilson's name was added to the story by an unrelated gossipmonger in response to her connection with Boccaccio House. But Annie Wilson was actually renting Madame Brussels' cottage in Casselden Lane when the mace went missing. Could she have been offering flagellation services there? The poor state of the cottage (and access to it) makes it an unlikely location for parliamentarians to be disporting themselves, but it is possible. Annie was probably occupying 22–26 Lonsdale (Boccaccio House) in 1893 when the rumour surfaced, but wherever she was located, she categorically denied ever having seen the mace, and there were never any rumours regarding other activities at her brothel.[19] Today it is often Madame Brussels' name that is associated with the missing mace, but no one has yet solved the mystery of its whereabouts, or hinted at secrets beyond rude games with parliamentarians.

14.

THE BUSINESS BROUGHT TO TRIAL

WHILE CAROLINE WAS SUBSTANTIALLY EXTENDING her business premises through Melbourne's booming real estate years in the 1880s, the reputation of the district where she was located was being increasingly maligned. By the middle of the decade the back lanes around Little Bourke Street to the south were succumbing to slum clearance, and many of the numerous occupants of those poorer brothels were moving a few blocks away into similar or slightly better accommodation off Little Lonsdale Street.[1] Over the decades from 1880 to 1900 Caroline's surroundings were gradually transformed from a place where working-class people of all degrees of respectability and criminality lived alongside a few sex workers into the place that became known as 'Little Lon', with hundreds of women working in brothels of varying classes and a reputation as a vile slum. During the day the area began to hum and chatter with an increasing number of Chinese cabinetmakers' workshops, banging and clanging with more and more industrial and mechanical factories, but at night it came alive with wine, women and the occasional song. And often, too, with violence and theft.

Along with the build-up of poorer people and sex workers in the community came the rescuers and the moral disapprovers; the Salvation Army arrived in 1882, the Little Sisters of the Poor joined them in 1884 and the Anglican Mission to the Streets and Lanes started in 1885. They all based themselves in the Little Lon area, and they all focused attention on the fallen women there, without relieving them of the burden of moral judgment or improving the level of women's wages.[2]

Located in the middle of it all, cloistered in her garden behind a tidy façade, Caroline went her own way, and – as we have seen – did some personal good for at least a few women after her own fashion. Keeping quiet and out of the public eye, though, was not enough to protect her from the machinations of Colonel Barker of the Salvation Army and the judgmental preacher Henry Varley.

The Reverend Mr Varley was an Englishman who first came to Victoria in the 1850s and made enough money working as a butcher to go home, take a wife and purchase a similar business in London; he had no formal religious training, but his belief in his own knowledge of God's intentions was unshakeable.[3] As his son wrote after his death, he had 'a spirit so self-reliant and independent' that he 'was not greatly given … to asking counsel of men when once he was convinced that his way was traced out before him by the finger of God'.[4] It was a finger that directed Varley to take his evangelical preaching all over the world. He was in America when W.T. Stead's campaign against Mrs Jeffries hotted up in 1885, but the decoy and ruination of young women was of particular interest to the 'Butcher's Evangelist', so he rushed home to take part.[5]

Varley – 'a fat-fingered man with a square face and stubborn countenance' – returned to Melbourne in 1887 preaching louder than ever against such vices as masturbation, prostitution and skating rinks that threatened to ruin otherwise able young men.[6] His style was, as one early observer noted, 'well adapted … to the taste and the comprehension of a popular audience in an English community', speaking as he did in 'the plainest Saxon language, displaying a mastery over those primitive elements of the English tongue'.[7] Clearly not everyone was swayed by him, since another journalist described him as a 'sleek, comfortable, egotistical, oily-tongued religious mountebank,' but his own certainties were enough to take him around the world fulminating.[8]

Henry Varley, c.1877

Back in Melbourne, Varley quickly identified Madame Brussels as the focus of his censure.

> During an interview he had with her [in 1888] she said she would not take £10,000 for her cottages, and under no circumstances would she receive any offer until after the closing of the [Centennial] Exhibition, as she could not let the golden harvest of that period slip past without availing herself of it.[9]

So by 1889 Varley was in full voice, lecturing to thousands at the Theatre Royal, ranting about 'a well-known procuress … prowling about in Bourke street accosting young girls in broad daylight' and threatening to reveal the names of 'some leading men holding professional appointments who were known to frequent brothels in Lonsdale-street'.[10] Varley's rhetoric and style of speech were aiming to achieve the kind of moral panic engendered by Stead's exposé of child prostitution, and in Colonel Barker he found a partner in outrage.[11] As one newspaper pointed out

Mr. Varley and 'Colonel' Barker of the Salvation Army appear to have constituted themselves as the censors of public morals … While Colonel Barker directs his energies to what may be termed the lower stratum of the social evil, Mr. Varley flies at the higher ranks of the demi-monde, and wishes to root them out lock, stock, and barrel. He is especially incensed against the 'upper ten' amongst the Phrynes resident in Lonsdale street.[12]

The 'upper ten', of course, included Caroline Hodgson. Her apparent wealth and the exclusive air of her establishment brought her to the particular attention of Varley and Barker, and in 1889 they set out to remove her from the business. They searched high and low to obtain evidence against her for procuring – the police believed there was nothing else they could charge her with, since she kept her house so well-behaved and orderly – and once the two men found some girls willing to give evidence they pressured the police to charge her.[13] The police were more careful after the Samuel Nathan case (it had only been five years since that debacle) and sent the briefing papers, including the evidence from the girls who were supposed to have been 'procured', to the Crown Solicitor for advice. His reply was very clear: 'The charge for procuring should not be attempted on the evidence before me'.[14] The political and public tide of opinion was turning, though, in response to Varley and Barker's verbal onslaught.[15] In *The Herald* Varley howled about the 'notorious improper house keeper in Lonsdale street' and how she 'injured, blasted and degraded' young girls in her 'moral cesspool'. With Barker threatening in the same newspaper to 'lay the whole matter before the public' if the police should decide that the evidence Barker had laid before them was insufficient, the police were caught in a cleft stick.[16] If they did nothing they would be seen to be colluding with Madame Brussels, but if they prosecuted her for procuring they were likely to lose. But in the meantime the Salvation Army and Henry Varley were proposing to launch a private prosecution of Madame Brussels under the vagrancy laws. Two senior lawyers were supposedly giving their 'professional services' pro bono to support the prosecution.[17] The police felt they could ill afford for a private prosecution to succeed, so they decided to use the legal advice obtained by Varley and Barker to prosecute Caroline Hodgson and a woman who appeared to work for her – Lottie Temple – for having no lawful means of support.[18]

Six women initially agreed to give evidence. When it came to the point, though, one woman said 'she had no evidence to give' and another 'declined to make a statement'. The police were also reluctant to use evidence from one of the younger women because she admitted she was not a virgin – 'she was suffering from venereal disease when she came to Madame Brussells [*sic*]'.[19] But their efforts to find more witnesses to support the prosecution were in vain. They had four young women with unsatisfactory evidence to carry the prosecution against both Caroline and Lottie Temple.

John Madden, who was shortly to become Victoria's chief justice, was one who offered his pro bono services to the government and provided an opinion about the evidence that would be required to prove the case against someone on vagrancy charges. His advice ran to more than two full handwritten foolscap pages and indicated that the ground had shifted, despite there being no change in the law.[20] While the General Sessions judge in Nathan's case in 1883 had been firmly of the opinion that 'a prostitute … has a perfect right to be a prostitute',[21] Madden's advice was that 'persons who live by prostitution … are (ipso facto) persons who have no lawful visible means of support'. That is, women doing sex work were, by definition, doing something unlawful, so if it could be proven that the women in Madame Brussels' houses were prostitutes the question of orderliness would not matter.[22] According to Madden, the prosecutors had to prove first that Caroline Hodgson was 'the tenant or the owner' of the house and that she 'exercised whole management' over it; second, that the women who habitually lived in her house were known to her as prostitutes; and third, 'that men resort there for the purpose of sexual intercourse' and pay for it. It would also be sufficient, he advised, to prove that she let bedrooms to men and women 'knowing they were not man and wife'.

The charge against Lottie Temple – for having no lawful means of support – was easily defeated when it was proven that she was married and that she and her husband ran a shop. When it came to the charge against Caroline, though, she was never placed in the witness box, and very few of the prosecutor's questions to witnesses seem designed to elicit evidence about any of the relevant matters. A policeman said he had seen 'men driving up to the house in cabs and waggonettes at all hours of the night', but no one was asked whether any of them paid for sexual intercourse, or whether couples who were not man and wife occupied bedrooms. Nor was any real defence offered; Caroline's barrister concentrated instead on two questions: whether the evidence of the young women was reliable, and whether it was right to close down Madame Brussels' houses when her business might simply move and become a nuisance elsewhere.

On the first question, the defence showed clearly that none of the young women were innocent virgins when they went to Lonsdale Street. The police knew this, and it should have helped their efforts to prove that they were 'common prostitutes', but a policeman from Footscray, where two of the girls came from, reported that he had 'no proof of their having solicited prostitution' even though 'their general behaviour is that of common prostitutes'. Once they were put on the witness stand one of the two admitted she had had an illegitimate child eighteen months previously, and the other that she had been seduced by a promise of marriage before going to Madame Brussels' house. The other two women stated decisively that they had not been coerced but had gone to the house of their own volition. It was as though the questions were aimed at proving the charge of procuring – which was actually never made – and somehow the young women's lack of innocence defeated the moral imperative of the case.

On the second question – whether Madame Brussels' houses should be closed down – rather than challenging the presumed nature of her establishment, the defence barrister had begun his cross-examination of the prosecuting policeman by asking him about 'the effect of the crusade some years ago on the suburbs', and then continuing with a description of how when brothels were closed down women were driven to the respectable suburbs 'like a stream of filth, where they became a great nuisance'. He agreed with Madden that 'technically no such houses could exist according to the law' but argued that 'it would be impossible to suppress them' before pointing out that Madame Brussels' house 'was one of the best conducted of its class; the police did not allege that any person had ever been robbed in it or that there had ever been any disturbances at it'. He also set out the government's view that it was best to keep the houses away from main streets, make sure they were kept in an orderly fashion and ban new houses from opening.

The barrister was framing the problem as a political rather than a legal one. Why had Madame Brussels been chosen for prosecution and not the other madams?[23] It was a clever defence because of the nature of this particular bench of magistrates. Under the rules at that time, justices of the peace were appointed to work at a specific local court but might also appear at any other court, and on any other case, of their choosing. Usually Joseph Panton, as the presiding magistrate of the Melbourne Police Court, was on the bench on his own, or perhaps with one or two other JPs. But on this one day, with the infamous Madame Brussels due to appear, he was joined on the bench by no fewer than ten other magistrates, several of whom were to prove in later years to have been keen clients of the brothels in Lonsdale Street.[24] Their decision – as Caroline's barrister well knew – would come not from the barrister's legal argument about whether she was guilty of an offence but from his ability to turn the question into one about where these houses should be located and whether Caroline Hodgson should have been singled out for punishment.

By appealing to the social questions of the acceptability of prostitution and what would happen if Madame Brussels took her business into

Miss Aspasia (to the District Court Bench): 'Now, Gentlemen, open your
eyes and imagine that I am the incarnation of purity and virtue.'
The Bench (in unison; fortissimo): 'You are, you are, we know you are.'

a 'respectable' area, her barrister effectively asked the magistrates whether
brothels should be allowed to exist at all, knowing what the majority answer
would be. For most of the magistrates sitting that day the barrister's argument – effectively that brothels cannot be eliminated and Caroline Hodgson's
brothel was a good deal better managed than most – coincided with their
own beliefs. In summing up, Panton affirmed the popular view that 'the local-
ity was known as one of the worst plague spots in Melbourne', but then
echoed the defending barrister by asking 'why one offender was selected out
of the many'. Having paid lip service to the idea of being in a court of law,
he went on to make an impassioned statement of his moral opinion that

more harm is done by the loose way parents look after their children and allow them to wander about the street at night frequenting these damnable dancing houses than in any other way. The free love encouraged in this country by these resorts, these holiday gatherings patronised by certain classes, is a disgrace to us. These things do more real harm than disorderly houses of the kind before us, and anyone with experience knows this is the case, and it is disgraceful that the disgusting sights at some of our public gatherings are not suppressed. The cases are dismissed.[25]

It was a split decision, but Caroline left the court a free woman, and she was no doubt flushed with relief and satisfaction. *The Daily Telegraph* reported the next morning that 'she, with a company of her dependents and allies, naturally enough celebrated the joyful event by rejoicing demonstrations in the street outside the Court!', and *Melbourne Punch* delighted in depicting her as having mesmerised the bench into doing her bidding.[26]

It was a win of sorts, but only for Madame Brussels' house, and only for a short time.

15.

A WIN FOR THE MORALISTS

IN THE 1880S MRS KEMP AND CAROLINE HODGSON were the cream of the flash brothel crop until Madame Vine came along late in the decade.[1] Hers was quite a different story, at least partly because of Henry Varley's fury over Madame Brussels' acquittal. Madame Vine was a peripatetic brothel madam who followed the big colonial events, and in February 1888 she was in Melbourne, setting up a café (named exotically after a spa resort in Europe) in time for the Centennial International Exhibition:

> **BADEN BADEN CAFÉ RUSSELL-STREET, MELBOURNE** The most elegant Café in the city, has been furnished with the greatest comforts for visitors. Best Brands of champagne, spirits and cigars.[2]

A short time later she was planning to move to the South Australian Club hotel on the corner of Lonsdale and Spring streets (Madame Brussels' 'local') but couldn't get a licence, so she moved to Carlton and took rooms above a tobacconist's shop in a brand-new and classy building.[3]

Plain-clothes constable Gleeson described her rooms as being 'fitted up in a very elaborate manner; in fact, in a similar way to those places of

Madame Brussel's, Charlotte Kain and Annie Wilson's. It was a "flash" house devoted to immorality.'[4]

But Madame Vine was a different character to Madame Brussels. Her entire history in Melbourne was one of shonky deals, skating around the edge of the law and obtaining credit and loans with apparently little hope of paying them back once the exhibition crowds had moved on. Her business judgment and ethics were substantially poorer than those of either Caroline Hodgson or Mrs Kemp, but she was unlucky too, having moved into the tobacconist's shop in Carlton at the exact time that Henry Varley was on the warpath over Madame Brussels.[5]

The newspapers were uniformly aghast at that acquittal, and *Melbourne Punch,* as we have seen, made the most of its opportunity to ridicule the bench, but Varley and his fellow crusaders were particularly incensed. Caroline's release increased Varley's invective against her, although she was not the only one to be abused; the magistrates' decision was questioned and denounced and ridiculed by the press far and wide, and Panton in particular came in for a drubbing, with *Melbourne Punch* accusing him of lacking the backbone to overrule the majority: 'a man standing six-feet-four in his stockings must be too long to be strong'.[6] But in his disappointment over the loss, Varley targeted Madame Vine. Varley might have failed to secure Madame Brussels' conviction, but he succeeded in having Madame Vine and her male business partner, Walter Reeder, charged with 'being idle and disorderly persons' occupying a house 'frequented by persons having no visible lawful means of support'.[7] Rather than facing Panton at the city court, they were brought before four justices of the peace at the Carlton police court. When the case came on for hearing, Reeder appeared but Madame Vine did not; she told her barrister that she was ill. The man who had rented them the house had to 'come off the Bench' to give evidence. He claimed (defensively) that he had thought his tenants were respectable, and then resumed his seat to pass judgment.[8] Reeder was sentenced to twelve months' gaol, and a warrant was issued for the arrest of Madame Vine. She did appear the following week, but 'during the hearing of the case the defendant went into hysterics and had to be removed from the court'.[9] In what must have come as a shock to her after Caroline Hodgson's acquittal, she was sentenced along with Reeder to twelve months' imprisonment, but her barrister gave notice of appeal and she was allowed bail. A short time later she was in the insolvency court.[10] When her appeal against the conviction for occupying a disorderly house came on for hearing the following week, Madame Vine was nowhere to be found. She had taken about £400 belonging to her creditors and gone to Sydney; from there she took a saloon cabin in a boat to Hong Kong.[11] One of Melbourne's policemen scored a sea voyage to bring her back.[12]

The punishment meted out to Madame Vine – prison for twelve months – would have sent a shiver up the spines of the rest of Melbourne's sex workers and madams, including Mrs Kemp and Caroline Hodgson. Mrs Kemp kept her house going for a time before retiring; she died in 1895.[13] Caroline kept her house going after her acquittal in 1889 but began preparing her path out of the business not long afterwards. All of them would have been watching the growth of Varley's influence with foreboding.

After the abortive trial of Caroline Hodgson in May 1889, while the case against Madame Vine was playing out, Henry Varley took his campaign to another level. He tried to institute a consumer revolt against the 'well known drapery houses who received large orders from Madame Brussells [*sic*] for expensive dresses', and set out to increase the pressure on the government.[14] The sale of drapery does not seem to have been affected, and when he (and 'certain Salvation Army officers') waited upon the Minister of Justice and asked him to review the decision of the magistrates, the minister simply replied that the Melbourne City Council had the power to legislate for 'the suppression of immoral houses' within city boundaries, so the reformers should talk to them.[15] Having gained no joy from the minister, Varley joined a deputation from the Society for the Promotion of Morality and waited on the attorney-general, this time pushing for urgent amendments to the criminal laws relating to immorality.[16]

The Society for the Promotion of Morality had been around for some time, and back in 1885, under the leadership of the Anglican Bishop of

Melbourne, it had pushed hard for legislation to raise the age of consent for girls and provide the police with a series of criminal offences they could use to attack brothels and brothel-keepers.[17] As we have already seen, the Protection of Women Bill was passed by Victoria's Legislative Council that year and sent to the Legislative Assembly for their consideration, but the Legislative Assembly discharged the bill from its order of the day without discussion and it was never seen again.[18] Not until 1891, that is, when most of it reappeared in the clauses of the Crimes Act Amendment Bill.

So, in 1889, when a deputation from the Society for the Promotion of Morality waited on the attorney-general, the legislative issues relating to brothels and sex workers already had some history, and members of the government were unwilling to enter that territory again. The attorney-general 'said that the Government having just passed through a general election had not yet had time to give the matter its attention, but he promised to lay before Cabinet the views which were expressed by the deputation'.[19] He may have laid their views before the cabinet, but nothing happened in 1889, and in 1890 – when an array of apparently new acts were passed, including a *Crimes Act* and a *Police Offences Act* – they contained none of the requested new provisions affecting sex workers.

Through the last half of 1889, 1890 and into 1891, though, the clouds of Victoria's post-land-boom crash had been thickening and turning dark; building societies began failing, investments were turning sour, and many parliamentarians were feeling the pressure of dread. In 1891, when the moral failings of their fiscal irresponsibility were staring them in the face, instead of introducing legislation to curtail unethical financial dealings and protect innocent investors, they found the will to concentrate their moral sensibility on punishing sex workers. They amended the *Police Offences Act* to make it a crime to solicit in the streets, and reversed the tenet 'innocent until proven guilty' by requiring women accused of having 'no lawful means of support' to prove that anything in their bank accounts had been obtained in a lawful manner.[20] They also turned 'procuring' into a crime punishable by up to two years' prison, but removed the major sticking point in the failed 1885 legislation by not threatening landlords with fines.[21] The legislation was presented to the Legislative Assembly, having 'already twice passed through the Council, after careful consideration'.[22]

To their credit the parliamentarians did amend the *Crimes Act* to raise the age of consent for girls from twelve to sixteen, despite objections from Captain Charles Taylor and other members of the Legislative Assembly. Apparently men (like themselves?) might unwittingly have sex with younger girls who looked older than they were and then be subjected to blackmail – 'in this country girls of fifteen years of age were as old as girls in a colder climate were at eighteen or nineteen'.[23] In 1892 Captain Taylor was one of the fraudsters who avoided prison over his unethical land dealings by making a secret composition with his creditors, but in 1891 he was worried about what fifteen-year-old girls might do to men.[24]

The 1891 acts were passed with very little discussion other than on provisions where members thought they might have an adverse impact on men. It was as though Varley's onslaught of invective had helped to turn the tide of men's financial irresponsibility against women on all fronts; the suffragettes wanting an independent voice in the shape of a right to vote were ridiculed, as were those working for temperance and protection against drunken, violent men, and women doing sex work for a living were turned into criminals as well as being vilified and shamed. As an independent and still apparently secure wealthy woman, Madame Brussels attracted the hatred and contempt of the fearful and the guilty, but they disguised it behind a façade of moral rectitude.

PART IV:
THE COMPLICATED YEARS

16.

A LOVER PERHAPS

While Henry Varley and Colonel Barker and others were abusing Caroline Hodgson from their pulpits and filling the newspapers with their denunciations, one lone voice was raised in her defence. Soon after the 1889 trial *The Herald* reported on a modestly dressed woman in black, with black kid gloves, standing 'right under the shade of the Young Men's Christian Association building [in Russell Street], … using the raised sidewalk as a platform' to deliver 'her candid opinions on the social evil in general and Mr. Varley, Madame Brussels, and one or two other prominent personages in particular'.[1] The woman's name was Louisa Clarke Wells, and along with Henry Varley she was a social purity campaigner, but her views were unorthodox for the time.[2] She believed that Varley's crusade was 'persecution, not reclamation', and that

> People only saw the girls flaunting, apparently hardened, on the streets; they did not see them as she had seen them, often weeping bitter tears of despair and heart-broken grief.[3]

Mrs Clarke Wells drew an audience of a few hundred people that day – nothing compared with the thousands that attended Varley's lectures – but they were mostly men, and the reporter was impressed that she 'was not greeted by one ribald remark, or immodest jest'. He also noted, respectfully, that 'at Mrs. Wells' right hand stood … a lady friend who had accompanied her, and on the pavement fringe of the audience was a small knot of well-dressed women, amongst whom was Madame Brussels herself'. Mrs Clarke Wells claimed that 'Madame Brussells [*sic*] was not at all the woman she was represented to be to the public', and she 'appealed for more justice for women in such matters, and to the chivalry of her hearers to deal more fairly with her sex, and to … use more common sense and reason in its treatment'.

It was an articulate appeal, in tune with the ideas that drove the reformers in England to oppose the contagious diseases acts of the 1860s, but Mrs Clarke Wells was no politician.[4] She never managed to advance her views through any means beyond pamphlets and street lecturing, and – like many women who stepped beyond the prescribed domestic role – she was quickly branded a 'nuisance' by the police and taken to court under the city council's move-on by-law.[5] The magistrate, again Mr Panton, thought a caution was sufficient punishment for this 'very tall, thin person, dressed in black, apparently about 50 years old' whose 'manner is very excitable'.[6] She appeared in his court twice, and then disappeared from Melbourne history.[7]

It is difficult to know how Caroline Hodgson would have felt about Mrs Clarke Wells lecturing in the streets using her name, because although she appeared to defend women such as Madame Brussels, at the same time she stood with Henry Varley in condemning the men who frequented her premises, including a man who – by later accounts – was close to Caroline's heart:

If Mr. ___ was to be Mr. Varley's sacrifice, Mrs. Wells suggested that his name should be bracketed with that of another name, and then she mentioned the name of a gentleman known by repute to everybody, one who moves in the very highest ranks of society.[8]

The identity of the man 'in the very highest ranks of society' is unknown, but the man she referred to as 'Mr. Varley's sacrifice' was without doubt Alfred Plumpton, who was at that time the music critic for *The Age*. To begin with, Henry Varley had only hinted at the identity of the well-known men supposedly frequenting Madame Brussels' establishment, but before the case against her went to court in 1889 he threatened to 'name names' if she was not convicted.[9] It was a strategy he had used with little success in relation to Mrs Jeffries in London, but that didn't stop him trying it again in Melbourne.[10] When the result of the case was not to his liking, he supposedly did name Alfred Plumpton, but the newspapers avoided printing it for fear of libel charges, despite *Truth*'s claim to the contrary.[11]

Alfred Plumpton, 1889

Even the police went to extraordinary lengths to avoid the name being mentioned; it has been cut out (not merely erased) from one record in the police archives.[12] The closest we come to confirming his identity from contemporary sources is in *The Ovens and Murray Advertiser*, where his newspaper affiliation was noted along with his connection to a recently arrived English singer:

> 'There is one man,' declared Mr Varley, 'who has been
> one of the many supporters of this notorious woman
> B – –, I mean —, attaché of the — ... I wonder that,
> in a large community like this, the proprietors of such
> a newspaper should retain him on their staff ... if
> that eminent singer, Mr Santley, had known the true
> character of this man, he would never have allowed
> him to be associated with his banquet.[13]

When it comes to the details of Plumpton's role in Caroline Hodgson's life, the police files relating to the 1889 trial only relay Varley's hearsay; the *Truth* newspaper fashioned its pieces from the same hearsay and were written over a decade after Plumpton left Melbourne.[14] Assessing the truth or otherwise of Varley's accusations is therefore hazardous, but the stories have been repeated so often that they need to be carefully examined, not least because they involve the parentage of a child. In 1903 the following appeared in both Melbourne and Brisbane editions of the *Truth*:

> Plumpton was a great man at the Madame Brussells' [*sic*] establishment. His large photo adorned the grand piano, and he was 'boss of the establishment.' Madame Brussells was really in love with Plumpton. She adored talent. When a female child was born, the event was celebrated with a great orgie. All the 'bloods' about town were invited, and a mock christening formed part of the disgraceful programme of festivities. The child was 'christened' in champagne, and the mock-priest named it 'Syphilia', ... and one of the principle actors in the salacious proceedings was a valued member of the staff of a Melbourne morning paper.[15]

The writer's claim was carefully phrased; he did not say 'when *their* child was born' or 'when *her* child was born', but only 'when *a* child was born'. Speculation about the identity of this baby has focused on two female children connected with Madame Brussels' establishment: Lily Grelcke, the 'adopted daughter' mentioned in Caroline's will under her adoptive name – Irene Maria Yvonne Hodgson – and Cara Plumpton, the daughter of Alfred Plumpton whose birth in Melbourne was never registered.[16] Lily, born in 1887, became Caroline's adopted daughter Irene Hodgson in about 1888, and Cara was born at the end of 1882.[17] We don't know when the 'orgie' was supposed to have taken place, so it might have been either one – or neither – of these children.

We know that Cara was raised by the Plumptons in Melbourne, because 'Miss Cara Plumpton' is recorded as performing in a theatrical production in 1890.[18] Cara's relationship to Alfred Plumpton is also stated, along with the place and date of her birth in her school record after they returned to England.[19] Despite this evidence of Cara belonging to the Plumptons and living with them in Melbourne, history enthusiasts have puzzled over whether she was actually the child of Caroline Hodgson rather than Alfred's wife, and a peculiarly worded obituary for Alfred in *The Australasian* does nothing to settle the matter: 'He has left behind him a sturdy, bright-witted, and gifted daughter to console his widow.'[20]

Was she not consoling her mother?

Alfred William Henry Plumpton came to Melbourne with his wife in 1878. He was a good tenor, but he preferred composing music to singing it. He had published numerous pieces before he left England, including an operetta, sacred songs and pieces for children, but his most popular fare was the British nineteenth-century equivalent of today's pop music, with sweet titles such as 'The Trysting Tree' and 'Like a Summer Shower'. He was also a more than competent keyboard player, and occasionally after they left England he performed duets on the harmonium with his wife on the piano. Alfred's wife was born Charlotte Elizabeth Ann Tasker, and they married in 1862 in London.[21] She was nineteen years old when they married and he was twenty-one; they were both professors of music – she of music and he of singing – but their skills were of a very different style and calibre.[22] Charlotte Tasker was a brilliant soloist on both the piano and the organ. At the age of thirteen she was appointed organist of St Dunstan-in-the-West, Fleet Street, and at sixteen she was elected as a King's Scholar of the Royal Academy of Music.[23] Charlotte went on to play at concerts in England 'with a brilliancy and finish which it would be almost impossible to surpass', but she never used the name 'Mrs Plumpton'.[24] Eliza Capner was the unwed mother who used that name. She gave birth to a baby called Alfred Ernest Plumpton in 1871 and named Alfred Plumpton as the father of her son.[25] Eliza and Alfred appear to have lived together as husband and wife for a time around 1875 when the baby was baptised, but it didn't last.[26]

The state of Alfred's marriage can be read in his wife's stage names, moving as she did from 'Madame Charlotte Tasca' to 'Miss' or 'Mademoiselle' Carlotta Tasca, and for a brief time Alfred Plumpton found himself performing on the other side of the world, at the Scandinavian Music Hall in Castlereagh Street, Sydney.[27] When he returned to England 'Miss Carlotta Tasca' was performing at the promenade concerts at the Royal Philharmonic Theatre in London, but in 1878 Alfred and Madame Carlotta Tasca went on a professional tour together, to India and Australia.[28]

They arrived in Melbourne on the *Assam* in June 1878, intending to commence their tour of the Australian colonies with a short season in Melbourne.[29] They began with Madame Tasca alone providing a private pianoforte recital for 'gentlemen belonging to the press and representing music'; she gave a performance of skill and musical knowledge that astonished Melbourne's music world.[30] At her farewell concert in Melbourne, Madame Tasca then chose to present her considerable talents as an organist.[31]

By the time they left Victoria for Adelaide in mid-August the gifted couple seem to have overawed the musical establishment, and by the end of September it was decided: Alfred Plumpton was to become the musical director at the Melbourne Academy of Music, and Madame Tasca would become the organist at St Andrew's Church, Brighton.[32]

Coming back to Caroline Hodgson, then, if Alfred Plumpton was Madame Brussels' fancy man – as Henry Varley called him – when and how did he meet her?[33] There is a range of possibilities. Alfred's position in the theatrical world gave him plenty of scope and opportunities for mixing with the women of the flash brothels. We know Caroline frequented the theatre – she was going there when the customs inspectors called and drank her champagne – and she was an eye-catching young woman.

Caroline Hodgson in her early days in Melbourne (1870s)

We also know that the chief commissioner of police, Frederick Standish, had on occasions introduced men to the expensive brothels, as his diary across the time of the visit of the Duke of Edinburgh in the 1860s shows, and he was a keen theatre-goer, as his extant diaries attest. He also knew Rosina Carandini, having taken her to the circus and accompanied the rest of her family on a picnic when they visited Bendigo in the 1850s.[34] Madame Tasca performed with Rosina Carandini at a concert in Melbourne in 1878, and Rosina was one of the vocalists who performed with the Academy of Music.[35] There were plenty of connections to lead Plumpton to Madame Brussels' establishment if he had been interested, and if Standish was the link then it is likely to have been in the Plumptons' early years in Melbourne because Standish died in 1883.[36] That would also fit with the suggestion that Cara Plumpton was 'Syphilia' from the mock christening at Madame Brussels' brothel. She was born on 29 December 1882.[37] But what would she have been doing at Madame Brussels' brothel?

If Madame Tasca was her mother, would her father have taken her there? It is highly unlikely that a man of that era would have been seen taking a baby anywhere in public, much less to a brothel, especially among 'the bloods about town'; babies were the domain of mothers and hired nannies, not men of Alfred Plumpton's standing. But there is no proof that Madame Tasca was her mother, so what if Cara lived there because Caroline Hodgson was her real mother?

The fact that there is no birth registration for Cara in Victoria's records makes the question a reasonable one, but Martha Burrell's twins were registered in 1880, so why would Caroline Hodgson not register a baby in 1882? However, if Madame Tasca was the mother, she may well not have known to do it. Cara's name is no help, either – 'Cara' being a nicely ambiguous derivation of 'Charlotte', 'Carlotta' or 'Caroline'. Going back to basics, then, what evidence do we have for pregnancy in either of these two women in 1882? None at all for Caroline Hodgson, but we would not expect to. She purchased her second property in Lonsdale Street East at the beginning of the year, but she would not have been pregnant then; she was prosecuted for selling liquor without a licence, but she did not appear in court; her name was mentioned at the Police Commission, but she was not asked to give evidence.[38] Otherwise she kept her house quiet and made no appearance in the newspapers. In 1882 Caroline was earning well and had successfully defended her business against a number of charges; there is nothing to suggest that she would have given birth to a baby and then given it up in favour of her career, especially since she adopted an abandoned baby later. Nor is there anything to indicate that she would have handed her own baby over to another woman – the wife of her lover – to treat as her own.

As for Madame Tasca, in December 1882 she was forty-one years of age – an unusual but not impossible age for a first pregnancy, and she was due to take part in the Melbourne Musical Festival at the Exhibition Buildings. The festival was a huge undertaking and loomed large in both size and importance for Melbourne, and especially her husband. Everyone who was anyone in the Melbourne music scene was involved, including her husband as one of six conductors.[39] The festival was to run across four days, the last being

27 December, but Madame Tasca was only on the program to 'do duty at the organ' on two of them, both at St Patrick's Cathedral: on Christmas Day she played the organ for the High Pontifical Mass (Alfred directed the musical service, and she played his Mass in G), and again the following morning when her husband was conducting his cantata, 'Endymion', which was 'specially composed for this festival'.[40] Cara was born two days later.

The question, then, is whether Madame Tasca could have done all this and given birth to her first child at the age of forty-one? Could a woman in the final stages of pregnancy have handled the physical demands of playing the St Patrick's Cathedral organ? That question was at least partly answered by the organist Ria Anjelika Polo, who recorded a video of herself playing the Scots' Church organ the week before her first baby's birth.[41] It shows how she was able to adjust her position at the organ to take account of her pregnancy and still reach the keys and pedals. As she pointed out, in 1882 the organ would not have had an electric action, so the pedals would have provided substantial exercise, and sitting for the required period may well have been uncomfortable, but it was not unusual for an assistant to arrange the stops during a performance, and Madame Tasca does not seem to have been physically delicate, or the sort of woman to give in to back pain or any other difficulty.[42] It would certainly seem to have been possible for her to play while undergoing a normal pregnancy, so is there any other evidence of her being pregnant in the preceding months or giving birth after Christmas?

Women of the Plumptons' class in nineteenth-century Melbourne did not give birth in hospitals; they were usually attended by an accoucheur (male doctor) at home, so we would not expect to find hospital records for Cara's birth. Nor would we expect to find any mention of Madame Tasca's pregnancy in the newspapers, even if she was heavily pregnant during a performance. Such things were simply not remarked upon, either in person or in print. The thing we might expect to find, though, is some reduction in her concert schedule in the last few months before her confinement. In the months after their arrival in Melbourne, Madame Tasca's concert schedule was heavy, but it reduced substantially in 1880 and 1881. Then, about the time in 1882 when she might have become pregnant she took on an additional teaching appointment, this time at Hamilton in the far west of the state.[43] She was also reported at an increased number of concerts, and in October and November her workload was particularly heavy, culminating in a report in *The Age* that she would not be participating in 'Mrs Cutter's benefit' because she had 'up-country engagements' (her school teaching in Hamilton).[44] In fact she returned to Melbourne by train four days before the concert and attended as a listener rather than a performer.[45] But on arrival she discovered that the solo pianist had been 'suddenly seized with acute rheumatism' and at a moment's notice she kindly agreed to fill the gap.[46] As *The Herald* reported afterwards, 'the concert was a very grand but a rather long one', and that would have been particularly so for Madame Tasca if she was eight months pregnant.[47]

Madame Tasca's workload in 1882, then, does not show much sign of her keeping out of the public eye, or seeking a restful pregnancy, but there is no record of her playing again between 25 November and the two Melbourne Musical Festival appearances. For a player of her stature, and the importance of the events in terms of her husband's musical reputation, the Christmas performances would have been not-to-be-missed occasions. But if she did get through those performances by the skin of her teeth, with a baby born two days later, can her schedule in the following month tell us anything about her recovery?

On 9 January 1883 Alfred set off for Hobart, and Madame Tasca followed two days later.[48] There is no sign of a child travelling with them, but that would not have been unusual for the time; it would be expected that the baby would be cared for at home by a wet nurse. They were away from Melbourne for two weeks and gave three concerts in each of Hobart and Launceston in that time. Towards the end of the tour the Launceston *Examiner* reported the first-ever criticism of Madame Tasca's playing: 'This lady possesses undoubtedly great digital skill, but she lacks to a certain extent grace of action.'[49] There were also complaints about her husband's accompaniments.[50]

So, could Madame Tasca have done all this and given birth to a baby as well? In the nineteenth century it was not unusual for women to work until the moment a baby was born, even through the first stages of labour, and to behave as though there was 'nothing to see here'. Georgiana McCrae, for example, tells of hosting a male guest without him realising that she was in labour.[51] By the 1880s it would have been unusual for a woman of Madame Tasca's class to be out and about as much as she was while clearly pregnant, but Madame Tasca was not an ordinary woman. She was thoroughly devoted to music, and determined verging on obsessive about her work; she was also seemingly energetic as well as gifted, and often played very long and difficult pieces from memory. Nevertheless, she did attempt to have a night off at Mrs Cutter's benefit, and despite playing very familiar pieces in Tasmania she and her husband made a few uncharacteristic slips; the existence of a baby could explain these incidents. For people like the Plumptons the baby would have made little difference to their day-to-day programs so as long as Madame Tasca survived childbirth without severe physical damage.[52] Despite the peculiar wording of *The Australasian*'s obituary, then, Cara was probably the Plumptons' child; she was certainly treated as part of the Plumpton family. So why was her birth not registered? Perhaps because the Plumptons were both absorbed by their careers, and either did not know it should have been done or simply never got around to doing it.

After Caroline Hodgson's trial in 1889, Henry Varley continued to put Alfred Plumpton under a good deal of pressure over his relationship with Madame Brussels. According to the *Truth* (presumably derived from Varley) Alfred actively supported her business:

He used to live in Victoria Parade ... Every morning, before going to Collins-street, he called at Madame Brussells' [*sic*], who would fill his sovereign-case with 'yellow boys.' That was his daily allowance for shouting expenses, and the money was well laid out on behalf of his inamorata's bagnio. He was one of her best travellers for enticing men of means to her house. These bagnios, it should be mentioned, have 'travellers,' men who are always about town, and are free-handed in 'shouting.' After a little supper, the traveller will propose a trip 'to the East,' to 'see life.'[53]

It made a good story, and Varley made the most of it. According to *The Bulletin*, his Sunday night addresses were 'creating something of a panic among the nobility and gentry of Smellbourne' because he had 'taken to "naming" the most prominent frequenters of Madame Brussels' bagnio, and a number of well-known citizens are now engaged in speculating as to whether their turn will come next'.[54] Alfred supposedly threatened him with libel – along with *The Daily Telegraph*, which published Varley's rants – but to no avail. As the *Truth* would have it, in 1891, 'Melbourne became too uncomfortable a place for Plumpton, and he left for London.'[55]

Whether the Plumptons departed Melbourne because of Varley's accusations or not, they left behind a puzzle that has teased anyone curious about Madame Brussels ever since. Was there a Syphilia? And if so, who was she? The wording of the *Truth* article means the baby could well have belonged to one of the sex workers and had nothing to do with either Plumpton *or* Caroline. In the context of a raucous party, with champagne corks popping, it was unlikely to be a visitor's child, but there were other women living in her brothels, and we know that Mrs O'Brien, at least, had children in the cottage next door; could Syphilia have been one of hers? A brutal husband like John O'Brien might have thought such a performance was amusing, but an unemployed working man was hardly likely to have been fraternising with the likes of Alfred Plumpton, and in any case his youngest child was a boy, Augustus.[56] Cara Plumpton too is unlikely to be Syphilia; aside from the fact that she was most likely Madame Tasca's child, she was also unlikely to have been taken to the brothel. Which leaves us with the abandoned baby, Lily. Nothing that we have learnt about Caroline Hodgson suggests that she would have allowed a baby to be treated in this way. But Caroline managed a number of brothels in Lonsdale Street, and she could not have been present all night every night at each one, although if she was as smitten with Alfred Plumpton as the *Truth* reporter claimed, she would probably have tried to be there on the nights when he appeared. So it might have been baby Lily who was christened, perhaps in the days before Caroline knew that Emilie was not coming back. The behaviour of 'the "bloods" about town' might even have been the catalyst that determined Caroline to advertise for her mother and then adopt the abandoned baby as her own, spending time and money to ensure she could provide her with a home away from the brothels of Lonsdale Street. At the same time, the christening of Syphilia might just have been another tale emanating from a *Truth* journalist's imagination.

For today's historians, chasing the story about Plumpton produces numerous intriguing details. The set of three conductors' batons held by Museum Victoria in Plumpton's name, for example, includes one inscribed with the word 'Savage' and engraved with dancing girls.[57] The Savage Club in London was founded in 1857 by George Augustus Sala, among others.[58] In its early days it was a club for bohemian writers and artists, the not-quite-respectable men of letters and the arts, but in 1871, when Plumpton's marriage was rocky and he was conducting an affair that resulted in an illegitimate son, the Savage Club expanded its membership to include musicians, and hired its first piano.[59] Plumpton and his music hall songs might have been an entertaining addition, especially in the year or two when he was composing, publishing and selling popular sheet music. Several of his connections point in this direction: in 1872, for example, Plumpton set to music the words of a poem by Lord Houghton, who was a member of the Cannibal Club along with Sala and Stud's uncle General Hodgson.[60] There was no Savage Club in Melbourne when Plumpton arrived in 1878, but the equivalent was the Yorick Club, which Plumpton joined along with Marcus Clarke, Curtis Candler and others.[61] Were these links with Sala and Lord Houghton coincidental, or was Plumpton a flagellator too? And did Plumpton introduce Sala to Madame Brussels' establishment when he was visiting Melbourne in 1885?

17.

RETIREMENT PLANS

'The Melbourne Baby Show' … Quite a picture was Irene Marie [sic] Hodgson in her quaint poke bonnet and Greenaway dress, and as she sat nursing her doll she forcibly reminded one of a recent Christmas picture entitled 'Now I'm Ready.'[1]
—*The South Australian Chronicle* (Adelaide), 19 October 1889, p. 16

1890 HAD DAWNED FAIR FOR CAROLINE HODGSON. Her business was blooming, as was her adopted daughter, Irene, and having escaped the trap set by Henry Varley and Colonel Barker she could have been forgiven for thinking that her future was secure and she might enjoy a weekend retreat at the beach. At the same time, she might have felt ready to start planning her retirement, especially since she would have known about the legislation that prohibited children under sixteen from living in a brothel.[2] Once she had decided to keep the baby and raise her as her own Caroline would have seen the need for a home for Irene far away from Lonsdale Street, and in the face of Varley's threats she may have been attracted by the prospect of a domestic family life for herself. On 3 March 1890 she purchased 'Gnarwin', a free-standing two-storey lace-verandahed Victorian house on Beaconsfield Parade in St Kilda, overlooking the sandy beach of Port Phillip Bay.[3]

'Gnarwin'; 39 Beaconsfield Parade, St Kilda,
when Caroline Hodgson owned it

Once again she may have taken advice about the location from people she knew: Agnes King, the widow of her long-time landlord of the rented brothels in Lonsdale Street, lived further along Beaconsfield Parade.[4] Soon afterwards a house adjoining the rear of Gnarwin came up for sale, so she purchased that as well.[5] But Henry Varley's ego was still smarting from his courtroom defeat in 1889; his imagination had kept him fired up and abusive towards her:

In this haunt of gilded licentiousness the summer nights have again and again witnessed ten or twelve young girls in a perfectly nude condition, entertaining numbers of prominent Melbourne and Victorian men in the garden and rooms of this protected vestibule of hell.[6]

Did Varley or any of his informants actually *see* these ten or twelve naked maidens? That is doubtful, because although he was right in saying that Caroline's garden was protected (at least partly by a brick wall), police records show that she had no more than six 'girls' working at her house at any one time, and usually no more than four.[7] But Varley never let facts get in the way of a good story; he was a master fiction writer. Here is his version of the tale of the white feather, addressing his audience of 'Men Only and Boys Over 16' in a pamphlet:

> Are you aware, Sirs, that some little time since you might have seen parading the 'block' in Collins-street, the accursed procuress, Madame B., in charge of a beautiful girl under twenty, with a white feather in her hat, telling by advertisement (the white feather), that maidenly virtue was to be had for price at her gilded den?'[8]

The unspoken context is that in the nineteenth century there was a common belief that a man could cure his syphilis by having sex with a virgin.[9] There were no antibiotics, and no cure for sexually transmitted infections, hence the supposedly high price for 'maiden virtue', and the implied evil of Madame Brussels in Varley's story of the white feather. The tale has been quoted many times without making this context explicit, and, despite the serious nature of the accusation, until recently it has not been challenged.[10] There is, however, considerable doubt about the veracity of the whole story.

There are three main problems. First, in the nineteenth century white feathers were not an advertisement for virginity in Melbourne. In newspapers they usually turned up in tales of men 'showing the white feather' to their opponents in a contest of some kind, with the reporter using the symbol to convey cowardice.[11] White feathers in this era were also common on clothing for women of all ages, especially on hats. One example, of 'a most tasteful head-dress', was illustrated in *The Australasian* not long before Varley wrote his sermon. It was described as 'arranged in a very becoming shape. It is composed of an ivory white ostrich feather on one side, and clusters of soft white marabout on the other.'[12] White feathers no doubt did adorn virgins at times, for example on the bridesmaids at a Melbourne wedding in 1888 who were 'dressed in white Liberty silk and lace … The tulle veils were thrown back and caught at the neck with a gold arrow set in diamonds, falling from a white feather and bow.'[13] But it was hardly an exclusive association, given that *The Australasian Sketcher with Pen and Pencil* reported the costume of the Princess of Wales the same year, who (in her drawing room) 'wore a dress of the most exquisite white and silver brocade, trimmed volante of lovely silver lace, looped with plumes of white ostrich feathers, corsage to correspond.'[14] The princess had been married since 1863 and had given birth to six children, so her costume was hardly indicative of virginity.[15] Any local association of the white feather with youth also has to be questioned given the report 'of the last Garden Party held by the Prince of Wales' printed by *The Gippsland Farmers' Journal and Traralgon, Heyfield and Rosedale News*; it described how 'her Majesty [Queen Victoria] appeared leaning on the Prince's arm. She was dressed in black with a white feather in her bonnet, and leant on a serviceable looking walking stick.'[16] The symbolism of the white feather for virginity was therefore either non-existent or not widely understood, which is probably why Varley chose to insert it in brackets in order to implant his chosen meaning in the reader's mind.

The second problem with Varley's story is that there is no evidence whatsoever that Madame Brussels conducted such a foul trade. Instead there is evidence to the contrary: of the four girls who were supposed to give evidence against her at her trial in 1889, none of the four were virgins when they went to Madame Brussels' house.[17] One of the policemen in the same case said that he had never 'seen in the house girls of tender years.'[18] None of the six policemen involved in the case against Caroline Hodgson made any accusations of the kind that Varley made, nor do any of the records from the police archives at the Public Record Office Victoria.

The same files, however, do provide evidence of a third problem with Varley's tale. In December 1890, the chief commissioner of police received a letter from a man called John Gibbs:

> I beg to ask for the sake of decency, also for the sake of those I love so dearly. I ask you to go or send to H. Varley in Collins Street, and demand all letter he [h]as received from me, and burnt them if they are not burnt already, for they have only been written under a fit of madness & I am not responsible for its contents.[19]

Gibbs' letter to the police contains a tale that bears a striking resemblance to the story of the virgin and the white feather which Varley had been telling in the months beforehand: 'I am led to believe one of my old sweethearts which is near and dear to me, [h]as been walked Collins Street flying the White Feather as the signal for Licentiousness ...'.

In dismay at the way Varley had twisted the tale that Gibbs told him 'under a fit of madness', Gibbs tried to retrieve his letters: 'I desire all notices taken down concerning Mad Brussels' case ... I have written asking for an interview with him, [but] receiving no answer I take it as a refusal.'

Gibbs wanted his letters returned or destroyed, but with no answer from Varley he turned to the police. He was concerned for his 'sweetheart', 'for though she [h]as fallen its anguish for me to see it made public', and asked simply for respect for the woman by suggesting that Varley 'should be cautioned to use a little more discretion in what he [is] speaking about for the sake of friends'. But respect for women of Madame Brussels' ilk was not part of Henry Varley's make-up. He abhorred prostitution, and she was the standard-bearer for all the vice he attached to it. Nor was a plea for discretion likely to influence Varley, especially from those who gave their address as Room 24E, Gordon Chambers – John Gibbs was living in a rooming house for single working men who could ill afford to live anywhere else. Gibbs wrote to the police again a month later, and this time the police interviewed him. They concluded that he was 'a man of weak intellect and his imaginings re the girl at Brussells [*sic*] &c is the result of a disordered brain'.[20] The police paid little attention to such people, just as Varley paid little attention to facts. John Gibbs said only that the white feather indicated 'licentiousness'; it was Varley's fiction that gave it the virginal twist.[21]

Varley's campaign against vice had been relentless since Caroline's acquittal in 1889, and his focus on her and Alfred Plumpton must have caused immense anxiety for them both. Plumpton was able to cut and run back to England, but Caroline's wealth was tied up in property and a business in Melbourne. In this context Gnarwin appears to have been part of a plan for her to retire from the business, or at least reduce her involvement. In December 1890 she took out a mortgage of £1000 with her solicitor, Samuel Gillott, on her property in Lonsdale Street despite not doing any building work there.[22] Nine months later she obtained more cash by mortgaging both the houses in Carter Street. There is no direct evidence of the purpose of these loans in the records, but in 1892 the police received a series of complaints from a solicitor about her house in Beaconsfield Parade. The first, written on 8 March, could only have emerged from a wealthy man's sense of entitlement. The writer was a solicitor, the son of Sir Archibald Michie, one of Victoria's respected elder statesmen:

> I have the misfortune to own a Terrace of Five two storied houses on the Beaconsfield Parade St Kilda next to a house named 'Gnarwin' in the occupation of a questionable character as I am informed known as Madame Brussells [*sic*]. Some of my houses are continually being vacated in consequence of the nature of the occupation of the occupier of 'Gnarwin'. I shall feel much indebted to you (as also will I am sure, the neighbours generally), if you instruct your local Sergeant of Police to take any steps possible to rid the place of the nuisance complained of.[23]

Michie sent his complaint directly to the chief commissioner of police; it was quickly passed down the line until it reached the superintendent of the area, who requested a report from Senior Constable John Thompson. Thompson's report on 14 March covered two foolscap pages, indicating that Madame Brussels' reputation had preceded her. He wrote that he had watched the house very closely ever since Madame Brussels bought it, and that it was 'done up and furnished in a most expensive style'. He went on to say that he could only imagine 'that the object of Madam Brussells [*sic*] in spending over £4000 in this place was to have a house of ill fame established, but in this she failed and there has never been anything seen by either me or the neighbours to lead to a belief that it succeeded for even a week.' The next day, before passing the report back to the chief commissioner, a more senior member of the same station added a file note to say that:

> When Madame Brussells [*sic*] purchased this property
> it is likely she had the intention of starting a brothel –
> but that intention was not carried out as she was told
> by the police that if she attempted any thing [*sic*] of the
> sort she would be prosecuted.

Caroline probably used the £1000 loan from Samuel Gillott to renovate Gnarwin. She probably also used the loan money from her Carter Street houses but it was seemingly not enough, as she took out a second mortgage on the same properties. The depression of the 1890s was no doubt beginning to affect her business by then, but she pressed on. Thompson's report included the fact that after it was done up 'a pair of ponies and Buggy [were] brought there', but 'after a few weeks watching they found that there was nothing to be alarmed about, and that it is without exception the quietest occupied house in Beaconsfield Parade'. In his view the house was 'only occupied by a man and a woman, the former only at night, the ponies Buggy and owner have gone back to Melbourne and are seen only about once in a month in St Kilda'. The 'man and woman', he said, were servants, and according to the St Kilda rate books they were 'out' every time the rate collector called.

In compiling his report Thompson interviewed the complaining solicitor's tenants, who said 'they saw nothing objectionable about Madam Brussells [*sic*] and did not leave for that reason'. Others he spoke to, including a JP, reported seeing nothing 'improper or unseemly' going on at Gnarwin, and Thompson was of the opinion that 'the police cannot interfere'. And so they didn't. Nor did they appear to know what was really going on at Gnarwin.

Caroline's purpose in renovating the house – despite the police assumption – was more domestic than professional. After 1891 Caroline ceased her tenancy of Robert and Agnes King's houses in Lonsdale Street and consolidated her business at 32–34. It may be that business had dropped off after the closure of the 1888 International Exhibition and the worsening financial situation in Melbourne, but her subsequent decisions suggest that she was deliberately scaling down her business with a view to retiring to Gnarwin. Like many other people in Melbourne at the time, though, her life was to be upended by events beyond her control.

18.

A POLICEMAN'S DEATH

STUD HODGSON WAS ANTICIPATING AN EARLY DEATH. On 25 May 1892, at the age of fifty-six, he made his will, and on 22 June he resigned from the police force. He had been stationed at Kerang in northern Victoria, but his health was steadily deteriorating.[1] He had tuberculosis.

In his will, Stud left £1000 and his clothes to Agnes Clatworthy 'in recognition of the great care and loving kindness she used in nursing me through a long and tedious illness'.[2] Agnes was a forty-three-year-old woman raising three teenage children on her own, and she had presumably been caring for him since he was transferred to Kerang towards the end of March that year.[3] When he made that will Stud had seemingly intended to die in Kerang, nursed by Agnes Clatworthy; but by Christmas he was living at Caroline's house in Beaconsfield Parade, cooled by the breeze off Port Phillip Bay. On 22 December he added a codicil to his will, removing Agnes entirely and redirecting her legacy of £1000 to his wife. It was not that his original will had excluded Caroline Hodgson; she was already the beneficiary of £2000 and his 'jewellery photograph album photograph and any article of my personal effects which she may desire in token of the love which I once bore her', so the extra brought her share to £3000.[4] The remainder of his property was to be converted to cash and held in trust for his widowed sister Katherine, who was living in Brussels. It has been speculated that perhaps Caroline had claimed a larger share of his estate in return for her hospitality, but in tidying up his debts his probate papers show a sum of £9 12s. 6d. paid to Mrs Jane Gadsen, Kerang, Nurse.[5] The break with Agnes Clatworthy appears to have occurred before he left Kerang, requiring him to employ another nurse before he left; perhaps it was also his reason for returning to Melbourne.

All the evidence points towards Stud Hodgson being an unusual man. He appears to have rejected the English boarding school system, along with his family's military tradition, yet he found a niche in the strongly hierarchical and physically risky Victorian police force. His police record shows that he did not get on with some men and showed insufficient deference to others, but he seemed to thrive on the solitude of small communities and remote country areas.[6] He was not inclined to blindly follow orders, but he was willing to stand up against cruelty or the mistreatment of animals or women.[7] His police record consistently notes his intelligence, as if it was an unexpected trait for a man occupying such a lowly rank, but he does not seem to have chafed against the lack of promotion. Altogether Stud seems to have been a man with a steady sense of duty and a strong capacity for self-reliance, but the evidence also suggests that in some fundamental way he did not fit neatly into the world of his birth family. The events surrounding his time with Agnes Clatworthy hint at a possible explanation.

It is doubtful whether Agnes was a widow. At least, she did become a widow when her first husband – the father of her first three children – died, but her second husband seems to have deserted her. Her obituary in 1917 does not mention him. By the time she was nursing Stud in Kerang, then, she was a mother in her forties, raising three teenage children on her own, having lost her only child by her second husband five years earlier.[8] Was she looking for a closer relationship with Stud than simply nurse and patient? It is clear from Stud's tone in his will regarding 'the great care and loving kindness she used in nursing me' that there was gratitude and a degree of warmth in his feelings for Agnes, but might she have misunderstood those feelings? Might she have mistaken his friendly thank-offering for love? A man in Stud's position would have been vulnerable, and there is little in his history apart from his marriage to Caroline to suggest that he was experienced in relationships with women; there is, however, another possibility. What if Stud was gay? And what if he realised that Agnes was hoping for a third husband, and knew that he could not reciprocate with more than friendship? In the context of nineteenth-century Victoria, Stud would not have – could not have – explained this to her. But, in the context of his marriage, Caroline might well have become aware of his sexual orientation and they may have chosen to go their separate ways because of it. If that were the case, and if she accepted his way of being, it would explain a whole raft of things, including why Caroline named her private residence 'Studholme Villa'. It would also explain why Stud left Agnes's nursing care and employed Jane Gadsen instead, and why he returned to Caroline when he was dying; apart from anything else he would have known that he would not have to explain himself to her.

Like pornography, homosexuality barely had a name until late in the nineteenth century, but in Britain and its colonial cultures it did have a moral and criminal judgment attached.[9] It could not have been spoken of openly in Victoria, and we would not expect to find concrete evidence of Stud's relationships if there were any. By marrying a young Prussian orphan in England he had satisfied one of the expectations of his family – that he would marry – without committing himself to the social circle his family occupied. He tried traditional marriage – at the late age of thirty-six – but it did not suit him.

If Stud had been a rebellious or self-indulgent gay man he might have lived a comfortably dissolute life in England on his inheritance; if he had been indolent or less self-respecting he might have bought a house in Melbourne and tried living in a fantasy of hetero marital harmony; but instead he joined the police force, broke with his wife and went up country to live a solitary existence as a mounted policeman. Yet he came back to Melbourne – and his wife – when he could not look after himself. If Stud was gay, and Caroline knew and accepted that, this would not be surprising.

Not long before Stud returned to Melbourne to take up residence at 39 Beaconsfield Parade, Caroline Hodgson had another visitor. When her brother-in-law, John Hodgson, sailed off to New Zealand with his family in the 1870s, Caroline and his wife, Lizzie Jane, had kept in touch. After a few years John's family had returned and settled in Sydney, but in the late 1880s John left his family and went back to England, leaving Lizzie Jane to raise their three children on her own.[10] The two women visited each other, although given the nature of Caroline's business she probably went to Sydney more often than Lizzie Jane travelled to Melbourne, if only because Caroline had more money to spend and the desire to explore the fashion and shops away from the judgmental eyes of Melbourne.[11] So Caroline would have known Lizzie Jane's son, Charlie, who, as a nineteen-year-old, was living at home with his mother and working in the haberdashery department of Anthony Hordern's, one of Sydney's biggest retail stores.[12] Caroline welcomed her nephew when he chose to come down from Sydney and stay with her at the brothel, and in return he treasured a letter from her, keeping it among his most precious and personal items.[13]

9 April 1892
32 Lonsdale St

My Dear Charlie

I expect you are quite at home again with your business, and that you like the new department by this time altho your Ma told me that you did not like it. I hope you quite understand the private mark by this time.

I expect we will see you again someday in Melbourne and I am glad that you like it, for after all Melbourne is a nice clean place.

We all miss you very much – Topsy sends her love to you hoping to see you someday in fact all the girls send their love to you. George and Mary as well also Walter in fact everybody sends their love. Mrs Burrell sends her best love to you and tell the old Irish gentleman in the shop that he will see me someday about the end of May or the beginning of June.

Now with love Charlie
I remain
Your Aff[ectiona]te Aunt
C. Hodgson

The letter is stilted in the way that letters from one generation to another can be, but it still conveys warmth, along with a sense of acceptance and the expectation that their relationship will continue. Charlie was a man of style, with a great interest in the theatre; after his death a family member donated eleven volumes of his diaries to the State Library of New South Wales, listing all the plays Charlie had seen in Sydney from 1885 to 1916 together with their plots and actors and his assessment of their merits. After discussion with the family, the library catalogued them with the subject heading – among others – 'Homosexuality – New South Wales'.

Charles Studholme Hodgson (1873–1950)

Was Caroline aware of her nephew's sexual orientation? At the age of nineteen, was Charlie experimenting with Topsy and 'all the girls', or enjoying some platonic friendships? As an observer of men and the madam of a brothel for two decades, it is unlikely that Charlie's preference escaped Caroline's notice over the period of his visit, especially since it has been suggested that she had other gay friends: 'Her clients were gentlemen in high positions in various walks of life, men of brains, and sometimes of "culture" – Greek culture – who were her guides, friends and counsellors.'[14]

From the tone of her letter to Charlie it is likely that she appreciated and accepted him as family and found him charming and fun to have around; his visit would also have given her something in common with Stud – a real family connection – when he turned up later in the year needing to be nursed.

There is no way we can know for certain whether Stud was gay, but there are small signs scattered through Caroline's history that together suggest she was very fond of him. She may have been angry, hurt and upset about his departure to begin with, but by the early 1880s she appears to have been making some attempt to protect him from her growing reputation.

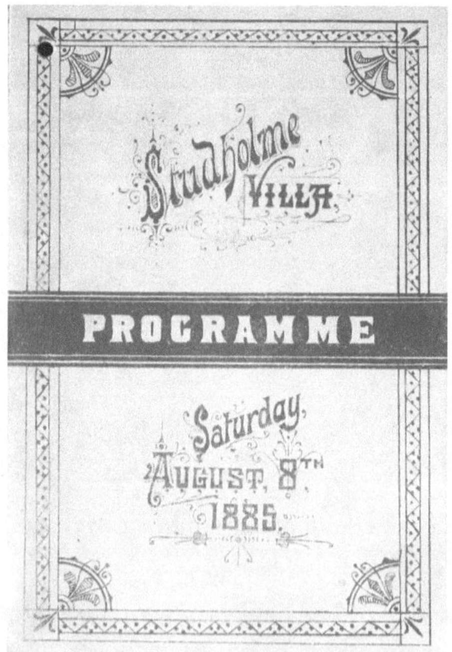

Front of dance card for an event at Caroline Hodgson's private house

The fact that Caroline's husband was a policeman appears to have been relatively common knowledge, with a poem being published mentioning 'Madame's husband – a trooper – away far / Awaits his promotion, and really there are / Some reasons to show / Why he should go / To the top of the tree, like a brilliant star'.[15] All through the Police Commission of the early 1880s, though, she is referred to under the name 'Bussel' or 'Bussells', and in 1884 when she wrote to the newspaper about the bootmaker's family she signed the letter 'C. Brussels'. Throughout the 1880s she appears in numerous court reports as 'Carrie Brussels', too, as though she deliberately shed the name 'Hodgson', and perhaps it was to protect her policeman husband. At the same time, by naming her private house 'Studholme Villa' she kept and nurtured his memory for herself.

Caroline Hodgson was a brothel madam, wicked and immoral by the standards of Melbourne's respectable society, but she tended her husband well in his dying months. The last doctor to attend to him was one of the best in Melbourne – Walter Balls-Headley might have been famed for his gynaecological skills in particular, but he was also president of the Medical Society of Victoria in 1889; Caroline brought him in for a final consultation, and then to certify Stud's death.[16] Stud died at 39 Beaconsfield Parade on 7 February 1893, when Caroline's adopted daughter, Irene, was a little over five years old.

In her old age Irene appeared to remember the time she spent with Stud in St Kilda; in her recollections she called him 'my father' alongside 'my mother' Caroline Hodgson, and her tone was natural and affectionate, like that of Caroline for her nephew Charlie.[17] The day after Stud's death the notice in the newspapers recited his pedigree: 'eldest son of Robert Studholme Hodgson, of Andover, Hampshire, England and grandson, of General John Hodgson, of the King's Own Fourth, and nephew of General Studholme Hodgson, of the 19th Regiment'.[18]

Caroline spared no expense on her husband's funeral. Stud was buried in a French-polished silk- and lead-lined oak coffin, mounted with solid brass fittings and covered with the best silk velvet. He was taken to his last resting place in a hearse drawn by four horses attired with plumes and cloths.[19] In the paper that reported his death, his friends were invited to join his funeral procession from the house in Beaconsfield Parade to the St Kilda cemetery.[20] Caroline spread the same invitation over several Melbourne newspapers, but it is unknown how many vehicles turned up to join the cortege.

Sorting Stud's affairs after his death was complicated. Not by his will, or his family, or his executor, but by the financial situation in Melbourne. Stud owned no property, but he had benefited from his mother's inheritance, so by the time he died he had a substantial amount of capital in bank deposits and shares. If Caroline had known about the contents of his will she might have expected that her finances would improve dramatically after Stud's death, providing as it did for her to inherit £3000, along with his goods and chattels.[21] Unfortunately, by the time his estate was wound up early in 1894 the bank failures of 1893 had wrought havoc with his savings.[22] In the end Caroline was only to benefit by £1792 plus £70 worth of jewellery, and clothing to the value of £5. His sister, Katherine – the widow living in Brussels – was meant to receive 'the ultimate surplus' from his estate after payment of the legacy to Caroline, but there was no surplus. His funeral, however, was a superbly expensive and showy occasion.

Caroline would also have lost personally through the bank and building society failures of the early 1890s. Having taken out a mortgage on her Carter Street houses from the Australian Deposit and Mortgage Bank Ltd in September 1891, the bank failed in March 1892.[23] She quickly took out another loan from a private individual.[24] Her share of Stud's estate may therefore have been a disappointment to her, but in terms of an ordinary working man's wage it was still a substantial windfall. On the anniversary of his death the following year Caroline placed a lengthy notice in all of Melbourne's four daily newspapers, including the conservative *Argus*, adding (quite truthfully) a baronet to the family story along with some nods to religion and poetry:

> **HODGSON.**—In fond remembrance of my beloved husband Studholme George Hodgson, who departed this life on the 7th February, 1893, eldest son of Robert Studholme Hodgson, of Andover, Hampshire, England, and grandson of General John Hodgson, of the King's Own Fourth, and nephew of General Studholme Hodgson, of the 19th Regiment, also brother-in-law of the Baronet, Sir Francis Wood, the brother of Sir Evelyn Wood.

'The Lord gave and the Lord hath taken away ;
blessed be the name of the Lord.'

Leaves have their time to fall,
And flowers to wither at the north wind's breath,
And stars to set – but all,
Thou hast all seasons for thine own, O Death !
We know when moons shall wane,
When summer birds from far shall cross the sea,
When autumn's hue shall tinge the golden grain –
But who shall teach us when to look for thee?[25]

(Inserted by his affectionate wife, Caroline Hodgson.
Home papers please copy.)[26]

Melbourne's post office directories list Caroline's private house in Lonsdale Street as 'Vacant' throughout the time Stud was living at Gnarwin, and Irene's memories of the time imply his presence in the house at St Kilda.[27] Together they suggest that Caroline set up home there during Stud's final illness and stayed while lawyers were clearing up his estate. The brothel continued, though, most likely under the management of her house-keeper, Martha Burrell. Then, within a year and a month of Stud's death, Caroline rented out Gnarwin and 'Mrs Studholme Hodgson' embarked from Sydney on the RMS *Britannia* bound for London.[28] Unlike the wife of a country policeman, though, Caroline and Irene travelled in cabins, and they took a nursemaid with them.[29]

19.

A NEW HUSBAND

IN 1903, THE *TRUTH* CLAIMED THAT after Alfred Plumpton left, Madame Brussels 'was inconsolable, and she made several trips to London', as though she had gone there especially to seek him out and continue their relationship.[1] It is true that she made two trips to Europe in the 1890s and both of the ships she travelled on were destined for London, but in those days that was the commonest route for people travelling from Melbourne to Germany. On the first trip Caroline took Irene and went home to Germany to spend time with her sisters – Maria Baum and her family at Scheiderhöhe, and Augusta Reifferscheidt at Braschoss.[2] Caroline could possibly have engineered a meeting with Alfred Plumpton in London or Paris on that first journey, a year after Stud died – three years after Plumpton left Melbourne – but there is no evidence that she did so.[3] It is unlikely that Caroline was chasing Plumpton on her second trip to Europe either, since she was accompanied by a new husband. After visiting her sisters the first time, Caroline left Irene with Maria Baum in Scheiderhöhe and returned to Melbourne;[4] very shortly after disembarking in April 1895, Caroline married a young man from Braschoss: Jacob Pohl.[5]

No passenger record has been found for either Caroline Hodgson or Jacob Pohl entering Melbourne in 1895, but it seems likely that they met in Braschoss and travelled to Melbourne together, because they married at St Patrick's Cathedral within days of her return, and (in an echo of her first marriage) they had no family at the wedding.[6] The two witnesses were Martha Burrell and the sacristan of the cathedral.[7] The couple then set up house at Caroline's property in Lonsdale Street.

During that first trip to Europe, when Caroline went to meet the women Irene referred to later in her life as her aunts, Martha Burrell took over as manager of the brothel at 32 Lonsdale Street and kept it operating until Caroline's return.[8] After her marriage to Jacob Pohl, however, Caroline seems to have closed her brothel and combined the houses into one private residence.[9] There are no police or newspaper records relating to incidents at her houses, and the rate books, for the first time, listed all of her properties together and named 'Mrs Hodgson' as the occupant. Similarly, the *Sands & McDougall* post office directory which had previously either not listed the address or described the house as 'vacant' or the occupant as 'out', began to name the occupant of her combined properties as 'Mrs Caroline Hodgson' and then as 'Mrs Catherine Poole' (it was corrected to 'Mrs Caroline Pohl' in 1898). In 1896, with Mr and Mrs Pohl in residence in Lonsdale Street, Martha Burrell, Caroline's long-time brothel manager, appears in the rate books as the 'occupier' (tenant) of another brothel altogether in Exhibition Street – the old Rosalind House, where she had previously worked.[10] With its eleven rooms and sizeable garden, 32–34 Lonsdale Street would have been a luxurious space for the newlyweds.[11]

By the end of 1895 Caroline was preparing to return to Europe with her husband; she applied to the chief secretary for a change of name on her travel documents.[12] Her application caused a small furore. Caroline was born in Prussia and first married an Englishman, which gave her British citizenship; her marriage to Jacob Pohl, since he was German, had changed her status as well as her name. In November she applied for 'Letters of Naturalization' under the name 'Caroline Pohl late Caroline Hodgson', and while her application was met without demur and signed by the governor on 28 January 1896, 'late Caroline Hodgson' was crossed out.[13] She applied again on 4 February to reinstate 'late Caroline Hodgson', but this time she ran into some resistance. She was asked first of all for her reason for desiring the change, and her reply is recorded in a file note: 'Mrs Pohl intends taking a trip to Germany and she states that the authorities are very particular in regard to travellers and to avoid inconvenience wishes to have her name described as asked.'

A later file note from the undersecretary to the chief secretary, Charles Topp, shows that he was unfamiliar with Caroline Hodgson's background.[14]

> The child of a natural born British Subject though born abroad (out of the Queen's domain) is not an alien and does not require naturalization, if Mrs Pohl's father (Hodgson) was an Englishman Mrs Pohl is a British Subject. Further inquiry should be made as to Mrs Pohl's reason for asking for the addition to the letters and as to her parentage.

That was on 6 February. 'Perhaps she might be asked to call', he added. She did call, and presumably answered his questions satisfactorily, because on 14 February she signed for the receipt of her 'Letters of Naturalization'. Someone, however, must have alerted the undersecretary to her reputation, because on the same day he forwarded the papers to the chief commissioner of police, Hussey Chomley: 'As there is reason to believe that the Caroline Pohl referred to in the attached papers cannot correctly be described as "a person of good repute", I shall be glad if the police can furnish any information in regard to her occupation and character.'

Chomley sent the request down the line until it landed with Senior Constable Canty at the Russell Street police station. Canty had been policing in the city since before Caroline's trial in 1889 and he was very aware of her business, though some of the details he reported are inaccurate:

The Caroline Pohl referred to in the attached correspondence has been the owner and occupier of a 'flash brothel' … for about twenty years. During the greater part of that time she kept six or eight prostitutes always on the premises, and as many servants to wait on them. I believe each prostitute used to pay Madame Brussels (the name Caroline Pohl was best known by) so much per week or month for her board and lodging, & that might be the reason she describes herself as a boarding house keeper, but she certainly made her living and a great deal of money out of her brothel and the prostitutes who lived in it.

Despite the fact that she was no longer running a brothel – confirmed by Canty's use of the past tense – it was Canty's opinion that Caroline Pohl 'could not be correctly described as "a person of good repute"'. His report was passed back up the line to Chomley, who returned it to the undersecretary on 21 February. Topp hurriedly sent the papers on to the premier, in an attempt to have Caroline's passport and papers cancelled. The premier replied that 'there was no power to cancel' but he instructed his department to refuse the passport. But that was on 27 February, and Caroline's boat had already sailed.[15]

The premier returned the papers to Topp, directing that questions should be asked about the magistrate who said that Caroline was 'of good repute'. Topp forwarded them on the same day to the solicitor general, which resulted in C.T. Plunket JP – the man who certified in 1896 that he had known Caroline Pohl 'for several years' – being 'severely censured for his carelessness and imprudence in giving the certificate'. 'Imprudence' it may have been, but was it 'carelessness'? Charles Thomas Plunket had been a pharmacist in Lonsdale Street since at least 1887, and on 10 May 1889 he had signed a letter published in *The Daily Telegraph* to say that he did 'heartily approve of the action being taken by Colonel Barker on removing objectionable characters who reside in this part of the City'.[16] There is no way he was unaware of Caroline Hodgson's occupation, and his letter to the paper suggests that he wholeheartedly abhorred it. So why did he sign her application? Had he changed his mind about prostitution between 1889 and 1896? Whatever his reasons, Plunket was seriously reprimanded, unlike the police magistrate who took her oath of allegiance. Charles Nicolson, the police magistrate, would also have been very well aware of who he was dealing with, but he did not challenge her status as 'a person of good repute' and he was not chastised for his oversight.

So, after ten months cohabiting at Lonsdale Street, Mr and Mrs Pohl had taken the *Culgoa* from Melbourne on 19 February, bound for London.[17] Martha Burrell accompanied them this time, apparently leaving the properties in Lonsdale Street unoccupied. In the weeks before they left, though, Caroline continued her annual tradition of reminding the people of Melbourne of her respectable connections by inserting an 'In Memoriam' notice for her first husband in *The Argus*, *The Age* and *The Australasian*. It was considerably less flowery and fulsome than her previous efforts, but despite being married to Jacob Pohl she signed it 'C.H.':

> HODGSON.—In loving remembrance of Studholme George Hodgson, who died at his late residence, Gnarwin, Beaconsfield-parade, St. Kilda, on 7th February, 1893. Home and Sydney papers please copy.
>
> Gone but not forgotten.
> —Inserted by his loving wife, C.H.[18]

Was Caroline attempting to build a respectable public persona on the footings of her past marriage? Her first husband may not have been interested in joining Melbourne society, but his family's status and titles provided her with an opportunity to claim respectability in her new role as a married woman with her second husband. After all, they were married at St Patrick's Cathedral and she was no longer running a brothel. But there appears to have been a cloud in the air. Caroline's income was not keeping up with her expenditure. Her first trip to Europe after Stud's death would have eaten up much of his bequest; return tickets for herself, Irene and a maid in saloon cabins would have been costly, and Caroline's taste would not have run to cheap hotels for the year they were away. Back in Melbourne she took out a mortgage on both Gnarwin and the house at its rear (Park Street) within months of her second marriage.[19] Six months after that she realised another asset by selling the house in Loch Street, St Kilda, to John Thompson – the police officer who had reported so fulsomely in response to the complaint

about a supposed brothel problem at Gnarwin. A month later again the
Pohls set off for London. When the group embarked on the *Culgoa* in
February 1896, Caroline left instructions to pay off her mortgage on the
Carter Street properties and transfer them to her long-time housekeeper
and shipboard companion: on 21 March both houses became the property
(at least on paper) of Martha Lamb Burrell. If Caroline had assumed that her
new husband would support her, and that she would have no further need
to run a brothel, then transferring the Carter Street houses to Martha could
be explained as a form of reward for her long and dedicated service, but if
Caroline had doubts about her husband's intentions, then transferring them
to Mrs Burrell would keep them safely out of her husband's reach.

If Caroline met Jacob Pohl in Europe, and they married soon after arriving in Melbourne, was her new husband aware of the nature of her business
before taking up residence in Lonsdale Street? He could hardly have
remained ignorant of it for long, because 'Madame Brussels' was notorious
in Melbourne, and after twenty years in the industry it would have taken
some time for news of the brothel's closure to reach all her clients; there
would have been knocks on her door at all hours for many months before
her visitors knew to go elsewhere. Perhaps that was an element in the Pohls'
decision to close the house and take another extended tour to Europe, or
perhaps Caroline felt it was time to bring Irene home. The youngster had
been away for nearly a year.[20] When they arrived in Germany, Caroline went
to stay with her sister Maria in Scheiderhöhe, and Pohl went to stay with his
parents in Braschoss. Their separation lasted for some time, because,
as Caroline wrote later:

> About two or three months after our arrival in Germany [Pohl] went
> to South Africa without informing me of his intention … The first
> I knew of his having done so was upon receipt of a letter from him
> from South Africa telling me so and promising that he would send
> for me in a couple of years.[21]

Caroline was obviously taken aback, both puzzled and peeved by her husband's behaviour. Had he gone goldmining? Chasing diamonds? Or simply adventuring with another woman? She didn't know. When she had applied to have the words 'late Caroline Hodgson' placed on her new passport she had given the reason that the German authorities 'were very particular', but Martha had told the investigating policeman a different story. She said it was because it would be 'regarded by her friends or relatives in Germany as proof of her previous marriage to Hodgson'.[22] If her sisters were doubtful about her first marriage, how could she possibly explain about the second? On her way home with Irene and Martha Burrell on the *Ormuz*, Caroline reverted to calling herself 'Mrs Hodgson'.[23] Her old passport, perhaps, came in handy when it came to repudiating her faithless second husband.

On their return to Melbourne at the end of 1896 Gnarwin was still occupied by tenants, but Lonsdale Street was unoccupied, so Caroline and Irene took up residence there, a mother and daughter together in their home. Caroline may not have spent a lot of time with Irene over the years, but she was determined to provide her with all the privileges that education and wealth could offer, so at the beginning of the following year Irene went off to school. It was not the local school with the rough children of Little Lon, though; Irene went to boarding school: a Roman Catholic school for 'ladies' – Star of the Sea Presentation Convent in Elsternwick, 'on the borders of Brighton Beach', where 'every care is taken of the religious training of the Pupils', and they 'have the advantage of sea bathing'.[24]

Why would Caroline choose Star of the Sea? Perhaps because the nuns taught German, or because it had an excellent music program (Irene learnt both piano and violin), but probably because it was a Presentation Convent, and Caroline had friends who were Presentation sisters. They were not located in Melbourne, and since they came from near her sister-in-law Lizzie Jane's hometown in Ireland they were probably more her friends than Caroline's, but one at least thought enough of Caroline to give her a birthday present.

The Presentation Sisters who arrived in Hobart in 1866 included 'Mother Xavier (Ellen) Murphy, Sisters Stanislaus O'Brien, Regis Murphy, Ignatius

Murphy and five postulants'.[25] It was Sister Ignatius ('Ig') who sent Caroline a gift on her birthday. 'With deep love and affection' she wrote, 'from her faithful friend'. The book containing 'Sparks of Light for every day' was sent for the birthday which occasioned the dance party in 1885. Presumably Ig was not able or tempted to attend in person, especially since by that time she would have known the nature of Caroline's business, but these nuns were women of the world and held sympathy for their sisters; perhaps that tolerance and compassion were the elements Caroline was looking for in Irene's education.

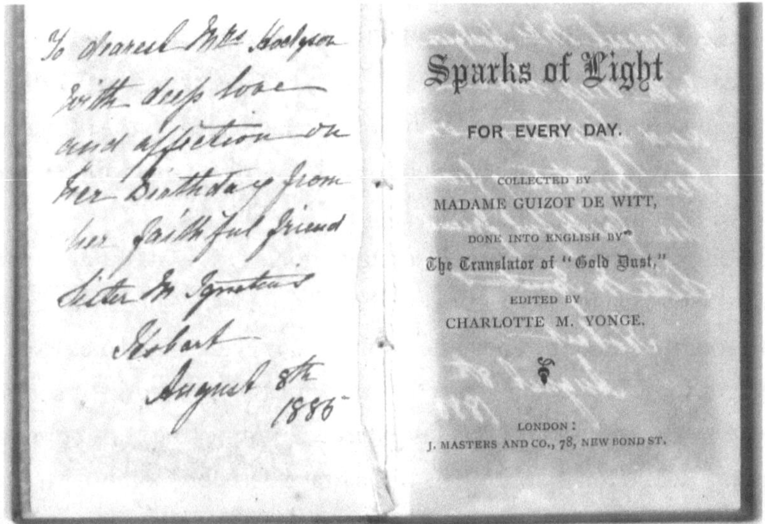

Flyleaf of gift from Sister Ignatius Murphy, 1885

After Irene went off to school in 1897, Caroline's 'In Memoriam' notice for Stud included poetry again, this time with a subtle note of envy as well as grief. Life had changed for her after Pohl's betrayal.

HODGSON.—In loving remembrance of my dear husband, Studholme George Hodgson, who departed this life at his late residence, Gnarwin, Beaconsfield-parade, St. Kilda, on the 7th February, 1893.

> Dear husband, sleep and take your rest,
> Your earthly cares are o'er;
> For you have left a troubled world
> To reach a peaceful shore.
>
> —(Inserted by his loving wife, Caroline Hodgson). Sydney
> and home papers please copy.[26]

Caroline held onto Pohl's promise to send for her 'in a couple of years', but in the meantime she needed an income. Her new husband had not provided for her, and during their marriage they had both been living off the rents of her houses plus additional loans she was able to raise on her properties, leaving her with a considerable debt to be serviced. As with all the other women in the sex industry, she had been affected by the financial disaster of the 1890s. She had never gone back to live at Gnarwin; instead she had collected rent on her beautiful home.[27]

Caroline Hodgson managed to stay afloat. On 8 December 1896 she arranged a mortgage with Samuel Gillott for the last of her three Lonsdale Street properties, and then at some point in 1897, with school fees to pay and mortgages to be met, she restarted her business. To begin with she rented the house next to hers in Lonsdale Street – number 26 – and opened up 32 again.[28] Reopening her brothels was a brave decision, because Melbourne had changed irrevocably since the permissive days of Chief Commissioner Standish and the boom years of the 1880s; instead of the police practising tolerance for quiet houses, the changes to the legislation in 1891 combined with increasing social pressures meant that police were beginning to drive the anti-prostitution barrow themselves, and Madame Brussels still had the name and reputation that set her up as the prime target for attacks from the anti-prostitution lobby, both within the police force and outside it.

20.

ON TRIAL
AGAIN

HISTORICALLY THE POLICE MAGISTRATE Joseph Panton had been sympathetic to sex workers and brothel owners (he presided over Caroline Hodgson's acquittal in 1889), but ten years later his attitude seemed to have been hardening. This suited the new inspecting superintendent of the metropolitan police district, Thomas O'Callaghan, who was brimming with anti-prostitution zeal despite his reputation for 'singing in low houses for the edification of gentlemen and ladies of the town' in his days as a lowly constable.[1] Police had often complained of magistrates' lack of support for their efforts in the courtroom, so when Panton remarked in a case that 'those undesirable places should be rooted out of existence by the police' it was taken by them as a sign that they could proceed effectively against the most disorderly of the women in the city.[2] The inspector at Russell Street station was pleased, noting that 'it is so long since these people have been removed that they seem to think they have got a lease of the place'. On 21 January he ordered Senior Constable Canty to provide a list of all the brothels and their keepers in Lonsdale and Exhibition streets, as well as 'their general character'. Canty provided those lists on 27 January 1898, together with a report that began:

Of many of the houses in Lonsdale St., the most that can be said against them is that they are brothels and that the prostitutes who live in or frequent them, are very often to be seen at the doors or windows, no doubt for the purpose of accosting some passer-by, and sometimes dressed only in white wrappers.

Canty admitted that there had been few complaints from the public about the women, and pointed out that whenever the police tried to have 'the worst of the prostitutes punished' by prosecuting them for 'vagrancy, insulting behaviour or soliciting prostitution' the charges were either dismissed or the women were given 'very light fines'. He then went on to categorise the brothels in terms of their class:

Some of the houses in Lonsdale St are quietly conducted such as Maud Millers 14 & 16 Lonsdale St where the prostitutes are never allowed in the doors or windows & at Bertha Morin's, 23 Lonsdale St a woman who lives always alone, and has no female frequenters, while the next best in that street are Dolly Harrison's 22 Lonsdale St and 'Madame Brussells' [*sic*] 32 & 34 Lonsdale St, but in both of these brothels the prostitutes are occasionally to be seen at the doors or at the gates and in verandah.

It would seem that, since her reopening, Caroline's business had not regained its pre-eminence. She had significant competition, and hers was no longer regarded as the classiest of the establishments in Lonsdale Street. Nevertheless, Canty's report went on to say that the brothels in Exhibition Street were 'of a lower class generally'; he suggested which of the houses were the worst and should be cleared 'if it is intended to try and purify the street'. Canty's report, with his list of the brothels, went all the way up the hierarchy to the Crown solicitor. The solicitor's legal advice was that: 'only the "Keepers" of brothels ... could be reached. Keeping a brothel is a public nuisance and an indictable offence.'

That is, under the legislation of the time the business of prostitution was a Supreme Court common law matter, not a police court matter. The Crown solicitor recognised that this made prostitution a political issue, and carefully avoided providing advice along those lines, while still making his view clear:

> I of course express no opinion on the policy of closing houses of ill repute in this locality where they have been situated for years with the possible result of distributing the occupants over the suburbs and apparently making it more difficult for the police to keep in touch with and controlling the women.

Meanwhile, the police had a galling experience at the City Police Court, when they proceeded against a number of women for soliciting, only to have Panton discharge the whole lot and tell them to prosecute the brothel keepers instead. Mr Panton's decisions were contradictory at best, but the lack of convictions would have provided some reassurance to Caroline, whose confidence can be seen rising again in her annual homage to Stud's memory:

> **HODGSON.**—In sad and loving remembrance of my dear husband, Studholme George Hodgson, who departed this life at his late residence, 'Gnarwin' 39 Beaconsfield-parade, St Kilda, on 7th February 1893.
>
> Dearest husband, thou hast left me,
> I your loss most sadly feel;
> But 'tis God who hath bereft me,
> He can all my sorrows heal.
>
> —Inserted by his loving wife, Caroline Hodgson.[3]

Panton's words against the brothel keepers were delivered on 14 February, so when the Crown solicitor's advice was received by the police on

22 February they immediately issued summonses to 'six of the worst of those in the front streets', the idea being to drive the women off the main streets and into the back lanes. But they were not charged with 'keeping a brothel', as the Crown solicitor had directed. Six brothel keepers – three from Exhibition Street and three from Lonsdale Street (not Caroline Hodgson) – were summonsed to appear at the City Court, effectively on vagrancy charges. David Gaunson defended the women, as he had done both successfully and unsuccessfully at times over the years, and when the police admitted that one of their aims was 'to clear the wide public streets of this class of houses', Gaunson launched into a colourful and racist denunciation of the policy:

> It would tend to degrade the unfortunates still further, and would force the more respectable of them to encounter the awful degradation to be found in the Chinese quarter. It was only making the outside of the platter clean at the expense of worse results from the inside.

The cases against four of the women were dismissed 'as they had vacated the premises occupied by them'. One was 'severely cautioned & told by the Bench if complained against again would be punished', and the last went to a separate trial, which gave Gaunson another opportunity to air his racist views. When the police ideal 'to keep such houses altogether in the back lanes' was repeated, Gaunson objected that there were 'some respectable people in the back lanes', and with regard to the woman's present location, since 'Chinese lived on either side and at the back of the defendant's place', he asked, 'What respectable Britisher would go and take up his residence between two Chinamen?' He went on:

> Which do you think preferable in the public interest, that the front street should be occupied by these women or Chinese, Syrians and Indians? Is it preferable for the glory and beautification of beautiful

Melbourne that one of its main arteries should be occupied by a horde of Chinese, as it will be when these women leave their houses?

Gaunson's arguments in support of the women reflected the changing nature of Melbourne's moral landscape. Having played the race card against 'foreigners', he then attacked the hypocrisy of the churches and argued that the police action was essentially 'terrorism over these women which he did not think was good either for the women or the community.'

The two magistrates on the bench that day represented different sides of Melbourne's debate about prostitution, and without agreement on their part the case was adjourned. Eventually the last woman, too, had her case withdrawn by the police, when she 'complied with Senior Constable Canty's instructions & left the house'. On 9 May, Canty was able to report that Exhibition Street was 'at the present time entirely free from houses of ill-fame', and by the end of May the number of brothels in Lonsdale Street had also been reduced from thirteen to eight.

This, then, was the context in which Caroline Hodgson reopened her brothels. She was not initially targeted by the police, but her turn came later in the year when hers was one of only three brothels left operating in Lonsdale Street. Again Senior Constable Canty was in the thick of it, and Caroline was taken to the police court rather than the Supreme Court, along with the other two women.[4] The three cases were all taken together on 5 August. Samuel Gillott's firm defended Caroline, and David Gaunson defended the two other women.

In some ways it was a repeat of the trial in 1889, although only five magistrates turned up, rather than the eleven who sat on the earlier case.[5] Once again argument centred on the rights and wrongs of allowing such houses to exist in the city. Caroline's barrister (the same one who represented her in 1889) argued the same line: if these houses were closed down, where would they go? He argued that 'it would be very much better to leave the defendants alone than to have the evil scattered into all the suburbs. The crusade conducted about 20 years ago did no good.'[6] The police, however, continued to argue that 'the idea was to relieve the main streets'. That is, to push the women out of sight. And once again racism was to the fore, except this time the police magistrate himself, Joseph Panton, was arguing David Gaunson's racist line with Canty:

> What manner of people are going to live in the house when you clear these women away – Syrians? – I don't know. They might be turned into boarding houses.
>
> Are you shifting them to provide room for the Greek gypsies? (Laughter) – No.

Gaunson followed up: 'Do you think Melbourne would be improved if a large street like that were filled with Syrians, Hindus and Chinese, and the usual draggle tailed crowd were there?'

The police – including Constable Stokes from the 1889 trial – brought witnesses to give evidence about the insults and abuse respectable church-going men suffered while walking up the street; they were working-class men attending the Wesleyan church in Lonsdale Street. The defending barristers simply ridiculed them. Then the presiding magistrate, Melbourne's mayor, Councillor McEacharn, pointed out that when it came to such houses 'there was no legislation to deal with the matter' so it was up to the police to deal with any annoyance to the public 'by taking proper steps to regulate the traffic'. Mr Panton, rather than taking the tough stance the police expected after his previous pronouncements, said that if cases of insulting behaviour were brought before the court the police would have a much stronger case, whereupon the mayor and his offsiders dismissed the cases. All three of them.

The prosecutors were not happy. Nor were some of the newspapers, for different reasons; it was pointed out that 'the magistrates had driven away all the poorer class of brothels, but the swell brothelkeepers were to be privileged'.[7] Mr Finlayson, for the Crown, indicated immediately that 'there would be further proceedings', but such women moved quicker than the law. The case was on 5 August, and Canty reported on 12 August that as a consequence of the cases being dismissed at least two women had returned to the old brothels in Exhibition Street. He subsequently obtained an order for the decision in favour of Caroline Hodgson and the other 'swell brothelkeepers' to be reviewed by a higher court, and after some legal toing and froing the Supreme Court effectively quashed the dismissal of the cases and sent them back to the lower court for re-hearing (that is, to convict the women).[8]

The Supreme Court decision pitted the mayor and Panton against the three judges of the Full Court, but they were not to be overawed. On 11 November 1898 the city bench was not only occupied by the mayor, the police magistrate and the three justices of the peace who had made the original decision to dismiss the cases, but they were also joined by another four JPs, including some suspected clients of the houses in question.[9] The same barristers covered the same territory, and the magistrates came to the same conclusion: that it would be unwise to force the women to take their business elsewhere, 'into districts where they will do a great deal more harm.'[10] Having been more or less directed by the higher court to convict the women, though, they did as they were required to do and found them guilty, but the sentence they imposed was creative if not arrogant: 'imprisonment during the sitting of the court'. As soon as the court rose the women were free to leave. Caroline walked out of court and back to Lonsdale Street with the backing of a number of men of influence to set about rebuilding her empire. The police watched on, smarting from yet another defeat. On 23 November the district superintendent reported to O'Callaghan that 'the Keepers of the houses have not left Lonsdale Street but they are keeping very quiet at present'. O'Callaghan replied with an order: 'On the first sign of any disorderly conduct let notice be served on these women to leave Lonsdale Street.' Caroline was no doubt fully aware of the threat, but she at least knew the extent of the influence she wielded among men with power. It's now time to examine that influence in more detail.

21.

INFLUENCE OR CORRUPTION?

Amongst the brothels which are the reproach and the curse of Melbourne is one of pre-eminently evil reputation. It is a 'respectable' brothel, with patrons in high places, and its keeper is a procuress of a singularly shameful type. Deeds have been done in this house, if all reports be true, which might shame the very devils. Many a girl, little more than a child, has been destroyed, body and soul, within those hateful walls. The place is open, notorious, familiar, as well known to the police and to all the circles of the 'fast' world as the Town-hall clock. Can anyone tell why this shameful establishment has been allowed to flourish untouched by the law for years? Are the police blind, deaf, or asleep in the matter? Now, it may be a mere baseless scandal, but it is a matter of common and notorious rumour that this vile house is allowed to flourish because its keeper pays black-mail to persons in high office, and because it is patronised by 'gentlemen' of influence. That Madam ----'s house is under official protection for con-sideration paid is a confident belief of all those who are best informed on the subject, of all newspaper reporters, of the entire police-court world, of all 'men about town,' and of at least three policemen out of every four. It is the almost universal belief in the force that any indiscreetly zealous officer who meddles with Madam ---- would find himself in difficulties with his superior officers, and would be transferred to some remote district where his zeal would occasion no inconvenience. Every constable in the City knows the house, and knows that ample evidence for its suppression might be collected seven days in the week. But the house has flourished for years, and its keeper boasts of the 'influence' she has in high places. This rumour, persistent and universal, may, of course, be baseless; but what greater scandal on the administration of our police can be imagined than that the keeper of a fashionable brothel – a woman notorious as a procuress – pays black-mail to the very servants of the law who thus shamefully sell to her permission to violate the law!

—*The Daily Telegraph*, 10 April 1889

IN THIS ERUPTION OF OUTRAGE regarding the case against Madame Brussels in 1889, *The Daily Telegraph* accused Caroline Hodgson of three things: employing young girls (meaning girls under the age of consent), blackmailing police and customers to gain protection against prosecution, and boasting of her 'influence' in high places. So how much evidence is there to support any of these allegations?

The first is easy to dispose of. The age of consent for girls in Victoria was only twelve until 1891, and sixteen thereafter, and despite the occasional flurry of investigation no evidence has turned up in police files, family records, newspapers or gossip rags so far to suggest that Caroline Hodgson ever knowingly recruited girls under the age of sixteen as lodgers.[1] One policeman's report in 1889 said that he had never seen 'girls of tender years' in her house.[2] The only case that has come to light was that of a fifteen-year-old who took herself to Madame Brussels' house in 1892. She was arrested there after her sister appealed to the police 'to rescue her from a life of shame'; it quickly became apparent that she had told Caroline she was nineteen.[3]

So many lodgers came and went in Lonsdale Street that Caroline Hodgson was unlikely to have closely questioned a girl who claimed she was nineteen before asking for a room. The police took the girl to court and she was sent home to her mother in Footscray. Similarly, Maggie O'Connor told the police she was '17 years and 6 months', and Caroline 'took her home to her mother'.[4] All of the women whose histories have been traced have been at least eighteen and mostly in their twenties, and there has been no suggestion of coercion on Caroline's part beyond dangling the lure of decent earnings.[5] If Caroline had enticed any of these girls under false pretences she could have been charged with 'procuring', but there were no such charges.

There are several snippets of evidence, however, that suggest that by design Caroline Hodgson's business model did *not* include underage girls, or even sexually inexperienced ones.[6] The four girls who gave evidence at the 1889 trial, for example, were chosen by the police because they were the only witnesses the police could find. One of the young women was nineteen and another was eighteen; they both said they had been seduced eighteen months previously. Another had been living with a man for a year before asking for a room at Madame Brussels', and when the last one, Maggie O'Connor, first asked Caroline for a room she did not immediately agree to take her in.[7] Maggie, apparently, returned to Lonsdale Street and took a room anyway, but she only stayed six weeks. After that she and one of the other girls 'went to Fitzroy to live with two "gentlemen"'.[8] It is difficult to describe any of these young women as 'little more than a child', and three of them admitted that they were not virgins – one had also had an illegitimate baby. One of the four girls was already suffering from a sexually transmitted infection when she arrived in Lonsdale Street, and it was Caroline who arranged treatment for her.[9] Like many others, if that young woman was 'destroyed, body and soul' by her sexual activities, her destruction could hardly be said to have occurred 'within those hateful walls' of Madame Brussels' establishment, but rather the contrary: by arranging treatment for sick girls Caroline Hodgson could well have helped many of them.

The second accusation against Caroline – that of blackmailing police and customers to gain protection against prosecution – is more difficult to address. There is certainly enough evidence in the police files to show that police on the beat frequented the back-street brothels at times, but whether they were taking advantage of the women, collecting protection payments or just taking part in the life of the back lanes is not always clear.[10] The police constables were not well paid, many of them were Irish like so many of the women, and some lived in the back lanes themselves, making poverty, culture and neighbourhood common to them all. Some residents of the area were adept at using complaints to or about the police for their own ends, too, and many were about local politics rather than police corruption.[11]

The situation for houses like Caroline's, though, was a little different. For the most part the women were not soliciting on the streets, and interactions between the madam and the police were likely to be more private, so we learn little about them. The only direct evidence of corruption relating to brothels such as hers comes from witnesses at the Police Commission in 1882, who gave evidence relating to the presence of Frederick Winch, the police superintendent for the Melbourne district, in a bedroom in Madame Brussels' house.[12] One constable said that he had found Superintendent Winch there once, and another said that he 'had been cautioned by some of the men not to interfere with that house because it was one of Mr Winch's places of resort'.[13] Could Caroline Hodgson have been blackmailing Winch over his use of the services in her house? The constable who found Winch there gave evidence that she attempted to stop him entering the room and finding Winch inside. It would certainly have strengthened her blackmail hand if she had been able to hide Winch's presence, but who would she have threatened to report him to? His superior at that time, Chief Commissioner Frederick Standish, was unlikely to object to his use of a discreet house, and protecting the identity of her clients (and therefore their custom) would be the natural instinct of a madam intent on avoiding disturbances and keeping the names of her clients away from the public.

The police commission concluded that not only had brothels become effectively immune from prosecution because of Winch's influence but also that he was actually blackmailing publicans (they were providing him with loans and goods).[14] The commission accepted the constable's story that Winch was not on police duty when he went to Madame Brussels', but came to no conclusions about the particular form his impropriety took: was he taking bribes, paying for services or blackmailing Caroline as well as the publicans? Rather than Madame Brussels blackmailing him, it seems far more likely that Winch was either charging her protection money or using his position as a police officer to avail himself of the women at her house for free.

In later years the *Truth*, for all its abuse of her, did not claim that Caroline blackmailed anyone or bought protection from the police, despite Senior Constable Laurence Gleeson's evidence in 1889: 'About eight months ago [Caroline Hodgson] asked if he was watching the house, and said if there was any complaint she would make it all right.'[15]

The hint of bribery is unmistakable, but *The Age* reported the same evidence differently: 'She said that if he was watching her house she would endeavour to keep her girls in order.'[16] Dishonest behaviour at Madame Brussels' was barely mentioned in the press until after the turn of the century. *The Daily Telegraph* said:

> Perhaps 'Madame' Brussels' reputed boast that she could always depend on 'official' protection, as hers was the brothel of the rich, is only a shameless lie; but it must be admitted that this confessed, and infamous brothel-keeper enjoys singularly good fortune.[17]

And while the *Truth* had no problem accusing her of everything else, it said only that 'There are numerous stories about how men were 'taken down' by women in league with unscrupulous lawyers. One wealthy man had to pay £5000 to escape exposure ...'

It promised that this would 'form the subject of another story in *Truth*', but that story does not seem to have been written.[18]

After the failed prosecution of Samuel Nathan in 1884, Caroline would have known that as long as she kept her house quiet she would be left alone. She may not have needed to blackmail or bribe anyone, but her anxiety about police activity increased as the decade wore on. You can see it on several occasions when she thought a policeman might be about to threaten her security. In 1887, as we have seen, a constable arrested her for insulting behaviour after she 'came rushing after him in a very excited manner, demanding to know if he was the constable 'who had dared to say he would report her house'.[19] You can see it again in 1888, when she asked Senior Constable Gleeson 'if he were watching her girls'.[20] With Henry Varley and the Salvation Army circling, she was right to be wary, especially if she was not paying for police protection. The idea of wielding influence through her clients, however, is another matter. Superintendent Winch might have been looking out for her interests prior to 1880, but towards the end of the decade the landscape around the women became much less tolerant. It was then that 'influence' with magistrates might have been invaluable.

When the trial of Caroline and Lottie Temple began in May 1889 there was 'a full Bench' adjudicating. Normally for the police court that would mean the police magistrate (Joseph Panton) and perhaps one or two other justices of the peace, but on this occasion it meant Panton and *ten* justices of the peace – it was what *The Daily Telegraph* described as a 'curiously crowded' bench.[21] At the end of the trial Panton said that 'a majority of the bench were in favor of both cases being dismissed, but he himself and two of his brother magistrates were of opinion that the charges had been proved'.[22]

That means that eight of the ten honorary magistrates were in favour of acquitting Caroline Hodgson against the advice of the presiding (in this case paid) magistrate. If she was wielding any undue influence among the men on the bench in 1889, her supporters are presumably to be found among the eight who voted for acquittal. But who were they?

The newspapers reported a variety of numbers and names for the men on the bench that day. *The Age* and *The Argus* reported ten justices of the peace sitting with the presiding magistrate, the *Weekly Times* said eleven,

The Daily Telegraph said nine, *The Ballarat Star* eight, and *The Herald* reported seven.[23] They are all consistent on the names, except 'Robertson', the eleventh member mentioned by *The Herald*, who is not mentioned in any other report and seems to be an error. The correct list is therefore: Joseph Panton, presiding magistrate; Francis Conway Mason, MLA; Bear Rappiport; William Bell; James Garton; James W. Peirce; W.D. Holgate; William Turner Moffatt; Dr Charles A. Stewart; A.J. George Walstab; and William C. Conroy.

As a police magistrate, Joseph Panton could be expected to be there, and Conroy, Mason, Walstab and Rappiport were all regulars too (though not sitting all at once), but there were men present who did not usually appear at this court, including Garton, who had previously sat for the adjournment. After the court's decision to acquit the women had been reviewed in July, *The Daily Telegraph* claimed to know how some of the men had voted:

> Messrs. Bell, Moffatt, and Rappiport concurred with Mr. Panton, P.M., in thinking that ... 'Madam' Brussels was clearly convicted ... Messrs. Mason, Holgate, Stewart, Price [*sic* – Peirce], and Garton ... held that this notorious brothel-keeper ... ought to be benevolently winked at by the law.[24]

Walstab later wrote that he had 'held the case proven, but ... a small penalty would meet the case'.[25] That leaves the votes of the bench divided as follows:

Convict	Acquit	Not Reported
Panton	Mason	Conroy
Bell	Holgate	
Moffatt	Stewart	
Rappiport	Peirce	
Walstab	Garton	

Panton, however, had been reported in most of the newspapers as saying that only two of his fellow magistrates had agreed with him, meaning either that he was lying or that something was askew. Some months later, after public gossip claiming that the numbers had actually been even and Panton could have given a casting vote for conviction, *Table Talk* redid the numbers. It concluded that Conroy had 'suddenly discovered that he voted for a conviction' but that he 'had been the victim of some delusion'.[26]

Conroy died in Carlton the year after the trial, and an obituary noted that he 'usually presided at the Carlton Police Court, where he will not be soon forgotten as a Magistrate who did his utmost to hold the balance of justice with an even hand, and if ever it did swerve a little, it was to lean to mercy's side'.[27]

Conroy, along with one or two others it seems, might have swerved a little and then changed his mind after the court's decision was challenged by all and sundry. So the question remains, who of these men might have supported Caroline Hodgson, and why?

Not William Bell: he was for many years the district secretary for the Independent Order of Rechabites and a vehement temperance campaigner; it is more than likely that he would have come from Hawthorn to sit on the bench in order to vote for a conviction (as he did). But there were others whose beliefs would have led them in the opposite direction. Francis Conway Mason often sat on the City Court bench, and his biographer described him as 'venal in a genial way, Mason was subject to rumours about his private life … Beatrice Webb described him as a 'worthy but vulgar individual'.[28]

Then there was James Garton,

who for years kept the well known hotel in Swanston street, was highly respected for his probity and liked for his genial manner. He had been a very powerful man in his day, and many stories are told of his encounters with the roughs who infested Melbourne in the early fifties.[29]

Having a 'genial manner' in the newspapers of the nineteenth century was often code for being 'a man about town', for whom brothels could be assumed to be part of their worldly experience. While Garton had the right to sit at the City Court he rarely did, so his appearance at both the first and second court hearings was unusual, and his vote to acquit is particularly surprising given that the day after the trial he signed the letter in *The Daily Telegraph* from 'the respectable residents in the neighbourhood' (including C.T. Plunket JP), saying he did 'heartily approve of the action being taken by Colonel Barker on removing objectionable characters who reside in this part of the City'.[30]

Garton ran a livery stable and horse bazaar at 227 Lonsdale Street; he and Caroline Hodgson could well have made mutual use of each other's businesses. James W. Peirce was in a similar situation, running a tobacconist's shop in Elizabeth Street and voting to acquit, but he did not sign the letter of support for the prosecutions. Garton's actions suggest duplicity, but he was at least sitting within his own bailiwick. A number of others were not. W.D. Holgate was the mayor of Collingwood, Dr Charles A. Stewart came from South Melbourne, and William Turner Moffatt came from Brighton. They were all part of Melbourne's middle-to-upper-rung businesspeople, with Holgate vice chairman of the Clifton Hill Mutual Improvement Society, Dr Stewart and his wife attending the South Melbourne mayoral ball, and Moffatt being an office bearer in the Philharmonic Society.[31] Holgate and Stewart voted for acquittal, Moffatt for conviction.

So, while the bench was clearly stacked, it was not all in Caroline's favour; some had presumably made a special effort to go and support her (Holgate, Peirce, Stewart, Garton), but others had gone specially to oppose her (Moffatt, Bell). Of the regular attendees at the City Court, Mason and Conroy appear to have been some of Melbourne's old-style believers in prostitution as 'a necessary evil', and hence voted to acquit, but the last two honorary magistrates, Bear Rappiport and A.J. George Walstab, were probably the ones added to Panton's original 'two of his brother magistrates' (Moffatt and Bell) to become what appears to have ended up as four voting to convict.[32] Why would they have wanted the public to believe they voted differently? Probably because the decision was howled about and ridiculed in the press, and they did not want to be seen to be in favour of brothels. Possibly also, since *The Herald* called them Panton's 'faithful henchmen', they might have changed their votes to support Panton.[33] Despite his bluff and bluster about the charges having been proved, Panton was notoriously lenient with women on vagrancy charges such as these, raising the question of whether Caroline could have been seen as wielding 'influence' over magistrate Panton.[34] That question arises again in relation to the 1898 trial, but Walstab had died and Rappiport had been brought low before then.[35]

In a system where magistrates were voluntary and not legally trained there was always the possibility of corruption, and in Melbourne it came to a head in 1895 when William John Lormer, a justice of the peace, made a series of accusations against other justices of the peace regarding bribery and bench stacking. The government was sufficiently concerned about the allegations to set up an inquiry board headed by a Supreme Court judge.[36] The Lormer Inquiry, as it became known, brought out charges of bribery and corruption against a number of honorary magistrates, including Bear Rappiport.[37]

The board found that Lormer was correct about what it termed the 'migration' of magistrates to courts where they were strangers, and that what occurred at Caroline Hodgson's 1889 trial was not unusual: 'whenever it is believed that the bench is going to be packed in the interest of one litigant or of one class steps are immediately taken for the purpose of meeting packing by counter-packing.'

Nevertheless, the board found that despite acting improperly, for many of the men ignorance was a sufficient excuse and they were let off. In relation to the specific charges against Rappiport and two others, the board was less forgiving. Rappiport and another magistrate from the central bailiwick, Allan Baxter, were found to be corrupt, having 'received bribes gifts and privileges' that were given to them for the purpose of influencing their judgment on the bench. These two were also found guilty of acting together in the interests of a litigant, and Baxter was found guilty of having visited brothels in Lonsdale Street, possibly including Madame Brussels.'[38]

The case against the third magistrate to be censured, George Bird, provides the most direct evidence regarding the influence of sex workers over the bench. Despite knowing May Blanch (also known as May Baker) and frequently being in her house (she was working in Lonsdale Street at the time of the inquiry and rented 6 and 8 Lonsdale Street later), Bird claimed ignorance about her occupation, and it was shown that 'upon two … occasions he visited courts in which he was not accustomed to sit and … adjudicated in the interests of women of bad fame and character with whom he had at the time immoral relations.'[39]

Importantly, one of the women who benefited from Bird's adjudication 'told a woman who charged her with stealing clothing that she could "do her no harm, as the Bench would be on her side, and it would be all right".'[40]

This was not Caroline Hodgson claiming 'influence', but it does illustrate the existence of that dynamic between the women and some members of the bench, and it is unlikely that Caroline would have been immune to the use of such influence if she had the opportunity. Given the class of her business, it is hard to see her *not* having the opportunity.

As a result of their enquiries the Lormer board recommended changes to the way the lower courts operated, but little had changed by 1898 when Caroline Hodgson was charged again 'with being the keeper of a house at 32 and 34 Lonsdale-street frequented by persons having no visible means of support'.[41] Once again there were two benches involved, and both appear to have been stacked in one way or another. For the initial hearing the bench comprised four men who all 'regularly appeared at the city court', so there was nothing unusual except the number who turned up all at once.[42] After that bench unanimously acquitted Caroline and the case had been reviewed by the Supreme Court and sent back for re-hearing, the new bench comprised the same men plus a few more.[43]

Given the voting history from previous cases (1889 and 1898), it could be expected that the votes of only three of these men are in doubt:

Convict	Acquit	Not Reported
Bell	McEacharn	Edwards
	Panton	Bent
	Cherry	Russell
	Lancashire	
	Power	

McEacharn, a man of old-fashioned ambition towards knighthood, and perhaps old-fashioned views about 'the necessary evil', was serving as chief magistrate because he was Melbourne's mayor. Panton was there as police magistrate and his vote is surprising given his stated views in 1889.[44] Robert Cherry and Samuel Lancashire travelled in from Hawthorn and both belonged to the class of men who regularly sat on committees guiding charities such as the Benevolent Asylum.[45] Henry Edwards, who floated in from the Carlton bench, was the chairman of numerous mining boards of directors, and was known to be harsh with sex workers.[46] Robert Power lived in Malvern, but regularly chose to sit at the City Court; he was described by *The Age* as 'a well-known supporter of the turf' and 'a fine type of sportsman',[47] but *The Tocsin* described him and Captain Russell from Toorak as 'two society swells'.[48] It was the presence of Thomas Bent, ex-MLA for Brighton, though, that raised eyebrows. Bent had lost his seat in 1894, and in order to recover his fortunes after the losses of the depression he had gone dairy farming at Port Fairy.[49] What was he doing at the City Court in Melbourne, adjudicating on Caroline Hodgson's case?

In the end the bench's decision was a compromise between those who wished to convict and those who would have preferred to acquit, and it's easy to see the hand of an experienced politician like Bent combined with the influence of McEacharn – 'a self-made man, a capitalist' – in the compromise. McEacharn's biographer describes him as a man 'always on the look-out for the main chance'.[50] In 1904, McEacharn saw the women of Lonsdale Street as 'the main chance' in his bid for election to federal parliament.[51]

McEacharn and Bent were just the kind of men to admire a woman like Caroline Hodgson. They convicted her as the higher court wanted, but the sentence was nominal; she was free 'at the rising of the court'. All the gentlemen (the 'society swells' and the old-timers who believed that prostitution was inevitable) knew that Madame Brussels would remain in business, and those who would have preferred to see her crushed knew that they were outvoted but at least they got a conviction. The interesting initial decision to acquit her came from Joseph Panton, the man who declared in 1889 that he had found Caroline guilty but had to defer to the decision of the majority who voted 'not guilty'. Had he changed his view of her business in order to acquit her this time, or was he perhaps emboldened by the mayor and Bent to act on confining the trade to Lonsdale Street? From Caroline's point of view it did not matter; again she had prevailed, and again she could carry on with her business.

22.

A MADAME'S ENTERTAINMENT PRECINCT

As soon as Thomas O'Callaghan became Inspecting Superintendent and was placed in charge of the Melbourne police, he started with a Pecksniffian snort to drive the Phryne and Messalinas of the city out of the drums which they occupied in Lonsdale-street and adjacent lanes. It was a most virtuous campaign, but failed miserably. For a space 'to let' notices ... were stuck in the windows of the deserted haunts of marketable vice, but gradually they were taken down, and the same old Pollies and Alices reappeared ...

—*Truth* (Brisbane and Sydney), 9 February 1902, p. 5

THE BUSINESS CAROLINE SET OUT TO BUILD in 1898 was essentially the same as the one she had been running before Jacob Pohl came into her life, with number 32 as a brothel and 34 as her private home. Police reports from that time describe four women employed there, often standing at 'the gate' and 'in verandah', suggesting they were all entering through the front door of number 32.[1] Her houses provided entertainment as well as sex, and she appealed to the wealthier members of the colony by recreating a fun version of their home environment, complete with grand piano (on which Alfred

Plumpton's photo supposedly once stood) and walled garden. She furnished her houses in high Victorian style, 'a lavish scramble of ebony, buhl and ormolu; buxom marble and alabaster nudes set a standard of female beauty . . . and the note was repeated in those large paintings of large women that Victorian artists produced.'[2]

This description is drawn from the *Truth*, but there was not a single nude – marble, alabaster or otherwise – in the sale notice of goods from 32–34 Lonsdale Street after her death, although it did include 'a set of six proof engravings by Gustave Dore'.[3] There is no doubt that in its heyday Madame Brussels' establishment presented an expensive, cultured retreat for drinking and dancing, singing and card-playing as well as more amorous adventures. There was also, it has been claimed, 'a safe in a corner which would have paid for burgling just as well as anything else of the same sort in this city', and 'a massive bed, "o'er canopied like an Imperial Throne" in Madame Brussels' "special boudoir"'.[4]

There is a story about one of Madame Brussels' beds which is possibly apocryphal. After Mrs Fraser died, her goods and chattels were sold at auction, and *Truth* reported two decades later that

> **T**here was great bidding for what was whisperingly described as '**THE DUKE'S BED**,' and even dames from Toorak made big offers for this precious article – this relic of royal debauchery. But it fell to Madame Brussells [*sic*], in whose house of ill-fame it occupies a distinguished place of questionable honor [*sic*] to this very day. The price paid for it was £9 15s. It was worth a pound.[5]

True or not, it was the kind of story that gave Madame Brussels' establishment a cachet that others lacked, and helped attract different kinds of clients from the usual. One of the girls who gave evidence in the 1889 trial, for example, told the police that while 'plenty of well known married men visit there to stop with the girls', there were also 'plenty of supposed ladies and gentlemen' who 'come to the Cottage for Short times but they don't stay all night'.[6] It seems that 32 Lonsdale was a sort of 'short-time' house for wealthy adulterous patrons, allowing couples to conduct extramarital affairs in discreet surroundings. Such clients were likely to have been people like Dr Robert Stirling, a surgeon who had rooms at 235 Lonsdale Street and whom Caroline employed to treat her boarders when they were unwell. It was brought to the attention of the court during Dr Stirling's divorce proceedings in 1900 that he was in the habit of hiring a hansom cab to pick up a girl in Richmond and take the two of them to various places 'where they stayed for an hour'.[7] Stirling was a surgeon, but he was to become Caroline's treating doctor towards the end of her life.[8]

After 1898, Caroline continued her business along the same lines, but the court case forced her to be ever more careful to avoid any suggestion of 'disorderliness'. From the time of her release 'at the rising of the court' in November, Caroline was not to be hauled in front of a magistrate again until 1906. For eight years she kept a low profile but retained her reputation as running the flashest of Melbourne's brothels, whether her business warranted it or not. 'Madam Brussels' appeared at 32–34 Lonsdale Street in the 1899 post office directory and stayed there until 1907. It might have been purely an advertising ploy, or it might have been an upraised middle finger to the police, but either way it was an act of confidence, and in those final years of the nineteenth century and the early ones of the twentieth Caroline needed all the confidence she could muster.

PART V:
THE NEW CENTURY

23.

AN ERRANT HUSBAND AND THE RISE OF *TRUTH*

IN NOVEMBER 1898, CAROLINE POHL became a convicted criminal for the first time, but she was also a businesswoman and a mother. She must have walked away from the court both chastened and determined: she had a daughter to raise. And the following year her usual homage to Stud revealed a touch of loneliness.

> HODGSON.—In loving memory of Studholme George Hodgson, who departed this life February 7, 1893, at his late residence, Gnarwin, Beaconsfield-parade, St. Kilda.
>
> Dearest husband, how I miss you
> Words of mine could never tell,
> But in Heaven I hope to meet you,
> Never more to say farewell.
>
> —(Inserted by his loving wife, Caroline Hodgson).
> Sydney and home papers please copy.[1]

Not long afterwards, returning home late one night she was attacked in the street.[2] It was an attempted robbery – described by the newspapers as 'bag snatching' – but the man she accused was a seaman and she was a fifty-year-old woman. It would have left her feeling vulnerable, especially since the jury did not believe her identification of the man; he was declared not guilty and released.[3] Perhaps that partly explains Caroline's response to the sudden return of Jacob Pohl.

After his first letter to her in Germany informing her of his flight to South Africa, Caroline received no further word from her husband, much less the promised invitation to join him. But in the late 1890s – 'about two or three years after her return to Victoria' – he turned up in Melbourne and called on her at Lonsdale Street.[4] It was the first she had heard from him since she came home, and she said afterwards that 'in answer to my inquiries as to his strange conduct in leaving me in Germany ... the only satisfaction I could get from him was that he wanted to travel about.'

She asked him 'what he intended to do about providing for me' – perhaps thinking she could retreat from the sex industry again – but having replied 'I will see what I can do,' he proceeded to do nothing at all in the way of supporting her. He had taken a room at Albert Street, East Melbourne, and Caroline 'frequently called there at his invitation and sometimes cohabited with him there about once a fortnight for about three months', but it proved to be a brief interlude with yet another unhappy ending. Jacob Pohl decamped again without telling her where he was going. She 'made repeated enquiries' for his whereabouts among his friends but was given no information at all.

If Caroline had hopes of retiring and settling into a domestic family arrangement with her husband and adopted daughter they were quickly and sadly dashed, but at least she had an income of her own to rely on and he was no longer drawing anything from it. From August 1899, Caroline returned to her business as Madame Brussels and her home life as a mother. Without the St Kilda house to go to, at least some of Irene's holidays from boarding school would have been spent at 34 Lonsdale Street, and with her developing interest in music and dance it can be imagined that she made the most of the piano during the daytime.[5] Irene's granddaughter describes her as a cheerful, elegant woman who was also broad-minded, but Caroline would not have sent her daughter to a convent and then allowed her to socialise with her Lonsdale Street clients at night. She was growing into a graceful, well-educated woman, learning German at school and in private lessons with Herr Martin Schmidt in the city.[6] For the next few years while Irene was at school Caroline ran the brothel as quietly as she could and mourned her lost husbands. After Pohl's departure she reintroduced the aristocratic members of Stud's family to her annual tradition of remembrance.

> HODGSON.—In loving memory of my dear husband, Studholme George Hodgson, who departed this life February 7, 1893, at his late residence, Gnarwin, 39 Beaconsfield-parade, St. Kilda; also brother-in-law of the baronet Sir Francis Wood, the brother of Sir Evelyn Wood.
>
> 'Tis just seven years since we were parted;
> Friends may think the wound is healed.
> But they little know the sorrow
> In my loving heart concealed.
>
> —(Inserted by his loving wife, Caroline Hodgson.)
> Sydney and home papers please copy[7]

Her instruction to Sydney papers to 'please copy' was for her sister-in-law Lizzie Jane Hodgson's benefit; the two remained good friends. The instruction to 'home papers' could only have been to let Stud's family know of her respectability and devotion.

> HODGSON.—In fond and loving memory of my dear husband, Studholme George Hodgson, who departed this life at 'Gnarwin,' Beaconsfield-parade, St. Kilda, February 7, 1893, brother-in-law of the baronet Sir Francis Wood, the brother of Sir Evelyn Wood. One of the best.
> Deeply loved and deeply mourned.
> Many a lonely hour,
> Many a sleepless night,

> I think of you, my husband dear,
> In your heavenly home so bright.
> Dearest friends may try to cheer me,
> Yet for you I still do call.
> None on earth could be so kind,
> When I lost you I lost my all.
> —(Inserted by his loving wife, Caroline Hodgson.)[8]

It was not until she took over 6–8 Lonsdale again in 1902 that Caroline's business began to recover; it never brought in anything like the profits she was drawing in the 1880s, but she was doing well again. Early in 1903, Lizzie Jane Hodgson brought her eight-year-old granddaughter Mary (known as 'Tottie') to Melbourne and met Nellie Melba on the train. The great Madame Melba was on a visit to Australia, and was returning to Melbourne for a week as a 'guest of the Governor and Lady Clarke' before her departure for London, while Lizzie Jane and Tottie were visiting Caroline in Lonsdale Street.[9] Melba's admiring comment on Lizzie Jane's jewellery gave Tottie a 'brush-with-fame' story to tell to her own grandchildren many years later, but her visit to Madame Brussels' establishment led to no recounted memories.[10]

Without hiding her background Irene also passed on few stories of that time to her children and granddaughter; she grew into a fun-loving musical young woman, but just as she reached her teenage years John Norton began taking notice of Madame Brussels' business. Norton had taken over the ownership of the newspaper *Truth* in 1896 and established a Melbourne edition at the beginning of 1902.[11] *Truth* has been described by one of Norton's biographers as running on 'the formula of sex, crime, radical politics and random muck-raking' that is typical of sensational journalism today.[12] Another biographer describes him as 'an assiduous historian of Melbourne prostitution', and Norton mentioned Madame Brussels in Sydney and Brisbane editions even before setting any type in Melbourne.[13] Norton's writings were generally scathing attacks on someone or something, but Caroline Hodgson was not his target that first time. It was Thomas O'Callaghan, the inspecting superintendent of Melbourne police, who drew his fire for hunting the sex workers out of '(S)Melbourne' and into the respectable suburbs. Norton's next mention of

Madame Brussels was more expansive, even if his journalistic flair did not extend to historical accuracy.[14] In October 1903 he posed the question 'Who is Madame Brussells [*sic*]?' in a Melbourne edition of *Truth*, and his answer is a curious melange of fact and fiction, mixing her first husband up with her second and not giving her a name. He provided the quotes that have been used to describe Madame Brussels ever since, including 'a pretty, slender, fair-haired German Gretchen'. In this, his earliest commentary on Caroline Hodgson, Norton also made some of the few positive observations about her on the public record, remarking that she was 'a perfect little lady', and

> her own superior understanding and excellent education were brought to bear on her peculiar, unsavory occupation. Don't think for one moment that it does not require brains, tact, cleverness, and business ability to run a large bagnio successfully. It does!

But his generous assessment of her capabilities was undermined by the misogyny that followed:

> It requires much cleverness to keep a company of 20 or 30 nymphs, of all temperaments, in order. It requires much ability to lick into shape some of the raw material, generally recruited from the kitchen and nursery, and make them presentable 'ladies' ... It was Madame Brussells' [*sic*] task to make the raw hoydens presentable to please men of taste and of considerable artistic refinement.

It may be that in the few days that the young women of the 1889 trial spent 'at the cottage' before beginning work at 'the big house' they were being 'licked into shape' in this fashion, but there is no mention of it in the young women's evidence apart from one of them saying that at the beginning of her time at the house 'Madame gave her money at her own request for to buy clothes'.[15]

By the time Norton was writing about her, Caroline had re-established her rented brothel at 6–8 Lonsdale Street, which perhaps explains why

Norton thought she owned 'four fine houses'.[16] Her two rented houses side-by-side formed a lower-class establishment than 32 Lonsdale, possibly catering to a different clientele or providing less in the way of food or accommodation, but the women moved freely enough between the establishments for Plain-Clothes Constable Porter to complain that he 'had seen her shameless hussies passing to and fro between the two places half clad, and one of them had been arrested at madame's door for soliciting prostitution, and had been fined at the City Court'.[17]

Caroline's boarders at 6–8 Lonsdale included Olive Douglas. Olive was the first person in Victoria charged with electoral fraud relating to the new federal government.[18] She was 'a tall, good-looking dark-complexioned young woman' who enrolled to vote at Jolimont in the Melbourne division, but when Sir Malcolm McEacharn's canvassers took a JP to Lonsdale Street to arrange convenient postal votes for the women, she applied under the name of one of her friends who had left Madame Brussels' house: 'Fanny Montgomery'.[19] Olive was not trying to vote twice, she just preferred to vote by post rather than having to find her way to a polling booth on election day. As she told the police, 'Fanny Montgomery' was not her friend's name any more than it was hers: 'I had as much right to sign that as she had. Her name is West. My proper name is not Douglas. Madame's is not Brussels. We all go by noms de plume here.'[20]

Despite the admission that 'Douglas' was not her real name, the case proceeded as though it was. As well as being 'good-looking', Olive was described in the newspapers as 'a fashionably-dressed young woman'; but when her case was sent to a higher court she pleaded that she was too poor to pay for a barrister to conduct her defence.[21] In her first trial at the City Court it was Madame Brussels herself – 'the keeper of the house in which she resided' – who stepped in and paid his fee, but she refused to pay more.[22] Luckily for Olive, the legal fraternity recognised the importance of this first case in testing the new legislation relating to federal voting, and there was provision for the attorney-general to fund the defence in such cases. Olive Douglas's case proceeded to the Criminal Court to be heard by a jury, which found her not guilty. As the chief justice pointed out:

a person would need to be very ignorant of the electoral law to think that a name being unattached could be used by anybody. However, if the prisoner's ability to judge was thought so weak she might be acquitted.[23]

Olive Douglas's ability to judge, apparently, was thought by the jury to be very weak, despite having chosen to vote. But in this era women had no experience of voting, and juries were always men, many of whom thought women were incapable of rational judgment about anything, and mere prostitutes (in their language) were even less endowed with intelligence and reason than most women. It was a view not necessarily shared by John Norton, but his quasi-positive description of Caroline Hodgson in 1903 turned to poison in 1906 when a wealthy man claimed that a woman working in her house had stolen his watch. *The Age* reported the incident with the headlines:

A SQUATTER'S TROUBLES.
WHOLESALE FLEECING ALLEGED.
HOUSE RAIDED BY THE POLICE[24]

It named the fleeced 'squatter' as Walter Harold Davidson and described him as '55 years of age, a widower' and the 'owner of the Coliban Park Station, in the Malmsbury district'. He also had a town residence at St Kilda, two cars and a chauffeur. Davidson told the police that

on a visit to a house of ill repute in Lonsdale-street a woman named Maude [*sic*] Gamble obtained possession of his gold watch, valued at £70, and only returned it to him on his paying £60. A day or two later she once more obtained the watch, and on this occasion a dispute occurred, which resulted in Mr. Davidson calling at the detective office.

The police went to the house, only to have Maud Gamble refuse to give them the watch, which, she said, had been given to her for safe keeping. When the police tried to pursue the matter with Davidson he refused to cooperate with them, instead returning to the house and paying £35 to retrieve his watch. He stayed another three days, running up another bill of £300. The police, however, were not to be put off: they were looking for an opportunity to close down the flash brothels of Lonsdale Street and they smelled blood; they obtained a warrant and went to the house where they

> arrested the persons whom they found on the premises with the exception of one young woman, daughter of the keeper of the house, who had just left school, and was found to have booked her passage for Germany by the steamer Friedrich der Grosse, which sails to-day.

At the age of eighteen Irene was off to stay with her aunts in Germany again. She was leaving behind the only mother she had ever known, freshly charged with being the 'keeper of a disorderly house'. Whether Irene knew it or not, it was a charge that carried the threat of gaol, and the financial burden was likely to be substantial given that the other eight women in the house were all charged with offences ranging from vagrancy to theft, and Caroline was paying their costs as well as her own. In the first instance she paid £10 bail for each of them at the City Watch House, before returning home to fare-well her adopted daughter. Irene steamed away in a comfortable saloon cabin on an ocean liner, dressing for dinner and dining with the captain, while Caroline, after keeping her house quietly out of the public eye for eight years, embarked on a journey through the courts that would eventually lead to the closure of her brothels. But first there was one last piece of land she wanted.

24.

COTTAGES AND COACH HOUSES

BY THE TIME MADAME BRUSSELS WAS SETTING herself up in business again in the late 1890s, Mrs Kemp was gone but other competition had arrived. Custom, it seems, had to be enticed in person more than in previous years, yet in 1902 John Norton still included her in his exemplars of Melbourne's flash brothels: 'Madame Brussels', Scotch Maud's, "Strathmore", "Mons"'.[1] But the following year he made it clear that despite her reputation Caroline's establishment was no longer at the top of the tree, and he related it to Plumpton's death in 1902. He said her establishment had 'been shorn of its profligate splendor. The surroundings are the same, but the class of women she harbors is of a more degraded and profligate type.'[2]

In 1903 'the surroundings' included the rented property on Casselden Lane. After Annie Wilson moved to Boccaccio House in the 1890s, Caroline incorporated the old weatherboard cottage into her main establishment.

When the brothel opened again late in the decade the gate between the Casselden Lane cottage and the garden fronting onto Lonsdale Street was opened too, increasing the number of rooms available for 'lodgers'. This gate can be seen – along with the brick walls that largely enclosed the

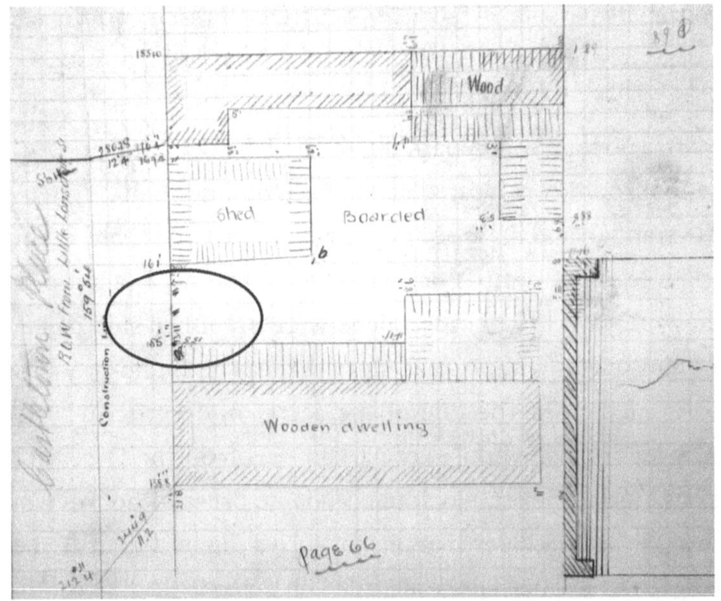

'Cottage' on Casselden Lane – a patchwork of old wooden buildings
with a gate to the main brothel

garden – on the survey which was carried out when the properties were sold
in 1908 after Caroline's death.

Norton was also unimpressed with the external appearance of the place,
describing it as having 'a mean appearance when viewed exteriorly from
Lonsdale St'.[3] Another historian more kindly described the house as 'discreet
rather than stately', supported by the rate collector's evidence that the house
was 'very private and secluded, with lattice work in front and standing back
from the street'.[4] These descriptions are at least partially borne out by the 1908
survey showing 'trellis' adorning a section of garden.[5]

Regarding Madame Brussels' £2000 bedroom, Norton claimed that it was:

connected with a secret passage leading through a beautiful garden
to a door in the high wall which separates it from Little Lonsdale St.
This door is used by the first-class customers, some of whom are
entrusted with the latchkey, by arrangement. The latchkey enables

a prominent person or favorite [*sic*] to let himself in unobserved from the back of the garden.[6]

There was no high wall separating the house from Little Lonsdale Street, and if her bedroom was located at the back of Studholme Villa, where an extended verandah and bathroom were built in 1886, it is hard to think of an asphalt path leading towards the privy at the rear as 'a secret passage', no matter how beautiful the garden beds were on either side of it.[7] Yet the description resonates with another story that has been told about the brothels in Lonsdale Street: the tale of the secret underground tunnels that supposedly led from the houses of parliament on Spring Street to the flash brothels of Lonsdale Street. No doubt Madame Brussels' houses would have been one of the favoured destinations for such a tunnel, but in all the archaeological digs that have been done at Little Lon not a single nineteenth-century tunnel has been found that could accommodate a parliamentarian striding upright towards a brothel.

Still, Norton was convinced enough of the value of the latchkey tale to retell it:

> The site is well-chosen for the purposes of private prostitution by public men and pillars of society, who are said to have frequented this baleful bagnio, by reason of the fact that access to it is afforded by a back entrance, a blind lane or 'cul de sac' leading out of Little Lonsdale-street.[8]

He went on to describe the alley at the rear of Caroline Hodgson's houses as 'the little lane by which her crapulous, concupiscent clients may enter and leave her lair of lechery practically unobserved'.[9] Historian Cyril Pearl took up the story and embellished it.

> At the back was a double coach-house and a pretty walled garden, with a door opening to Little Lonsdale Street. Favoured clients,

including the more regular Parliamentary visitors, had a key to this door, and made their entrance, circumspectly and picturesquely, through the cloistered garden.[10]

The plans drawn up for Melbourne's sewerage survey only partially support this romantic picture. There is certainly a shed (with a verandah marked 'V') which might be a 'double coach-house' at the dog-leg end of Gorman Alley, and several garden areas around the summer house that might be 'pretty'; but the plan also shows houses all the way along Little Lonsdale Street, an electric light pole ('E.L.P.') at the entrance to Gorman Alley, and another on the corner right outside her back gate. Her clients – especially if they were well-dressed – could hardly have been expected to come or go unobserved in a locale where many of the residents were labourers, sex workers or tradesmen, and the houses were small enough for a lot of socialising to be done on the streets at night. But 'unobserved' by labourers is not the same as 'unobserved' by one's peers, so the latchkey story remains believable for men who did not want to be exposed to gossiping eyes by going in the front door. The nearest thing to a 'cloistered garden' is the long walk from her private house to the privy, but when the owners built on the adjoining property,

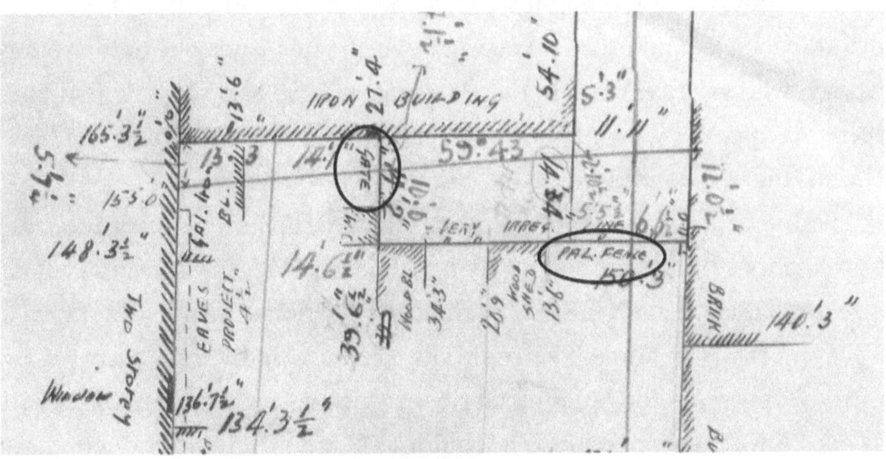

Rear of Caroline Hodgson's properties in Lonsdale Street leading to Gorman Alley

the new buildings had overhanging eaves and windows overlooking this cloister. It was not the place for a circumspect entrance. Nor is there a 'door' leading to Little Lonsdale Street: the plans show a more prosaic 'gate' leading past an outdoor 'W.C.' (water closet), or privy, and it was probably large enough to admit a buggy, and locked against thieves. Again, unlikely to facilitate sly, exotic access in semi-darkness.

Despite these inconvenient facts, access by use of a 'latch-key' became part of the mythology surrounding Madame Brussels' establishment.

By the 1900s the inside of Caroline's houses was probably as tired and worn as the outside. The 'great wealth and sumptuousness' was of a heavy Victorian style, with curtains of guipure lace and costly rose satin window valances.[11] Her customers could relax in a luxurious 'Chesterfield covered in saddlebag' (leather), or warm themselves by a fire protected by a brass fender beneath the matching rose satin drape across the mantelpiece. The furnishings were designed for men ('splendid saddlebag suite' for their masculine frames and 'black walnut hall-stand' for their hats) but also for eating and drinking ('diningroom suite in walnut and ash' and 'black walnut sideboard'). Somewhere there was still a piano tinkling, too, since Caroline was employing Madam Blanch at the rate of 12s. 6d. per week as a pianist.[12] If the stories about Alfred Plumpton are true, the piano would initially have been of a respectable (and probably expensive) character, since one of the young women who gave evidence in the 1889 trial said she had 'seen Mr [cut out] there playing on the piano', but by the turn of the century it may not have been in the best condition.[13]

Fashions in furnishing were changing with the new century, too, and Caroline was ill and focused on paying off her mortgages. She is unlikely to have been updating her furnishings in the way that her wealthy clients were updating theirs at home. She could not keep up. So by 1904, after nearly thirty years of use, the building fabric was rundown, if not crumbling, and as one of her clients remarked, he couldn't tell the time there because 'there is no daylight in this house.'[14] Caroline's rental of 7s. per week for the buildings on Casselden Lane suggests that any light there may have been coming through the walls.[15] When the widow who owned them 'in trust for her life-time' died, though, Caroline still decided to lash out £200 and buy the collection of shanty structures beyond the 'very dilapidated irregular fence'.[16]

In 1906 Norton commented: 'The glory of Brussel's has departed of late years, and so far as there is any elevation in the way of swell harlotry the Cardigan-street brothel is now in the ascendant, while Brussel's is on the down grade.'[17]

This assessment accords with the evidence in Caroline's probate papers, where the carpets 'like meadow-grass' had been replaced by linoleum.[18] Yet Madame Brussels' public profile had not declined. In a court case against a woman charged with stealing from a man 'down from the country', the man was asked by her defending barrister where he stayed that night. 'Did you stop at Madame Brussels?' he asked, insinuating that the man's evidence was untrustworthy.[19] 'Madame Brussels' had become the byword for 'brothel' in Melbourne, for a man of any class.

The purchase of the cottage on Casselden Lane was finalised in March 1906, at the same time as Caroline was in court over the matter of Walter Davidson's gold watch.[20] It would seem that the glory of Madame Brussels' clients had diminished too; Davidson might have been wealthy, and by marriage and occupation connected to the upper crust, but 'one of his sons has described him as "The Outlaw," and [he] is certainly outside the pale of decent society'.[21] A wiser head than Caroline's might have decided it was time to contract rather than expand.

25.

ANOTHER TRIAL
AND A DIVORCE

IN 1906 *THE AGE* COVERED THE FIRST part of the trial of the women from Madame Brussels' house in about 500 words. *The Herald* spent 1000. *Truth* splashed about 4500 words across five and a half columns.[1] The man whose watch was supposedly stolen was a wealthy squatter, but Melbourne's most popular conservative newspaper, the squatters' rag *The Argus*, said nothing; *Table Talk* reported that 'desperate efforts are said to have been made to keep these events from the public'.[2] In terms of the supposed theft of the watch and other items, *The Age* reported concisely that the squatter 'was now convinced that the girl [Maud Gamble] did not intend to steal the articles. He believed she removed the watch from his waistcoat under superior orders, and handed it over to 'Martha' [Burrell, Caroline's second-in-command] as security.'

When asked by the police whether he made inquiries about his property he replied: 'I didn't bother my head about them, because I knew where they were.' The squatter was quite clear that when he reported the matter to police: 'I only wanted to frighten [the women], because they wanted more money than I was going to pay.'

The Herald reported the exchange in different words, but confirmed that the women asked for £60, but that Davidson was only willing to pay 'about £15 or £20'.

In other words, the squatter went to the police in an attempt to blackmail the women into reducing his bill. After bringing the police to the house but failing to recover the items, the squatter managed to negotiate a £35 settlement of his debt; he then spent another three days at Madame Brussels' house, shouting champagne for all and sundry and paying another £300 for his pleasure.

The case was widely reported throughout Australia, mostly including the squatter's testimony that his watch was held as security for his debt rather than stolen. In his summing up the defending barrister pointed out that the watch was in the hands of Martha, not the girl accused of stealing the watch, yet the police had not charged Martha with receiving stolen goods. But Joseph Panton, the presiding magistrate this time, said he had 'never listened to a clearer case' and sent Maud Gamble to trial on a charge of larceny, with bail of £50 (presumably paid by Caroline Hodgson). Panton went on to hear the evidence against the two women charged with keeping a disorderly house. David Gaunson was defending Caroline and Martha for the first time, but he used the same arguments as his predecessors in 1898 and 1889. Madame Brussels' establishment had been there for thirty years, he said, it was quietly conducted and not a nuisance to the neighbours, and since the city council had the power to regulate these houses but chose not to do so, her house was effectively located in a part of the city set aside for the purpose. Panton, however, had already made up his mind and turned the blame away from the squatter. He said it was not the only accusation of blackmail he had heard against 'this particular house', and 'when a house takes to this sort of thing it is time it was wiped out'. So he ignored the squatter's attempted blackmail of the women, sent Maud Gamble off to be tried for theft even though the squatter said she did not steal anything, and postponed his decision on Caroline and Martha until the higher court had made a decision about the theft. Caroline and Martha had to pay another £50 for bail, but all the young women of the house were discharged without Panton needing to hear any evidence from them at all.

When the charge of theft against Maud Gamble was heard again, the squatter confirmed his attempt to beat the women down: 'I thought I would get my jewellery back by paying a moderate rate for it.'[3] Justice a'Beckett went through all the evidence and without hesitation – despite Panton's opinion that it was a 'clear case' – directed the jury to return a verdict of not guilty.

After the acquittal, Caroline and Martha were again brought before Mr Panton to hear their fate. David Gaunson argued again that the house had been quietly conducted, and 'asked that a small fine might be inflicted, instead of imprisonment'.[4] The magistrate retorted that 'when harpies conduct themselves in the manner of which we have had evidence in this case, it is time the police stepped in to protect the public'. Caroline wept and 'asked the bench to "give her a chance," declaring that she would not be seen in court again.' Panton admitted that nothing 'in the shape of robbery' had taken place in her house before, but repeated his claim that it was a 'clear case', and 'Men of the world knew exactly what took place. When such harpies are allowed to parade, it is quite enough.' He then announced a curious decision: 'We think the publicity given to the case will be sufficient punishment, and will let you go.'

It was not the first time that Panton had been strangely strong on rhetoric and weak on punishment, especially when it came to Caroline Hodgson.

The release of Caroline and Martha without a fine or imprisonment was reported in *The Herald* in over 400 words, in *The Age* in less than half that, and completely ignored by *The Argus* and *Truth*. Having reported the earlier trial in great detail, leaving the reader with the pleasure of a titillating story without a proper conclusion, John Norton chose not to bother enlightening his readers with the news of the women's lack of guilt. He had had his fun with Madame Brussels for the time being. But in his 4500 words headlined 'Madame Brussels' notorious bawdy house – her junketing Jezebels', Norton had set the tone for his future writing about Caroline Hodgson.

It has been argued that under Norton's editorship, *Truth* 'consistently campaigned … in favour of greater protection for the weak and oppressed – slum dwellers, exploited workers, women and children',[5] but his writing about the women of Lonsdale Street in general and Caroline Hodgson in particular was always tainted by his alcoholism and his appalling attitude and behaviour towards women.[6] Assessing the truth or integrity to be found in his writings about Madame Brussels, then, is a fraught endeavour, but his work still provides us with information that cannot be found anywhere else. The sketch of her, for example, that appeared as part of the report of the Davidson trial in *Truth* was the only known depiction of her until family photographs were donated to the State Library Victoria in 2018.

Madame Brussels as drawn by *Truth* in 1906

His descriptions of her, too, are some of the few contemporary portrayals we have:

Madame certainly was quietly attired. The spectacled, middle-aged woman, with her reticule* on her arm, and her fan languidly waving, had more the appearance of a benevolent midwife than the keeper of a notorious brothel.

Caroline Hodgson (otherwise Madame Brussels) ... was accommodated with a chair on account of her great age, her gold-rimmed spectacles, and her fascinating black bombazine fan.[7]

A drawstring handbag or purse.

Norton also described Martha Burrell (appearing as 'Martha Atkinson' in the 1906 trial), characterising her as 'a dowdy, elderly person' who 'looked as though she might have just come from a love feast in connection with the Wesleyan Conference, so simple was her attire and demure her demeanour'.

Martha Burrell (aka Atkinson) as drawn by *Truth* in 1906

These court cases took place before Norton's blood was truly boiling against Madame Brussels and her workers. He did describe them outside the court as an 'undistinguished company of undesirables', and commented on the crowd's 'envious animadversions upon the wearers of the silks and satins, the laces and embroideries, and the resplendent millinery' of the women, but he also admired the young workers as 'bobby-dazzlers. Their millinery left nothing to be desired – except immunity from payment of the bill. Their rustling silks and scintillating satins had been made up by past mistresses in sartorial art. And everyone of them bespoke a remarkable expenditure of Chinese laundrymen's patience.'

In 1958 Cyril Pearl was to write that 'Norton's degree of drunkenness at any time can be measured with remarkable accuracy by the amount of alliteration in his prose', so we can assume that he wrote the last article in a reasonable state of sobriety. The next thing he wrote about Madame Brussels, though, had the stamp of an alcohol-fuelled hate-fest, but before that storm broke over Caroline's head there was the matter of a divorce to be sorted.

After the turn of the century Caroline's business seems to have gradually picked up, at least in terms of income. She transferred the houses in Carter Street back from Martha Burrell's name to her own in 1903 and paid off the mortgage on them, and then paid cash for the cottage in Casselden Lane in 1905. By then she had also taken back the house in Beaconsfield Parade for her own use. Irene had probably lived there after she left school, but after she went to Germany Caroline used it herself. She might have needed a safe haven during the court cases, but it is also possible that she was too busy with business at Lonsdale Street to go there much – the newspapers had provided her with a lot of free advertising and Norton inadvertently introduced another path for customers to follow to Madame Brussels' door. There had always been curious men noseying through the back lanes, but the tourism trade would have increased as a result of his story about Alfred Plumpton taking young men there to 'see life'.[8] By 1906 Lonsdale Street, and perhaps especially Madame Brussels' houses, had an air of olde-worlde vice about them, making it a place for tourists to go – and brag about having gone – to experience the pleasures of 'the East'. Even if it was not profiting the way it had in its boom years of the 1880s, Caroline's business was solid. She had paid off all of the mortgages on her Lonsdale Street properties, and that is possibly why she chose to initiate divorce proceedings.[9] In July she had learnt that Jacob Pohl was living in Fitzroy, but he had not contacted her; if he had suddenly made claims upon her hard-won property, as his legal wife she could not have prevented him from fleecing her again.

On 3 October 1906 David Gaunson applied to the Supreme Court for a divorce for Caroline Pohl on the grounds of desertion. Jacob Pohl, she swore, 'has without just cause or excuse wilfully deserted [her] and … left her continuously deserted during Three years and upwards'. Her sworn statement sets out the story of their marriage and her desire to rekindle it. 'I have always been ready and willing to live with Respondent if he had provided me with a home,' she wrote, and 'I have until quite recently been hopeful that I and the said Respondent would have been able to come together again.' It was a sad admission of failure, but as divorce proceedings go the details were not at all sensational and thus barely worth reporting. *The Age* spent barely a hundred words on it, and *The Argus* even less. No one at that stage, it seemed, had realised that 'Caroline Pohl' of the divorce court, boarding house keeper of 39 Beaconsfield Parade, was the notorious Madame Brussels of Lonsdale Street. The address was a handy disguise, but it didn't last long. A decree nisi was granted and costs awarded to Caroline without the respondent ever appearing in court, and a fortnight later all hell broke loose in Victorian politics. Madame Brussels' name was at the centre of it.

26.

A POLITICAL STORM AND THREE MORE TRIALS

THE BANK CRASH OF THE 1890s had burst upon Melbourne like a mudslide. The destruction was dirty, widespread and seemingly indiscriminate in terms of the lives lost, but the mud only stuck to those with insufficient wiles and arrogance to rise above their creditors. The idea of social responsibility took a beating in financial and legal circles (where the irresponsibility was greatest); instead of demanding financial probity and legal accountability from the many wealthy speculators who caused the disaster, Melbourne's leaders and legislators became embroiled in arguments about prostitution and off-course betting. Instead of legislating to protect workers and provide liveable wages for working families, they argued about whether libraries and art galleries should be open on Sundays. Demands for temperance and women's voting rights, too, distracted the masses; they also challenged the prevailing attitudes towards women's role in society, putting the ideas of respectability and domesticity in direct conflict with the old idea of prostitution as a 'necessary evil'. All those social developments thrust Caroline Hodgson's business onto the front line of the morality wars. John Norton was on the front line too, but his attacks were more like a barrage of loose cannons than a carefully planned offensive. His main targets were the wowsers – the anti-drink, anti-larrikin, anti-gambling, anti-nudity (even in art) fraternity – but he could find a good target anywhere, especially when there was a touch of hypocrisy about. Hence his attack on Sir Samuel Gillott, who, as Chief Secretary and Minister for Labor in Victoria's government, was 'an important member in a Ministry which proposes to legislate against the Drink, Traffic and Gambling, and, indeed, against vice in every shape and form'.[1]

As Norton pointed out, there was certainly a case for Gillott to answer regarding a conflict of interest between his public duties and his property and professional links with publicans and bookmakers, but it was Gillott's loans to Caroline Hodgson that fired up Norton's fury, and with his gift for alliteration he erupted with a blazing blitzkrieg of bilge.

> You have lent money over and over again to the worst and wickedest woman in Melbourne – to 'Madame Brussells' [*sic*], the immoral monster who for many years past has lived on the shame of her sisters in sin, and whose bagnio has been a black blot on the boasted morality of Melbourne for over a quarter of a century.

He was aiming for Gillott, but his shots were hitting Caroline too, describing her as 'this Princess of Procuresses', 'this morally putrescent prostitute's pimp', 'this female Minotaur' who 'has for many years carried on her body-blighting and soul-damning business as a brothel-keeper right in the heart of this great Christian City of Melbourne'. He described the 'crapulous, concupiscent clients' who visited 'her lair', 'her house of horrors', her 'cunningly contrived crib for carrying on the bestial business of a brothel', and published a plan of the boundaries of her establishment. He then set out the fine details of Gillott's loans from 1877 onwards that had enabled Caroline Hodgson to purchase her properties: the mortgage numbers, the dates, the amounts and the time she took to repay them.

There was no praise for her financial probity, only abuse for her morals. 'This feculent fiend in female form' was, he said, 'an infamous and notorious procuress' and 'a hellish harridan'. The business of 'this disgusting drab of Lonsdale-street', he wrote, was 'the systematic degradation of the bodies and damnation of the souls of frail fallen girls' whom 'this vampire' had got into 'her cruel and crafty clutches'. 'That wicked woman, "Madame Brussels," he wrote, carried on a 'damnable traffic in human bodies and souls [that] would be a capital crime against decent Democracy.'

Anyone would think that Norton's soul was white as snow, and that he was a paragon of protection for the proper purity of women, but his history of domestic violence and sexual conquests says otherwise. The power of his writing, though, lay in his ability to deflect the reader from such considerations by speaking powerfully for those 'many thousands of lower-class readers living unenviable lives at the base of the social pyramid':

Who, I ask you – who is it that has kept 'Madame Brussels" bagnio going and flourishing on the sin and shame of the daughters and sisters of the People during so many years? Who, I ask you, are they who have protected this pestiferous procuress from police interference, prosecution and legal punishment for so long? Has it been the Workers, the Wage-earners, the Labor Leaguers, or the much-maligned Socialists? No ... It is the rich and influential scallywags, who sweat the workers and sneer and scoff at their aspirations and efforts towards industrial emancipation and social regeneration. These are the clients of 'Madame Brussels'.

The labouring workers who bought *Truth* in enormous numbers 'genuinely regarded Norton as one of their few true defenders', so by aligning Caroline Hodgson's business with the 'rich and influential' he cleverly turned the argument back towards the misbehaviour of the 'capitalistic cliques, club coteries, and "smart sets"' rather than his own.[2] If Cyril Pearl's assessment of Norton's alliteration is accurate then he had obviously been drinking copiously during the production of this 3000-word dose of invective.[3] But there was more to it here than alcohol. As his wife said in court after he was charged with indecently assaulting another woman, 'when he was drunk he was a lunatic', and even the more sympathetic of his biographers called him 'a gifted megalomaniac constantly teetering on the brink of sanity'.[4] In this case, though, Norton's mental struggles were not confined to personal or domestic issues; they had broad implications. The information he published on 1 December was spouted from the pulpit by the Methodist reformer William Judkins on 2 December, and taken up by *The Argus* the following day.[5] Within a week of the publication of Norton's poisonous article Sir Samuel Gillott had resigned from all of his public duties and embarked on the *Grosser Kurfurst* heading for Europe.[6] Norton then turned his rage onto William Judkins.

Judkins was a lay preacher who, like Norton, was 'vigorous with the pen'.[7] And like Henry Varley before him, Judkins was loud in his condemnation of the 'social evils' he saw all around him, including 'prizefighting, gambling, racing, drinking, dancing, and even barmaids'. In 1906 he was particularly focused on John Wren and his illegal Collingwood betting shop and blamed Sir Samuel Gillott for not dealing effectively with the problem. He, too, used the information about Madame Brussels' property loans primarily as a means to attack Samuel Gillott, but Caroline's reputation suffered collateral damage.

Norton could have seen Judkins as an ally, fighting the same fight, but instead he was incensed. Judkins, after all, had had the effrontery to claim that he had done his own research, and that he was the first to have 'revealed' the information. Norton was a journalist, and his horror at having someone else lay claim to his scoop led to another alliterative rant even longer than the first. Most of it was aimed at the 'sanctimonious, shekel-snaring snob', the 'snide snufflebuster', the 'pusillanimous pietist, and canting cowardly "Christian champion"' Judkins, but in the process of attacking Judkins, Norton doubled down on 'this Brussels bawd', 'that wicked female whore-monger, "Madame Brussels"', 'this stale strumpet'.[8] He described her 'bad, black bestial bawdy business' as having been for many years the principal place for purposes of prostitution for politicians and other prominent public men, including not a few fashionable pillars of 'Society' of the tough Toorak type. Here have been ruined, body and soul, scores of women and girls: here have the fathers and husbands, brothers of good women and innocent children, been robbed and ruined; here, too, have parsonical denouncers of impurity among the people degraded their nature and disgraced their holy calling by frequenting this seraglio of sin in disguise; and here, also, have been perpetrated some of the most hideous outrages, cruel crimes, and rascally robberies ever perpetrated in a community boasting of its Christian piety, and of its police precautions for the promotion and preservation of public morality.

It was a stinging attack, but Norton quickly returned to the primary object of his displeasure, the 'holy hypocrite and howling humbug' Judkins. He likened him to a jackal, then to a chameleon, Norton turned and gave praise to his earlier victim.

I tell you, Judkins, that the conduct of Sir Samuel Gillott since 'Truth's' exposure last Friday has been dignified and decent compared with yours, which, I repeat, has been cowardly and contemptible.

It is possible that Norton did have some sympathy with Gillott, but he had no such change of heart about Caroline Hodgson. Having accused Judkins of dishonesty on page one of that day's *Truth*, he produced some of the same opportunism himself on page five in a 1500-word article on Caroline Hodgson's divorce. 'No one in the court had the slightest idea,' he pontificated, 'that the petitioner was the notorious "Madame Brussels",'[9] despite the fact that it had been reported in both *The Age* and *The Argus* at the time, and the connection to Madame Brussels reached as far afield as Perth.[10] In that interstate report it was said that Caroline 'appeared as a most benevolent looking old lady, and quite secured the sympathy of the court by her demeanour and recital of the story of her wrongs'.

Norton, however, was having none of that sympathetic nonsense. He was in the mood for ridicule, and he dished it up in prime style.

She wept copiously in the witness box over her marital wrongs, and gave one the impression that she was simply a decent, respectable German frau who had been badly used by a brutal husband. Fat and fifty-five, she filled the witness box like an elephantine Niobe.[11]

He published her entire affidavit telling the story of her marriage – was it a public document, or did he obtain it by stealth? – and then followed it with an exchange between a witness and Caroline's barrister, Mr Woolf:

Albert Muller ... was present when the divorce papers were served on [Jacob Pohl].

MR WOOLF: What did he say?

WITNESS: He said, 'Come and have a drink, old man. That is the best news I have heard for a very long time. She's too old for me.'
Respondent had a gaudily-dressed young woman with him at the time. When he said, 'She's too old for me,' respondent added, 'I want something like this,' pointing to the young woman who was with him.

Truth was the only newspaper to include this choice morsel of gossip, and since Norton was not there to hear the evidence we must take it with a large grain of the salt that belongs with every statement of fact in *Truth*. Norton concluded shamelessly that 'the curious part of the whole affair is that no one in court recognised, or, at least, pretended to recognise, in the sedate, elderly, black-dressed and unostentatious Caroline Pohl the notorious woman of evil fame, "Madame Brussels."'

A few weeks later Norton published another article claiming the credit for Samuel Gillott's resignation and heaping more abuse on Caroline Hodgson.[12] One can hear his sense of superiority over this 'lecherous, blasting blight' of a woman, and his pride in *Truth* having created the national profile of 'Madame Brussels, the most notorious pimp, procuress and harridan in Australia'. He might well have taken his own advice, though, that 'he who seeks to cleanse public impurities should himself be clean and sweet, with no hidden undercurrent and connection with the profits accruing from vice and misery'.

Caroline, too, might have taken more heed of Panton's warning regarding her method of extracting payment from her clients. It was not long before she found herself in trouble once more, and this time there was no escape.

It began with another grazier, this time from Dandenong to the east of Melbourne rather than Malmsbury to the north, but otherwise very similar circumstances.[13] Henry Pallenberg arrived at Madame Brussels' establishment one Sunday night with a few pounds in his pocket, separated from his wife (he said) and keen for some entertainment. He handed over his gold watch and chain as security for his debt and went on a spree. A beer, champagne, women and whiskey kind of spree spread out over the rest of the week. 'There was dancing, and a sing song going on at the time. I gave the pianist some money,' he said.[14] When it came time to pay, halfway through the week, he wrote out a cheque for £150 and Martha Burrell caught the train out to Dandenong to cash it at his bank. The women thought the cheque was for them so they divvied the cash up between them, but the grazier claimed later that he had expected to get some change. About £100 worth of change, in fact. According to Pallenberg he had been so intoxicated the whole time that he didn't remember much about anything; according to the women he had never been very drunk and had been sober enough to sign a cheque for £125 poorly and then destroy it and sign a cheque for £150 more clearly. He himself said that he was 'lucid' when he signed the cheque, although he was not sober. When his friends came and collected him on the Friday morning, he left without collecting either his watch and chain or his cash. He subsequently recovered his watch and chain through his solicitors.

When Pallenberg brought the matter to the County Court he wanted his £150 back; he was asked a lot of questions about whether he had been to the house before (about a dozen or a dozen and a half times, the last about a fortnight ago for a few hours) and how much it cost to stay there (about £16 last time for those few hours, but £10 to £12 per day without wine). When he was asked how much he thought he owed the women for his stay this time, he replied 'about £40' because he didn't drink. He said he didn't drink because he was ill. He also said that when he gave the pianist some money he was too drunk to remember how much, when he signed the cheque he was 'three quarters drunk', and when he left the house he didn't collect his watch and chain or wait for the change from the cheque because he was drunk at the time. The women's defending barrister asked, 'You now want to get the whole of your money back without allowing defendants anything?' Pallenberg responded: 'Oh, no, I will pay my bill.'

The barrister asked Pallenberg why he was not shouting the women wine, and he replied 'because I was ill with dysentery.'

Did this dysentery last while you were in bed?—Yes.

And did one of the girls tell you you had spoiled a nightdress of hers that cost 10 guineas?—I cannot say.

Pallenberg's memory was very poor when it came to such details. He couldn't remember telling some of the women that his wife had an account at a shop where they might go to get 'some dressing-gowns and other things they wanted', and he definitely didn't remember the women telling him that Madame would not allow them to do that.

The prosecutor began by admitting that 'his client was a fool' and 'a man who, if he took liquor, behaved in a most foolish manner', yet his client told the court that he didn't drink while he was there because he was ill. Much fun was had by Norton on the basis that Caroline had repeatedly warned the grazier that 'he had been going lemons', and his supposed reply that 'he didn't kill a pig every day' – a reference to his recent success in mining speculation. The woman who entertained him said that he admitted 'he had given a lot of trouble, and didn't care what he gave'. Yet Judge Eagleson, without hesitating, ordered the women to pay the grazier the full £150 plus costs. He was not prepared to concede the women's right to be paid for their work or hospitality. The case ended on 8 April, and on 25 April Mr and Madame H. Pallenberg (the supposedly separated couple) left Melbourne on the *Armand Behic*, bound for Marseilles and London.[15] Nothing further was reported about the grazier paying what he owed to the women who had entertained him for nearly a week.

The end of the Pallenberg case was not the end of Caroline's worries for even a short time, because while she had been facing the hostility of Judge Eagleson in the County Court, one of her neighbouring madams in Lonsdale Street had been brought before Joseph Panton at the City Court.[16] He, too, had turned against the women. When Sarah Russell of 14 to 16 Lonsdale Street was charged with being the occupier of a disorderly house she faced almost the same bench of magistrates as Caroline had stood before in 1898, with Panton presiding instead of McEacharn.[17] Sarah's barrister used the same arguments to defend her as Caroline's had successfully employed in 1898 and 1889, pointing out that it would be 'an invidious thing to pick out one keeper and prosecute her, while the rest go scot-free'.[18] But Panton was not impressed this time.

> Whatever the state of these houses may have been years ago I know from experience sitting here that they are a disgrace to the community. They are nests of vampires. I see unfortunate women from the streets brought here day after day, but these horrible vampires are allowed to go and rob at large in these dirty filthy dens.

Instead of sentencing Sarah to 'imprisonment during the sitting of the court', Panton announced that 'this has been going on too long, and it is necessary to deal with it severely'. The day after Caroline was ordered to pay Pallenberg his £150 Sarah was sentenced to three months' gaol. Sarah's barrister sealed Caroline's fate by remarking to Panton: 'Well, your worship, I hope now that every keeper will be brought up before you at once by the police.'

A week later his hopes were realised when seven more women, including Caroline Hodgson, were charged with being the keepers of disorderly houses.[19] By the time she faced Panton on 18 April, Caroline had seen the writing on the wall and given up her lease on 6 to 8 Lonsdale Street. According to her barrister she had also sent the women away from her own house and put it on the market.[20] *Truth*, of course, was quick to trumpet the news of Caroline's downfall. The fact that there is barely an alliteration in sight suggests that it was not written by John Norton himself, but there is a sense of history in the making.

THE PASSING OF BRUSSELS.

LEWD HOUSES IN LONSDALE STREET.

Madame Stricken with Diabetes – She undertakes to Sin No More.

Crocodile Tears in Court.

Her Houses Closed.[21]

The tears shed by Caroline Hodgson in court that day, according to *Truth*, were not in response to 'remorse for her long and despicable career as a brothel-keeper' but were instead 'for her own suffering body'. She had diabetes, for which there was no cure.

Caroline's barrister pointed out that she had relinquished her rented houses and cleared the women out of the houses she owned. She had, he said, decided to give up the trade altogether. Given that this would satisfy the objective of the police, he suggested the case be adjourned for a month to prove her intentions. Mr Panton agreed. *Truth* noted that Madame lifted her veil, 'and removing her spectacles, wiped the tears away with a dainty lace handkerchief.'

But *Truth* was not finished with its obituary of 'Madame Brussels':

She has made a name that will outlive even her 'blocks of buildings,' a name that many a girl has wished to God she had never heard. Not all young women who go astray have the brothel to blame. 'Truth' is well aware of that. But once on the down grade, they were often dragged to the bottom by establishments such as those over which Madame presided. 'The passing of Brussels' means the extermination of at least one plague spot in the city, and the greatest one of them all.

And so the myth of Madame Brussels – 'the worst and wickedest woman in Melbourne' – was delivered to Melbourne's history books through the pages of John Norton's *Truth*.[22]

Panton agreed on a month's adjournment because he was waiting to see what became of Sarah Russell's appeal against the gaol sentence he had handed her the week before. As it turned out, the higher court set aside her sentence of imprisonment and imposed a fine of £10 instead, but when the other cases came back to Panton, all of the women except Caroline had already left Lonsdale Street.[23] Her barrister asked that she be allowed to remain there since 'she could not leave the premises untenanted' and was no longer operating the business. No conviction was recorded against Caroline, but Panton insisted that she get rid of the house in fourteen days.[24]

PART VI: THE END

27.

CORRUPTION AGAIN

The success or failure of a high-priced parlor house ultimately rested on the central figure of the establishment, the madam. Viewed from an occupational point of view, the position of a madam required extreme competence in business and political matters as well as managerial, personnel, and communication skills … A reputation for absolute silence was essential … she had to protect the identities of her customers … In some cases, some madams became silent partners in the local power structure; they knew too much for any local politician to shut their establishments down.

—Ruth Rosen, *The Lost Sisterhood: Prostitution in America, 1900–1918,*

1982, p. 87

JOSEPH PANTON WAS THE PRESIDING MAGISTRATE in the last three cases against Caroline Hodgson, one in 1906 and two in 1907. In 1906 Panton was accompanied again by Lancashire and Cherry from the 1898 case, with one other magistrate. They made the extraordinary decision to both harangue the women as though they were guilty, and then let them go because 'we think the publicity in this case is punishment enough'. As we have seen, *Table Talk* suggested that there was a conspiracy to protect the wealthy squatter rather than the women: 'One paper with a reputation failed to publish the story, but it has all leaked out through another channel.'[1]

But John Norton chimed in through the pages of *Truth* to blame Caroline:

> It is said that the police have in the past been in the pay of
> 'Madame,' and that at critical junctures some of the police were
> regularly subsidised by her to keep watch over her 'Business,'
> and to ward off prosecutions, menacing witnesses, or 'whisper-
> ing' them away: and even, as it has been alleged, manufacturing
> false evidence themselves in defence of 'Madame'.[2]

Given that Norton claimed in the same article that 'a small mob of drunken members of Parliament "swollen with lust and wine"' had stolen the parliamentary mace and 'marched in procession to "Madame Brussels"' bagnio' – known now to be complete untruths – his claims about her buying police protection are likely to be of the same gossipy ilk; but equally they might contain a grain of truth.[3]

In the first case of 1907 Panton was accompanied on the bench again by Power, Lancashire and Bell, along with another JP; this case was a matter of money as well as morals, and Caroline was believed to be wealthy.[4] The decision satisfied both sides of the bench by denying the women payment for their services and making Caroline pay the money back. In the last case of all – the one that caused her to close her house – Caroline was one of six women to be charged with being the keeper of a disorderly house, but the other five women simply packed up and left. Caroline sent all her lodgers away, but still had to face court because she remained in possession of the house.[5] It was not reported who sat on the bench with Panton for that last hearing, but his decision was far more lenient than three months' gaol; he gave her fourteen days to leave the house.[6] Panton retired six weeks later, and Caroline died, still in her house, the following year.[7]

Before the case in 1906 *The Age* expressed the opinion that 'among the questions likely to provoke interest in official and legal circles will be the constitution of the bench', and that 'certain members of the force are said to have been in the habit of visiting the raided premises and availing themselves of the hospitality and the motor cars of [the plaintiff] to pay calls at other houses of no better reputation'.[8] Curiously, neither of these accusations made any further appearance in the press, and no evidence of police corruption relating to brothels or Caroline Hodgson's influence over the magistrates came to public notice during the police commission of 1905–06.[9]

Over the years Panton was often (though not always) more forgiving and lenient than the police would have liked towards sex workers, and there is no doubt that his decisions favoured Caroline despite his sometimes harsh rhetoric. The closer he came to retirement, though, the less leeway he was willing to give her. There is no evidence that Caroline had any unseemly influence or hold over him, or over the other magistrates who voted against convicting her on numerous occasions, but rather it seemed as though they liked her and didn't like many of the others. Some of the magistrates could have been her clients, but we have no access to her visitors' book if she ever had one. Her good fortune may simply have been due to certain kinds of powerful men, who held practical views about the inevitability of prostitution and the need to manage it somehow, feeling strongly enough about her fundamental decency to oppose those with a deeply held desire to close down *any* woman operating in the industry. Madame Brussels' business was at the confluence of these opposing views.

Apart from Laurence Gleeson's statement to the court in 1889, and *The Daily Telegraph*'s claim about '"Madame" Brussels' reputed boast', nothing else has come to light suggesting that she was protected by her contacts. It is entirely likely that she felt she had some influence and that she wielded the power of bribery at times when she felt it was to her advantage, especially to silence police on the beat, but it was always of more value to her business to look after her clients and rely on their loyalty. The *Truth* acknowledged this when it claimed (in 1903) that 'nobody has ever been robbed in her place of his cash' and 'Madame Brussells [*sic*], indeed, prides herself that she has had for safe keeping at a time as much as £2000 of a man's cash whilst he "enjoyed" himself at her house for a fortnight; and although the man was drinking, "his money was safe".'[10] For all her efforts and influence and money, though, and despite winning numerous small battles, in the end she lost the war.

28.

WORKERS AND CLIENTS

GOING BACK TO THE QUESTION OF THE 'class of women' who lodged with Caroline Hodgson, in 1889 she was drawing young women partly by word of mouth through her longstanding reputation and the contacts of her lodgers themselves, and partly from what were called 'registry offices', or employment agencies.[1] We have no evidence to suggest whether she actively employed women to scout for likely lodgers among the girls who went to such places looking for work, or whether it was simply that women like Lottie Temple (who was charged along with Caroline in 1889) had their own reasons for keeping Madame Brussels' rooms full.[2] Temple ran a shop with her husband and supplied goods to the women in Madame Brussels' houses; she might have taken a commission for chatting up young women looking for work and then 'introducing' them to the house, but even without such active recruitment the benefit to her business is obvious.

For all the women – Caroline, Lottie and the boarders – the issue was money: how to earn the 'best' living. The likely boarders were therefore mostly working-class women for whom the usual jobs that were on offer were poorly paid; one of the girls who gave evidence in 1889 said she was offered a position 'in an india-rubber factory at 5s. a week to learn the business, but refused to take it because the wages were too small'.[3] Five shillings a week was not a liveable wage, but factory owners could keep women working for six months or more on such pitiful amounts while they 'trained'. Another one of the girls had been working in a draper's shop for 9s. a week, again not enough for a young woman living out of home to survive on.[4] These were poor young women, looking to earn enough to make their own way, and we can assume that throughout the sorry financial times of the 1890s finding work would have been even more difficult, if not impossible for them.

Sex work was primarily an economic decision, but that is not to say that Caroline did not at times take advantage of young women. She did try to influence the ones who went to her house thinking she wanted servants by emphasising that they 'could earn plenty of money [as sex workers] instead of working hard for it'.[5] Young women may have gone there with no intention 'to lead a bad life' but with the promise of 'as much money as [they] wanted' from Caroline and 'the persuasion of the other girls in the house and the dress and jewellery they showed [them]', they stayed.[6] And some, like Lizzie Emmanuel, regretted it. She 'went out for a walk and never went back', claiming that 'I am living a respectable life now thank God for it'.[7] Others, too, like Olive Douglas's friend who called herself 'Fanny Montgomery' before going back to being a laundress, doubtless found the life not to their taste and left.[8] But does that make Caroline 'the worst and wickedest woman in Melbourne'?[9] Does tempting girls with material goods and letting them choose whether to grasp them or not make her a 'morally putrescent prostitute's pimp'?

There is no suggestion that Caroline's boarders were ever trapped into staying and working, or coerced by anything other than their own taste for 'finery'. Dressing well, with diamonds, silks and satins, would have been beyond the wildest dreams and expectations of these young women if they had kept to factory and domestic work, but boarding at Madame Brussels' gave them the opportunity to buy such things or be given them. Mary Lawrence, for example, said that in the few days she was at Madame Brussels she 'took about £5 and paid £3–10 for board and the rest was spent in clothes'.[10] £1 10s. was therefore pure profit – at least three weeks' worth of ordinary wages, with no rent or food to be taken out of it. What joy for a young woman with a taste for fine things! But the downsides of the industry – the risks of disease and unwanted pregnancies for example – were such that many of the women only worked in it for a short time before either marrying or taking up other work. There was a frequent turnover of boarders at most of the brothels, and constant changing of tenants in houses around Madame Brussels'.

International research indicates that the price of sexual services was generally dependent 'on the class of the client' rather than the refinements of the sex worker.[11] The high rate of turnover would have worked against the provision of any formal skills instruction in Madame Brussels' houses, but the workers were required to be fashionable, so it was up to Caroline Hodgson to ensure that the young women had the means to dress appropriately. When she was charged with being 'the occupier of a disorderly house' in 1906, she was 'quietly attired' herself when she attended court, as was her housekeeper. The women from her house who accompanied her, however, were 'bobby-dazzlers', dressed no doubt to arouse desire in the male onlookers.[12] Those court cases might have cost Caroline a small fortune in dressmaking if she was paying, but it was all part of running her business and the early appearances at least would have been good advertising. Sometimes, though, the investment might have been a poor one, if women left without paying their board, or took clothes with them. One of the young women who gave evidence in the 1889 case, for example, was in debt for her board when she left.[13] Unlike some other madams, there is no indication that Caroline Hodgson ever took an ex-boarder to court to recover any costs. There is plenty of evidence to suggest that the women were not relying on Caroline for their clothing, though; both Davidson and Pallenberg gave the women access to accounts at local shops to buy clothes, and men were also known to give women orders (that is, nineteenth-century gift vouchers) to purchase at certain stores.[14]

Regarding the character of the women working in the brothels, one comment from a senior policeman stands out. It came after an advertisement was placed in *The Age* for a pianist at a place known to be a flash brothel. A constable was sent to ensure that no respectable woman was hired. The madam assured the policeman that she had no intention of doing such a thing, and that the woman who was there at that moment was a friend of hers. The constable reported that the friend was 'a middle aged woman, and one evidently accustomed to brothels as she was inclined to be impertinent'.[15]

Impertinence – not knowing one's place – was a common complaint about sex workers. They were too sassy and independent, which is something that Caroline Hodgson seemed to understand about her boarders. As one of the girls told the police before the case in 1889, 'she said we could please ourselves as to what we did'.[16] Three of the four girls in that case 'declared they had acted with their eyes open; knew exactly what they were doing, and gave one the impression that they would not return to the paths of morality, even if that were possible'.[17]

The case against Olive Douglas for electoral fraud provides more direct evidence about the kind of women who worked in Caroline's houses after the turn of the century. The friend whose name Olive took was a laundress, and they both chose to vote.[18] It was not compulsory to vote in Australian federal elections until 1911,[19] but at that second-ever election in 1903 Martha Burrell ('cook') registered to vote, as did eleven other women in houses managed by Caroline Hodgson.[20] Caroline herself did not enrol (perhaps in response to the kerfuffle over her nationality in 1896), but the women managing the other well-established brothels of Lonsdale Street – Margaret Gordon, Emma Westcott, Bertha Morin and Louisa Bisgrove – all enrolled, along with many of the women working in their houses. All of these working women were listed with the occupation 'home duties'. In 1905, in preparation for the third federal election, Caroline Hodgson ('home duties') also enrolled; she appears along with Martha (still described as 'cook') and eight women at number 32.[21] Again, the women recognised by the police as managers of the other Lonsdale Street houses were all registered. They generally called themselves 'boarding house keepers', but the women who worked in their houses referred to themselves meaningfully as women 'of Lonsdale street'.[22] They might have been poor and ill-educated, but they had a sense of themselves as deserving to have their vote counted.

For all these women, names were a moveable feast, though the older women seemed to be more consistent – and therefore more traceable – than the younger ones. Those like Olive and her friend Fanny knew to distinguish between their real names and what they called their working noms de plume, but in the common way of women in that era they often went on to adopt the name of the man they were living with, whether inside or outside marriage.[23] The view that names could be changed at will depending on a person's circumstances was part of the social reality of many people in Melbourne at that time, especially women, for whom the use of 'Miss' or 'Mrs' was often matched with circumstances unrelated to formal marriage. For John Norton to describe the women as 'a more degraded and profligate type' than those of the boom years of the 1880s was therefore probably less a reflection on the women themselves than on the expectations of the world around them (or John Norton). Throughout the nineteenth century there were few negative consequences for such deceptions, but the broadened franchise, among other things, had sharpened the need for a stricter view of 'identity', and the development of newspapers such as Maurice Brodsky's *Table Talk* through the 1890s and John Norton's *Truth* in the 1900s increasingly pandered to the taste of Melbourne's public for stories about disreputable behaviour; they took pleasure in exposing what their subjects might prefer to hide.[24]

In the understanding of respectable judges and men on juries, most of 'the women of Lonsdale Street' were seen as 'weak in their ability to judge'. They nevertheless made the effort to vote and they were seen as a valuable constituency by some candidates. Sir Malcolm McEacharn (knighted since he presided over the court that acquitted Caroline Hodgson in 1898) had vociferously opposed women's suffrage, but in 1904 he was most definitely in favour of harvesting women's electoral numbers for his own benefit, which is how Olive Douglas got herself into trouble.[25]

Regarding the men who frequented the flash brothels, Cyril Pearl said that 'Madame Brussells' clients included Cabinet Ministers as well as eminent squatters, business men and lawyers'.[26]

We can confirm from the 1906 and 1907 cases that at least one squatter and one mining speculator visited her houses, and we can suspect the likes of Malcolm McEacharn and Thomas Bent (was he Pearl's 'Cabinet Minister?' and if so, was that a fact or a rumour?) visited them too, but it is possible that Pearl's information on this (as on many other things) came from the ever-unreliable John Norton. Early in 1906, at the time of the Davidson debacle, Norton said:

> Men who have since achieved very distinguished positions have been known as 'Brussels' men,' have entertained in Brussels' house, at Brussels' cost; and such circles of gents as many a Toorak swelldame or beldame would give her head or anything else marketable to bring together under her roof.[27]

Being a man among men, though, with certain (double) standard scruples, Norton refused to publish their names, because 'it is not fair to name them. Alcibiades and Socrates sought solace, escape from the silly, inane affectations of the polite society of their times in similar companionship.'

He went on to include musicians, military men, doctors and lawyers, 'and the fat men came along and paid up, right glad of the chance to see a bit of life and good company.' Later that year he took in certain churchgoers as well, 'the "Saints of Society," ... some of the most wealthy and prominent of the puritans of the Collins-street congregations.'[28] Since Norton did not name any of the prominent puritans, it is as likely as not that the hints he threw around were as much gossip and hearsay as they were truths. But Mrs Kemp's probate papers provide us with an interesting prompt to our conjectures on the matter of clientele for the flash brothels.[29] Included in the receipts by her executors are the following entries:

<pre>
F.K. Terry on a/c pchse money for policy
over life of Garnet Walsh [sic] £25
" "   "   " " (Bal.) per Aust. Alliance
Assce Co £165 4s 3d
" "   "   propn of prem. re Garnet Walsh [sic] £2 17s 8d
</pre>

And in the disbursements is the entry:

<pre>
Aust Allce Assce Co intst on £160 @ 8%
21 June got D/D £4 5s 4d
</pre>

The Australian Alliance Assurance Company was a life insurance company in the nineteenth century, and Francis King Terry was a merchant,
an unmarried man who gave the Australian Club as his address in 1895.[30]
The Australian Club was a gentleman's club whose clientele were largely
well-to-do businessmen. Francis King Terry was working with the firm
McIlwraith, McEacharn & Co Ltd – that is, the firm of Malcolm McEacharn
of city bench fame.

The Garnet Walch whose life insurance policy was being arranged by
Mrs Kemp and F.K. Terry was an author and dramatist who lived in
Melbourne through most of Mrs Kemp's brothel heyday of the 1870s and
1880s. According to his biographer, Garnet Walch 'seems to have enjoyed
a somewhat raffish reputation. He was a member of a bohemian circle in
Melbourne which included Marcus Clarke . . . [he was] a tremendous talker,
"shabbily dressed and distracted looking".'[31]

While that may position him well as a client of Mrs Kemp's house,
Garnet Walch was also a man with a family; beginning in 1868 his wife bore
him four sons and four daughters, but in 1880 – after resigning from his job
in 1879 to write a book – he was declared bankrupt. His wife would have
needed the charity of friends to keep the household fed, and even more so if
her husband had died when the children were young. Was that the purpose
of the life insurance policy? To help his wife if things went wrong? Walch

lived on until 1913, long after Mrs Kemp and F.K. Terry had passed away, so the full story behind this curious life insurance policy will probably never be known, but the connections between Garnet Walch, the Australian Club, Malcom McEacharn and Mrs Kemp's flash brothel are suggestive.[32] Were the flash brothels in some way aligned to particular social elites among Melbourne's male population? The squatters of the Melbourne Club with Madame Brussels, perhaps, and the mere (wealthy) men of trade in the Australian Club with Mrs Kemp? But if so, what should we make of Alfred Plumpton's Yorick and Savage Club connections?

No matter where their business came from, Madame Brussels is the only one of the flash madams to be commemorated today with a city thorough-fare named after her, but it was more likely to have been notoriety than admiration that brought her the attention. By the time her establishment was closed down in 1907 she was very ill, and the house was somewhat taw-dry compared with its heyday in the 1880s. The evidence that came out about the business during the court cases involving the squatter and the mining magnate have the hallmarks of a household run by an elderly woman not quite on top of her game, rather than Caroline Hodgson in her prime.

29.

DEATH OF A WOMAN

The complete story of this Princess of Procuresses would be a theme for a Balzac, so full is it of garish incident, human nature, and raw material for the epigrammatic moralist. ... in 'The Harlots Progress,' as in other volumes in the Human Comedy of the great French author, will be found fine descriptions of the ups and downs, sham pleasures, pathetic pretence, squalid degradation, and final hapless misery which mark the prostitute's passage from the time of her first fall, through the period of her womanhood's sexual prime, to the hour when her faded charms become a scoff for roués ...

—'A Broken-up Brothel. The Story of a Sale', *Truth* (Sydney),

5 October 1902, p. 6

JOHN NORTON HAD SUCH A JAUNDICED VIEW of sex workers' lives that when he wrote about Madame Brussels' predecessor Sarah Fraser in 1902 he could well have been writing about Madame Brussels herself. In 1903 he described Caroline Hodgson as being 'in her advanced middle life' and having 'developed into flesh, but still retains a certain sweetness in her face'.[1] Reporting on her divorce proceedings in 1906 he was less kind, and ignorant, perhaps, of her diabetes: 'Fat and fifty-five, she filled the witness box like an elephantine Niobe', adding that this 'sedate, elderly, black-dressed and unostentatious Caroline Pohl ... looks much older'.[2] Newspaper reports that include any kind of description of her invariably remark on her 'stylish' or 'fashionable' attire, and the few photographs we have of her confirm that she dressed well.[3]

Caroline Hodgson [about 1875–1879]

But when it came to the first of her 1907 trials in April, Norton was more focused on her gold-rimmed glasses and her German accent than her dress sense. He represented her as speaking faulty English, quoting (or misquoting) her:

He was drinking of liquor a little every day, and pressed the ladies to drink his health, also myself, but I do not drink. I ... said, 'My, you have been going lemons: you been having a big spree, and hope you won't go away and "weep" the cat and say we have robbed you.'[4]

Norton also mentioned that she was having difficulty with her mobility; the court had provided her with a chair when she was giving evidence early in 1906, and it did so again in April 1907 when she needed to lift her veil to remove her spectacles and wipe away her tears.[5] The spectacles, like her decision not to drink alcohol, were most likely related to her diabetes, for which there would have been no effective treatments available, and the tears that Norton so mercilessly ridiculed as being only for herself rather than 'for the girl-lives she had ruined' could well have been from the excruciating pain caused by her chronic pancreatitis. She had been working 'in the house every night till 3 or 4 o'clock in the morning' for decades, and suffering for six years by then.[6]

In May 1907 Mr Panton demanded that Caroline leave 32 Lonsdale Street within two weeks. Irene was still in Germany, and Caroline's health was deteriorating, but she was a proud and determined woman. Either she did not want to let go of the property she had accumulated so carefully in the face of so many trials and so much abuse, or she was too ill to arrange it, and despite Panton's insistence that she get rid of Lonsdale Street, Caroline held on. She probably moved to Gnarwin for a time and enjoyed her beautiful house and its magnificent view of Port Phillip Bay while she could, but she did not sell her Lonsdale Street properties. She rented 51 Park Street (the house behind hers in St Kilda) for 11s. a week, and had a tenant in one of the Carter Street houses for another 8s. a week.[7] The other Carter Street house was rented to Martha Burrell's family for a nominal shilling a month. That gave her less than a pound a week to live on, and with rates to pay, gardens to be maintained and domestic staff to employ it was obviously not enough. Instead of selling some property to make up the shortfall, over the following year she borrowed, mortgaged or pawned almost everything she owned, beginning with her jewellery. About a month after she closed her brothels she pledged it with a pawnbroker for almost £300, and before the end of the same month she mortgaged the Carter Street properties for another £215.[8]

By the end of 1907, though, Caroline was again running short of cash; she arranged a bank overdraft on the strength of the Lonsdale Street titles (her last remaining unmortgaged property) and carried on. Presumably part of the amount she borrowed was used to bring Irene home; the young woman arrived in a saloon cabin on the *Gneisenau* from Bremen on 2 May 1908. Caroline died at home in Lonsdale Street on 12 July, attended by Dr Stirling, the man whose extramarital dalliances had been reported in the newspapers during his divorce proceedings.[9]

In those last few months of her adoptive mother's life Irene was not only adjusting to being back in Melbourne after more than two years living in Germany, she was also facing a completely different home life. No young women around, no partying in the brothels, no visiting up and down the street, and a very sick woman to be nursed. And, to make things worse, no way of paying the bills. Caroline had established all the usual accounts – for bread, milk, meat, groceries and the rest – serving both her Lonsdale Street and St Kilda residences, and at the time of her death they all had substantial debts awaiting the attention of her executors. Caroline's immobility meant that whenever she needed cash for other things in those last months it was the people around her who borrowed money on her behalf. Martha Burrell borrowed £10 from Rosalie Hart, a pawnbroker around the corner in Exhibition Street.[10] Martha's daughter-in-law, Maud Burrell, lent her £44. Someone arranged promissory notes for her with local tradespeople, while some of her staff simply waited for their pay. The executors' sale of furnishings and effects from Lonsdale Street do not include any 'ebony, buhl and ormolu' or 'buxom marble and alabaster nudes', or 'large paintings of large women', suggesting that any readily saleable items had already been sold before Caroline's death.[11] So, besides dealing with her grief when Caroline died, Irene would have found that she had a funeral to arrange, and executors to negotiate with over the denuded contents of Caroline's estate, and no cash. Not least of her concerns would have been the realisation that her mother was not as wealthy as she appeared.

When Caroline made her 'last will and testament' on 7 July 1908, just five days before her death, Irene was living at Gnarwin and probably expected that it would remain her home for the foreseeable future.[12]

Caroline herself believed that she was still wealthy enough to be buried in 'a polished oak coffin', and for her mortgage on the Carter Street houses to be paid by her estate before bequeathing them to Martha Burrell, 'my house-keeper (now residing with me)'. Caroline also expected that after paying her debts, including her funeral expenses and probate duty, the value of her estate would still be above £3000. In that case, she said, it should be divided into three equal portions, one for each of her two sisters in Germany and Irene. If it was less than £3000, she said, £1000 should go to Irene, and the remainder shared between her two sisters.

In the process of paying the estate's debts and expenses, the properties were all sold or disposed of and there was an auction sale of her goods and chattels. Despite Henry Varley's claim in 1889 that 'the furniture in one room of her cottage would be worth from £500 to £600', the furniture from both of her houses realised only £514. In the end Caroline's estate left her sisters with nothing and Irene with no home. But among the items of furniture offered for sale from Gnarwin was a 'Very handsome imported Sheraton bedroom suite of Inlaid rosewood (cost over 200 Guineas)'.[13] Perhaps this was part of the £2000 bedroom.

The months following Caroline's death would have been extremely difficult for Irene. She had no income apart from the £6 she received for caretaking at Gnarwin for six weeks, and unlike Martha Burrell she made no other claim for wages. Martha not only claimed £6 for six weeks of caretaking at Lonsdale Street, she also claimed an additional £70 for wages and inherited two houses as well. Irene eventually received £658 0s. 5d. in cash, plus £21 14s. 6d. worth of clothes and lace and £372 16s. worth of jewellery and trinkets, but the cash wasn't in her possession until 23 December 1909, and she had been married for eight months by then, and had a six-week-old son.[14] Irene was obviously resourceful, and an early photograph shows a confident young woman dressed in an expensive and elegant mode. It reflects her upbringing, which in turn displays what Caroline made of her life and experience.

In 1896 when Caroline Pohl had applied to have the words 'late Caroline Hodgson' added to her passport, it was apparently because she wanted

Caroline Hodgson's adopted daughter, Irene, about 1909

written proof of her first marriage.[15] But what was there about her story that would have made her friends and family in Germany doubt her marriage to Stud? The most likely reason can be seen in the 'In Memoriam' notices that she placed every year in the newspapers, including *The Argus* (Melbourne's conservative daily newspaper, and the one most likely to be read by her wealthy clients). Caroline claimed (rightly) that her husband was 'brother-in-law of the baronet Sir Francis Wood, the brother of Sir Evelyn Wood', and earlier she had claimed him (also rightly) as a 'grandson of General John Hodgson, of the King's Own Fourth, and nephew of General Studholme Hodgson, of the 19th Regiment'.

If Caroline had told her sisters at the time of her first visit to Germany in 1894 that she – the illegitimate daughter of a labouring miner, who had left home as a poverty-stricken orphan – had married a man with aristocratic connections, would it have seemed a likely story? Probably not. But she would have been a picture of wealth when she arrived with her seven-year-old adopted daughter in 1894; well-dressed, travelling first class, and flashing gold, diamond and sapphire jewellery. Irene, too, would have been stylishly dressed; even as a two-year-old she was taken to a baby show dressed à la mode, in a 'quaint poke bonnet and Greenaway dress'.[16] So, would Caroline have told her sisters about her brothels? She could have told stories – mentioned names – of the men she mixed with that might have indicated that she moved among Melbourne's elite, and even as a child Irene could have vouched for the significant amount of property she owned. Caroline would have protected the young child from any knowledge about the business in Lonsdale Street, so if on that first trip she had decided to explain her wealth by reference to Stud, Irene might not have known enough to contradict her or accidentally let the truth slip. After Stud's time at Gnarwin and his expensive funeral, Irene would have been able to verify his presence in Caroline's life, and support the story about her 'mother' and 'father', as she called them. It is likely that Caroline explained her wealth to her sisters by referring to her husband's aristocratic background rather than her brothels. And Caroline's sisters could well have caught a hint of something odd about her story and doubted the marriage as a result.

If it was important enough to Caroline Hodgson to try to convince her family and friends in Europe of her husband's elite lineage, we can assume that social status and the material gains she had made were of some significance to her. She was hugely successful through the 1880s in her chosen business, having worked her way up from running a boarding house in a rented property to owning numerous properties of her own and employing a number of workers. She had taken a beating through the attacks from Henry Varley and Colonel Barker, but Caroline's story in the 1890s shows a woman trying to stand up straight, hold her head high and claim a measure of respect from a world that paid homage to aristocracy and domesticity. She would have been fully aware that as a brothel madam her position in Melbourne society could never offer her any more than the fleeting respect offered by wealthy men within the privacy of her own dwelling, and the illusory nature of that respect would have been obvious to her once she was out in the street, yet she was not prepared to hide from public view when it came to her husband's funeral. She withstood the lies and moral barbs and attempted to create a different kind of life – a more respectable version, with a husband and a daughter in a domestic setting – but her efforts were foiled by circumstances and personalities. Nevertheless, she went on to raise a well-educated bilingual daughter who was affectionate and cultured in her tastes, even when she swore (she resorted to German on those occasions, suggesting that she learnt it from her aunts rather than Caroline).[17] John Norton's *Truth* was at least willing to concede that she had done well on that score:

> If there be one bright spot in her family it is that her youthful daughter has never been allowed to step within the bounds of the contaminating influence of her mother's environments. She has been kept at a distance, and brought up and educated as any girl of her age should be. We repeat, that, at least, some credit attaches to the dead woman for this.[18]

It is a nice admission – that *Truth* could actually find one redeeming feature for the woman it had branded as 'the wickedest woman in Melbourne' – but family history says that Irene did visit Lonsdale Street when it was operating as a brothel, and that she was fully aware of Caroline's business.[19] According to *The Age*, as we have seen, Irene was actually present when the police raided the house as a result of Walter Davidson's complaint in 1906.[20]

Family memory also says that Irene shared what the nineteenth century would have regarded as another one of Caroline's vices. They both smoked.[21] Irene used cigarette-holders; her granddaughter says they were 'her trademark'.[22] One of the few lost-and-found newspaper advertisements placed by Caroline in the nineteenth century was also for a cigarette holder, to be returned to Studholme Villa.[23] It was not an ordinary cigarette holder, it was meerschaum, which made it expensive, and the reward she offered – £1, the equivalent of a week's wage for a labourer – meant that it was in some way very special for her. It paints a picture of her in her heyday in the 1880s as a sophisticated brothel madam, elegantly wielding a cigarette in a long, carved meerschaum holder. There may be truth in the image, but it's still a caricature, which can be seen when we add the contents of another one of her advertisements to the picture. A year after she advertised for her cigarette holder, she was looking for her dog.[24] Not a well-dressed poodle or a handsome show dog, but a 'Lost, rough Terrier dog', the sort they used for rat-catching. Once again she promised that the finder would be 'handsomely rewarded'. It might have been a pampered pet, or a valuable working dog, but the chances are that it was simply a companion – a treasured companion, perhaps, for a woman sorely in need of the kind of unconditional love that a dog can provide.

30.

END OF AN ERA

MADAME BRUSSELS' BUSINESS THRIVED in the whirl of social and moral ambiguity that prevailed throughout the British colonial world in the late nineteenth century. Alongside a plethora of new material goods and engineering marvels, the industrial revolution produced unprecedented social disruption, with huge waves of migration from Prussia, England and beyond creating entirely new communities in places like Australia. In Melbourne the melange of people of different nationalities – convicts and ex-convicts, pastoralists, goldminers, traders, farmers and all of their families – produced even more social uncertainty, and the extraordinarily random distribution of wealth produced by the gold provided a challenge to the old moral framework too. Melbourne passed through a relatively libertarian era up to the mid-1850s, due at least partly to the overabundance of single men of marriageable age; even when Caroline and Stud Hodgson arrived in 1871, Melbourne's demographic make-up in terms of age, class and ethnicity was unlike most other cities of the world. There was still a disproportionate number of men, and there were no aristocrats demanding obeisance on the basis of their birthright; it was a city of self-made men, and although there was plenty of poverty it was neither as extensive nor as entrenched as that of industrial cities such as London and Liverpool.

The response to this upheaval from the men governing Melbourne was initially to cling ever more tightly to old structures and ways of arranging security in their world, but too much happened too quickly and money (made by any means) soon bypassed the traditional measures of a man's worth to create a different kind of social elite. The thing that didn't change was the British habit of sweeping uncomfortable social issues under the carpet and stepping around the resulting lumps. Prostitution and the need for women to be able to earn a living for themselves and their families – especially widows, deserted wives and single mothers – was one of the wrinkles that society kept tripping over but refused to look at with a clear eye. Some women were able to take advantage of the opportunities to be found under the carpet and Caroline Hodgson was one of them, but for most women working in the sex industry it was a hand-to-mouth existence, as the network of money lenders and pawnbrokers around Bourke and Lonsdale streets testifies.

All these working women, though, rich and poor, contributed to Melbourne's economy in myriad ways. Caroline's probate papers, like those of other madams of the nineteenth century, reveal her integration in the local community.[1] It was not just the milliners, dressmakers and jewellers who benefited from her business, there were also the milkmen, the bakers, fruiterers and poulterers as well as the man providing wood and coal for her houses in both Melbourne and St Kilda. With such deep roots in her community it is easy to see why she refused to be cowed when people like Varley tried to straighten the pile. It is also easy to see why the manufacturers, property owners and legislators (who were often the same men) were more inclined to blame the victims of their decisions than to change the system. Hence the flash brothels of Flinders Street in the early 1870s were swept aside, and popped up again in Stephen Street; when they were mopped up in time for the International Exhibition of 1880 they moved around to Lonsdale Street.[2] And so it went on.

By the late 1880s the middle classes were fast adopting the habits of British respectability, putting establishments like those of Madame Brussels on the frontline of social tensions relating to sexuality and women's place in the world. The economic depression of the 1890s then produced a kind of moral fervour in Melbourne society that had not been seen before. The shame of greed, and the fear of exposure among those of Melbourne's elite who had first benefited from the land boom and then crashed, ruining both themselves and their families in financial terms, fed into the maelstrom of anger and outrage and desperation among those who had been burned through no fault of their own. Henry Varley's campaign, for all its ugly hate-filled rhetoric, contributed to the uncertainty by helping to shift the idea of male sexuality as uncontrollable and in need of slaking like thirst to that of self-control being a normal part of mature masculinity. It was a difficult transition for some, and everyone was looking for others to blame. As always, it was the ones who owned the carpet who took it upon themselves to straighten the wrinkles, but rather than raising the old rug and cleaning the floorboards beneath they decided to nail it down harder at the edges, trapping those below.

In 1907, after Caroline's last court case, Victoria's parliamentarians passed new legislation aimed at eradicating prostitution.[3] It became not only illegal for women to do sex work, and for madams to conduct brothels, but also for men to live off women's earnings, and – most importantly – landlords were prohibited from letting houses to sex workers. Predictably, though, without legislation to lift women's wages and provide support for widows, deserted wives and single mothers, and without addressing the root causes of poverty and inequality, instead of eradicating prostitution the legislation made the sex industry more dangerous for women. It did force the business off the main streets, which is what the police had been trying to do for at least a decade, but it largely drove the industry into the realm of bullies, pimps and corruption. Caroline Hodgson chose instead to close her 'boarding houses' altogether. The other women in Lonsdale Street closed their houses too, but some merely moved to less iconic locations.[4] Whether through stubbornness, pride or naivety Caroline refused to give in or play the role of victim; even in her last year, when she was ordered to leave her house, she stayed. Is this why Madame Brussels is the only one of Melbourne's flash madams to be remembered today? Sarah Fraser is occasionally referred to, but only because of her brush with royalty, and there is no hint of a royal coat of arms hanging in Exhibition Street now. Madame Brussels has an inner-city bar and a laneway named after her.

In some ways Madame Brussels' fame is due to her first husband. If he had not returned to her in his final months, but instead died as a retired policeman in Kerang, she would not have had the opportunity to try out a domestic family life in St Kilda or enter the public realm by giving him a fancy funeral. She might still have placed annual memorial notices in the newspapers, but without being able to trumpet his presence at her own address it would probably not have given her the same sense of stature in her attempts to become respectable. She knew that social acceptance was all about perceptions, but her attempts to shape her position through claiming aristocratic connections – and probably the marriage at St Patrick's Cathedral – were transparent, and ultimately risible once her second marriage failed and she opened her brothels again. Melbourne society might have been susceptible to name-dropping and a proximity to titled English families, but any suggestion of involvement in the business of prostitution would have quickly undermined her efforts.[5] After introducing a new poem every year for a decade, Caroline chose to repeat the 1901 'In Memoriam' every year until the February before her death in 1908, when she neglected to publish anything at all. She was ill by then, so perhaps she forgot; but it was also her first year of not running a brothel, so it is possible that the notices had just been advertising after all. Yet there is no doubt that she loved Stud. Why else would she insist in her will that she be buried beside him? Even if she died 'in any part of the Commonwealth of Australia other than Victoria' she wanted to be brought back and placed next to him.[6]

Caroline Hodgson was loved by many who knew her, especially women related to Caroline's housekeeper and friend Martha Burrell. Martha's niece Sarah named her baby 'Carrie' after her, and Maud Burrell, Martha's daughter-in-law, inserted an 'In Memoriam' notice in *The Age* a year after her death, mourning 'our dear friend … Gone, but not forgotten'.[7] Most tellingly, as a mature woman Irene spoke fondly of her mother to her daughters, acknowledging that Caroline owned brothels, but never uttering a bad word about her.[8]

The ironic part of Madame Brussels' story is that it is probably her bitter enemies Henry Varley and John Norton who are responsible for keeping her memory alive, quoted as they were by journalists such as George Meudell, Montague Grover, Cyril Pearl and Keith Dunstan throughout the twentieth century.[9] These writers' love of language – and Norton's incomparable alliteration – meant that Caroline Hodgson, 'this feculent fiend in female form', continued to hold the public's sniggering attention. On the strength of those writings, too, history walks through the St Kilda Cemetery include her on their itinerary, even though there is no grave to visit now. Caroline was buried there – as she wished – next to her first husband, Stud, but, perhaps because no headstones were ever erected, the graves were apparently illegally on-sold to others in 1951, and unrelated people were buried on top of them.[10] Without Varley and Norton's colourful words, ugly as most of them were, Caroline Hodgson would probably be as invisible as Mrs Kemp, who was only found in one police reference (with the wrong given name) and proved very difficult to locate in the records. Should we be grateful, then, that these powerful men paid her so much attention? Is it wise to bang your head against a brick wall because it's so good when you stop? If Varley and Norton's poisonous prose has ensured her memory, it has also ensured the longevity of their misbegotten malevolence towards sex workers; the long-term damage of the attitudes conveyed through their writing is incalculable. Some of the speeches made against Victoria's Sex Work Decriminalisation Bill 2021 in both the Legislative Assembly and the Legislative Council, for example, reveal how prevalent those nineteenth-century attitudes remain. And given that decriminalising sex work requires changes to many other pieces of legislation, these attitudes will continue to be aired in our parliament for some time. Instead of banging our heads we need instead to remove the brick walls that sex workers face and accept that everyone should have the right to make decisions about how they use their own bodies.

In considering the lives of sex workers historically there is always the question of 'why did they do it?', given the heavy social penalties entailed. The answers tend to be about the structure of society and its attitude towards women, interleaved with individual circumstances, mostly relating to money. Women most commonly did – and still do – sex work because they need an income and sex has a commercial value, but as recent research has shown, that is not confined to the struggle for survival. Sex work 'is a way of reaching or maintaining a certain standard of living', and that can mean – as it did for Caroline Hodgson – creating an income surplus.[11] In her case there is also an added curiosity: 'did she ever do sex work herself?' Most of what we have been able to learn about Caroline has come from records relating to her time as a madam – a 'boarding house keeper' as she styled herself – making this the most intimate of questions, and probably the most difficult to answer, but we do have one important clue.

Caroline was in her mid-twenties when she set up her boarding house in North Melbourne. She had been married, and was therefore presumably sexually experienced; a gay husband was no bar to heterosexual pleasure, as Oscar Wilde's marriage and children attest. Her subsequent history suggests that she had a sociable nature and the capacity to love and care for others, but she was an orphan and motherless at the time of puberty. Her relationship with Stud was unusual, even more so if he was gay, but his declaration in his will, leaving her a substantial legacy 'in token of the love which I once bore her', shows that the relationship was built on more than convenience. She reciprocated, with her own will – made in the week before she died – stipulating that she wished to be buried beside him.[12] Her second marriage had been a disaster of a different kind, suggesting that her capacity to create strong loving relationships with men was limited. If her heart desired a traditional marriage, then her decision to try providing 'superior board and residence for gentlemen' at Peel Street rather than taking all comers might have been an attempt to find a mate. In which case perhaps there was someone like Jacob Pohl among her first boarders; someone who took her heart and then left her, but spawned the idea that her sexuality could be utilised for making a living. Perhaps she also learnt about using a bent coin for contraception.

Archaeologists have found coins in numerous American brothel sites and presumed that they had been used as an early form of cervical cap, by affixing the coin to the cervix using something like quinine or Vaseline.[13] They were usually copper coins, especially pennies, because pennies were the right size and copper supposedly diminished the survival rate of sperm. In this context bent coins could be expected to provide better coverage than flat ones, and therefore more reliable contraception. Like a Dutch cap in a later era, such an item would be a valuable part of a woman's personal belongings, and depending on the memories it evoked it might also become a precious memento. Which brings us to Caroline Hodgson's probate papers; along with the diamonds, pearls and sapphires, and the gold fob watches and trinkets, there is this curious entry:

> Silver mounted purse (Bent coin inside) [value] 10 [shillings].[14]

There is no indication of what kind of coin it was, or whether it was copper, and there is no proof, of course, that it was her personal cervical cap. But it was kept carefully, housed in precious silver, and placed in with her most valuable belongings. We can only surmise that it meant something special to her, and what could be more significant than a contraceptive device for a former sex worker?

Caroline Hodgson, though, is not remembered as a sex worker, but as a brothel madam. She was not lauded for offering a handsome reward for the return of her lost dog, or looking after a woman who had been beaten by her husband, or treating the women who worked for her with respect, or taking in an abandoned baby.[15] She was accused instead of being a moral monster. Her story reveals how these contradictions were part and parcel of Melbourne's social and cultural world in the nineteenth century, and how the ordinary ebb and flow of money and the law, sex and women's rights, played out in relation to sex work in Victoria. We hope that by telling this much of Caroline's story the balance of respectful history might be tipped a little more her way. Let her legacy be less tabloid ridicule for sex workers and more appreciation for the nuances of people's lives.

We learned things which made us think better of our fellow-man and -woman, though he might be criminal and she prostitute. We learned of great deeds – noble deeds judged by any standard – done by those who were beyond the gates of Respectability. More than that, we learned that Lonsdale-street was a cosmos in itself, obeying the conventions of vice, but otherwise very much like any other community, self-sacrificing, self-ish, venal, altruistic, snobbish, democratic, brave, cowardly.

—Montague Grover, 'Big Lon, and Little Lon: Sinister Streets of Other Days', *The Bulletin*, 7 June 1933, p. 36

APPENDIX 1: SUMMARY OF PROPERTY TRANSACTIONS

Compiled from:

Victoria, Registrar-General's Office, Old Law Memorial Book 299 no. 696

Victoria Certificates of Title:

> [32 Lonsdale] Volume 911 Folio 182193; [34 Lonsdale] Vol 1668 Folio 434; [Beaconsfield Parade] Vol 2240 Folio 911; [75 Carter] Vol 1972 Fol 211; [77 Carter] Vol 1912 Fol 230; [Casselden] Vol 3099 Fol 720; [Park] Vol 2265 Fol 990; [York] Vol 1625 Fol 819

PROV VPRS 460/P0 Applications for Certificates of Title, unit 833 file 9740; PROV VPRS 460/P0 Applications for Certificates of Title, unit 37699

1876	19 September	Paid £50 cash deposit for 169 Lonsdale Street, which became 32 Lonsdale Street when the numbers changed in 1888
1876	20 October	Paid £200 cash deposit for 169 Lonsdale Street
1877	26 February	Mortgaged 169 Lonsdale Street to Samuel Gillott [SG] £600
1881?[1]	10 March	Discharged mortgage of 169 Lonsdale Street to SG
1882	8 February	Bought 171 [30] Lonsdale Street; mortgaged to SG 1896, discharged 27/9/1906
1884	30 October	Bought house in Park Road (subsequently 76 Loch Street then 26 York St) South Melbourne [never mortgaged]
1885	10 March	Bought 167 [34] Lonsdale Street; mortgaged to SG

1886	10 April	Discharged mortgage on 167 [34] Lonsdale Street to SG
1887	27 April	Bought first of adjoining houses at 75–77 Carter Street, Middle Park, no mortgage
1887	19 November	Bought second of adjoining houses at 75–77 Carter Street, Middle Park
1890	3 March	Bought 39 Beaconsfield Parade, St Kilda
1890	31 May	Bought adjoining house at the back of 39 Beaconsfield Parade – 51 Park Street, St Kilda
1890	3 December	Mortgaged 51 Park Street, St Kilda, to the London Chartered Bank of Australasia [discharged 29/12/1890]
1890	12 December	Mortgaged 169 [32] and 167 [34] Lonsdale Street to SG [discharged 27/9/1906]
1890	29 December	Discharged mortgage on 51 Park Street, St Kilda to the London Chartered Bank of Australasia
1891	16 September	Mortgaged both of adjoining houses at 75–77 Carter Street, Middle Park, to Australian Deposit and Mortgage Bank Ltd

[March 1892 Australian Deposit and Mortgage Bank Ltd suspended payment]

1892	24 March	Second mortgage on both adjoining houses at 75–77 Carter Street, Middle Park, to William John Butcher
1895	24 June	Mortgaged 39 Beaconsfield Parade and 51 Park Street, St Kilda, to Saunders Benjamin
1896	3 January	Sold the house in Park Road (subsequently York Street), South Melbourne, to John Thompson, a St Kilda police officer
1896	21 March	Discharged second mortgage on both adjoining houses at 75–77 Carter Street, Middle Park, to William John Butcher and transferred both houses to Martha Lamb Burrell
1896	8 December	Mortgaged 171 Lonsdale Street to Samuel Gillott
1899	3 February	Caveat placed on adjoining houses at 75–77 Carter Street, Middle Park
1903	23 May	Caveat lapsed on adjoining houses at 75–77 Carter Street, Middle Park

1903	23 May	Discharged mortgage on both adjoining houses at 75–77 Carter Street, Middle Park, to Australian Deposit and Mortgage Bank Ltd
1903	23 May	Adjoining houses at 75–77 Carter Street, Middle Park, transferred back to Caroline
1906	14 March	Bought adjoining property to 32–34 Lonsdale Street in Casselden Lane from Anne Cunningham's executors – never mortgaged [been renting it since 1886]
1906	27 September	Discharged mortgage to Samuel Gillott for 171 [30], 169 [32] and 167 [34] Lonsdale Street
1907	27 July	Mortgaged adjoining houses at 75–77 Carter Street, Middle Park, to Leah Abrahams
1908	23 November	Caroline Hodgson estate sold 167, 169, 171 and Casselden Lane to Lugtons
1909	16 August	Executors cleared mortgage on adjoining houses at 75–77 Carter Street, Middle Park
1909	22 February	Executors cleared mortgage on 51 Park Street, St Kilda
1909	23 February	Executors sold frontage of 51 Park Street
1909	??	Executors cleared mortgage on 39 Beaconsfield Parade
1909	1 September	Executors sold 39 Beaconsfield Parade and rear of 51 Park Street

APPENDIX 2: LOHMAR/SCHULZE FAMILY TREE

NB: For clarity the following locations relate to the equivalent modern boundaries rather than how it would have been contemporaneously. Placenames have been anglicised if there is one in common usage.

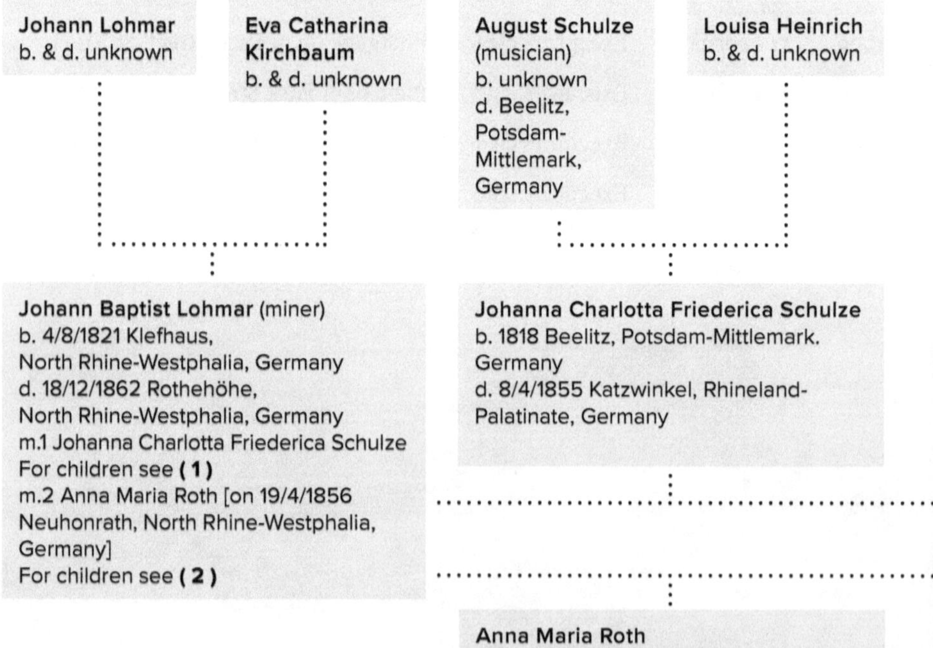

1. Children of Johann Baptist Lohmar & Johanna Charlotta Friederica Schulze [Caroline and her half-siblings or siblings]

Friederike Auguste Amalia Schultze
aka **Maria Lohmar**
b. 27/9/1844 Beelitz,
Potsdam-Mittelmark, Prussia
d. 6/3/1914 Kreutzhauschen,
North Rhine-Westphalia, Germany
m. 15/5/1874 Scheiderhohe, North
Rhine-Westphalia, Germany
Peter Baum
b. 18/7/1843 Lohmar
d. 19/7/1906 Kreuzhauschenh
North Rhine-Westphalia, Germany
For children see **(3)**

Caroline Lohmar
b. c. 1846 Beelitz, Potsdam-Mittelmark,
Prussia
d. 1908 Melbourne, Vic., Australia
m.1 Studholme George Hodgson
b. 20/9/1835 Appleshaw, Hants, UK
d. 7/2/1893 St Kilda, Vic., Australia
[in 1871, London, UK]
m.2 Jacob Pohl
b. 1870, Braschoss, Germany
d. 1946, Melbourne, Vic., Australia
No issue

Hubertina Henrietta Lohmar
b. 1849
d. 2/10/1852

Anna Frederica Lohmar
b. 22/6/1851
d. unknown

Auguste Gertrudt Lohmar
b. 4/8/1854
d. unknown
m. unknown Reifferscheid, Germany

2. Children of Johann Baptist Lohmar & Anna Maria Roth [Caroline's half- or step-siblings]

Margaretha
b. 9/4/1857
d. 3/2/1858

Johannes
b. 12/12/1858
d. unknown

3. Children of Peter Baum and Maria Lohmar

Johann Peter Baum
b. 19/1/1876
d. 9/4/1889

Anna Maria Baum
b. 13/12/1877
d. unknown

Joseph Baum
b. 2/11/1879
d. 10/11/1879

Bertha Baum
b. 27/3/1881
d. 29/8/1894

Friedrich Georg Baum
b. 2/7/1883
d. unknown

Heinrich Baum
b. 27/3/1886
d. 1/4/1886

Wilhelm Baum
b. 16/9/1887
d. 5/5/1889

APPENDIX 3: HODGSON/DUKE FAMILY TREE

All UK except where noted

Studholme Hodgson (field marshal)
b. 1705 or 1708
d. 20//10/1798, London, Middlesex
m. 28/6/1756

Lady Catherine/Katherine Howard
b. 1734?
d. 16/4/1798
m. 28/6/1756

Six children, including:

John Studholme Hodgson (general)
b. 16/3/1759 Westminster, London, Middlesex
d. 10/1/1846, London, Middlesex
m. 26/6/1801 Hanworth, Middlesex

Catharina Maria (Catherine Mary) Krempien
b. unknown
d. unknown
m. 26/6/1801 Hanworth, Middlesex

Six children

Catherine Elizabeth Hodgson
b. c. 1801 Southwell, Berkshire
d. 6/7/1879 Kensington, London, Middlesex
Did not marry

continued overleaf

Studholme John Hodgson (general)
b. c. 1803 Hadleigh, Suffolk,
d. 31/8/1890 Newton Abbey, Torquay, Devonshire
De facto relationship: Princess Laetitia Christine Wyse
nee Bonaparte
b. 1/12/1804 Milano, Lombardia, Italy
d. 15/3/1871 Viterbo, Lazio, Italy
3 illegitimate children
m. 9/8/1853 Paddington, London, Middlesex
Lady Caroline Chichester nee Thistlethwayte
b. c. 1818
d. 1897 Southwick, Hampshire
No children

John Studholme Hodgson (major-general)
b. 28/4/1805 York, Yorkshire
d. 14/1/1870 London, Middlesex
Did not marry

Elizabeth Catherine Hodgson
b. 1806 Ipswich, Suffolk
d. 28/11/1878 Cambridge Square, London, Middlesex
m. 19/3/1831 Marylebone, London, Middlesex
George Sandby
b. 1798 Denton, Norfolk.
d. 23/11/1880 Marylebone, Middlesex
3 children

Louisa Howard Studholme Hodgson
b. c. 1809
d. c. 17/1/1869 Reading, Berkshire
m. 29/11/1827 Lyminge, Kent
John Hambley Humfrey
b. c. 1805
d. c. 14/2/1885 Folkestone, Kent
6 children

Robert Brownrigg Studholme John Hodgson
b. 1810 Bermuda
d. 5/2/1884 Boulogne-Sur-Mer, France
m. 2/4/1833 Appleshaw, Hampshire
Selena Mary Duke
b. 9/5/1798 Quebec, Canada
d. 6/5/1891 Brussels, Belgium
For children see over

Family of Robert Brownrigg Studholme John Hodgson and Selena Maria/Mary Duke

Louisa Mary
b. 19/5/1834 Woodford, Wiltshire
d. 13/6/1910 Westgate-on-Sea, Kent
m.1 20/2/1854 Westminster, London,
Middlesex
Sir Francis Wood, 3rd Bart of Hatherley
Hall
b. 20/2/1834 Cressing, Essex
d. 21/4/1868 Witham, Essex
5 children
m.2 6/5/1874 Mayfair, London,
Middlesex
Lt Col Lewis John Fillis 'Inkerman' Jones
b. c. 1835, Portsmouth, Hampshire
d. 14/6/1906, Westgate-on-sea, Kent
3 children

Studholme George
b. 20/9/1835
d. 7/2/1893 St Kilda, Vic., Australia
m. 1871 Mayfair, London, Middlesex
Caroline Lohmar
b. c. 1846, Beelitz Potsdam, Germany
d. 12/7/1908, Melbourne, Victoria,
Australia
No children

**Selena Katherine Mary
(known as Katherine)**
b. 10/2/1837 Appleshaw, Hampshire
d. 20/3/1898 Ufford, Woodbridge,
Suffolk
m. 7/7/1854, Appleshaw, Hampshire
Henry Theodore James Bagge
b. 28/2/1824
d. 19/11/1861 Munich, Bavaria, Germany
2 children

John Studholme
b. 17/11/1837
d. 28/3/1895 at sea
m. 12/4/1866 Newtown, NSW, Australia
and also
9/5/1869 Sandridge, Vic., Australia
Elizabeth (known as Lizzie) Jane O'Brien
b. c. 1840 Ballincollig, Cork, Ireland
d. 31/10/1920, Paddington, NSW,
Australia
3 children

Georgina Emily
b. 12/2/1840 Constance, Baden-
Württemberg, Germany
d. 31/3/1863 Christchurch, Hampshire
Did not marry

Charles
b. c. 1842 Frankfurt, Germany
d. unknown, but after 1851

AFTERWORD

Philip Bentley

To the best of my recollection the first time I heard of Madame Brussels was during a guest lecture by historian Chris McConville as part of a third-year history course on colonial Melbourne, taught by Marian Quartly, at Monash University in the early 1990s. I may have come across her previously in one of the sensationalist articles that cropped up in the press from time to time, but this was the first occasion I had heard about her in any depth, as Chris had done research on her as part of his PhD thesis on 'outcast Melbourne'.

Part of the assessment for the course required a biographical essay, and seeking a challenge I cast around for someone who may have had reason to cloak their past. Madame B. seemed to fill the bill, although when I suggested it to Marian I was half expecting her to scoff at the notion. Instead she thought it was great idea, rang Chris on the spot for some initial direction, and so sent me on my way that day for a long and involved journey into some of Melbourne's more shadowy corners over thirty plus years.

The essay went over well, so I expanded it into an honours dissertation the next year ('Edifices of Venereal Renown and Gilded Palaces of Sin: A Life on the Margins in Mid-to-Late-Nineteenth-Century Melbourne'), although that turned out to be more of a slog given much of the easily accessible information had been obtained the year before. Especially in those pre-digital times, seeking information from newspapers required long hours fighting motion sickness as one slowly scanned rolls of microfilm.

Following that I revisited the subject several times. First, a revised version of the thesis was included in a multimedia CDROM (*Vanished Communities: Interpreting history at 'Little Lon'*, La Trobe University, 2002) although thanks to some programming glitches it ran anonymously. Then I was asked to prepare the *Australian Dictionary of Biography* entry on her published in the Supplement of 2005 (now online at http://adb.anu.edu.au/biography/ hodgson-caroline-12986). After this, though, I thought my days of chronicling her had passed, even though there were a variety of questions that remained outstanding. Issues such as what her family background had been, what the circumstances surrounding her adoption of her daughter Irene were, and then what of the child's fate, and just why a German woman would adopt a nom de guerre from a city in Belgium best known today for its bureaucrats, were just some of the queries that I thought would probably never be answered. Certainly they weren't in the small biography of her that was released in 2009 (L.M. Robinson, *Madame Brussels: This Moral Pandemonium*, Carlton, Vic., Arcade Publications).

But with the passage of time have come some more powerful tools with which to further investigate the past. In particular the digitisation of information and the internet have been game changers in this regard, allowing key words to be searched across newspapers, public records and genealogical information worldwide.

So in the mid-2010s an idle search for Madame Brussels and those connected to her showed that there was much more information to be gleaned than I had found originally. I was particularly taken with the amount to be found on her first husband, Studholme Hodgson, whose family has been something of the 'gift that keeps giving' in research terms, although regrettably only a portion has been able to be included here. Then in 2019 I happened across a news report detailing the coming to light of pictures of the couple from a Hodgson descendant. Prompted as the result of an article in *The Conversation* by Sarah Hayes and Barbara Minchinton, as detailed by Barbara in the introduction, these photographs and family mementos are now in the State Library Victoria (Caroline Hodgson collection,

MS Box 4985). Sarah (an archaeologist) and Barbara (a historian) had been working on interpretations of the various archaeological digs that had been conducted since the 1980s in the Little Lon precinct. While they had encountered Madame Brussels during this research, the uncovering of the cache of unlabelled photographs brought them a lot closer to her and led Barbara, in particular, to research both Caroline and Studholme as she sought to identify the people in the photos.

A meeting between the three of us ensued that led to Barbara and I deciding that the time was ripe to put our heads together towards producing an as exhaustive biography as we could manage. In this we were driven on by our conviction that Caroline, and many of her sisters of the demimonde, had not been treated well either at the time or during many of the years that had followed. Given the lack of hard evidence regarding her character and actions I had always maintained an open mind as to just how decent a person she may have been, but Barbara's more recent investigations (some of it presented in her book *The Women of Little Lon*, La Trobe University Press, 2021) had tilted the scales considerably.

So we redoubled our research into Caroline's life and times, revisiting all previous research, then seeking to add to it through searches into any other aspect of her life or associates we thought appropriate. Here we used digitised newspapers; public records relating to births, deaths and marriages, property occupation and ownership and public utilities; as well as such work that had been published in relevant areas. The recollections of the two descendants of her and her husband, who had contacted Barbara as a result of the *Conversation* article, were further solicited. We commissioned a researcher in Germany to see what could be obtained there, and spoke to others here and overseas to clarify any outstanding points. Most importantly we began an exhaustive email correspondence that continued over the next four years on all aspects relevant to her life.

Often with biographies one has a fulsome archive of diaries, letters and other writings to use in terms of divining your subject's impetus, personality and inner life, yet here there was little along those lines, just facts from the public record, some jaundiced reporting and a small amount of family ephemera. Hence as well as a 'front on' approach to research through elements directly related to her life, we have often had to take a more oblique stance targeting elements related to those who had some connection to her.

Given the above, the project has benefited greatly from our discussions allowing us to prosecute every morsel of information we had rigorously. Through this approach details previously unclear came into sharper focus, such as her possible trajectory through Europe to London in her teens, the derivation of her sobriquet, the fact that she had multiple locations for her establishment and how she used them, and her decision to close her business for a time in the mid-1890s.

How we would collaborate with the writing was made clearer when a health issue in 2021 meant that I needed to absent myself from the writing for a time and by my return Barbara had already accumulated many thousands of words. So the book you hold in your hands combines the accumulated research of three years, adding to that from earlier, filtered through our exacting email discussions of somewhere around 1000 pages, then distilled through Barbara's keen mind and deft turn of phrase. Given I have been to this well three times over I think the project has benefited from having another voice involved in this way.

While I have been pleasantly surprised – and at times astonished – by just how much information on obscure doings from 150-odd years ago we have been able to claw back, some elements have still remained beyond us. In particular, I don't feel we have unpacked Caroline's personality as much as we would have liked. She appears to have had a more modulated temperament and a better business head than many of 'the women of Little Lon', and was capable of performing appropriate social graces when required, but evidence for claiming more than that is slim. Nevertheless, we have remained resolute in our desire for all conjecture to have a basis in fact and so have resisted the temptation to speculate on how she overcame her early education towards 'moral earnestness, humility, self-sacrifice and obedience to authority' in order to become Melbourne's most famous brothel madam of the nineteenth century. That said, we do feel that we have managed to shine a light into some previously dark places, delineating elements of the workings of Melbourne and its inhabitants not previously known, and presenting a person formerly largely characterised either as a monster or as a figure of fun in much more rounded terms.

Philip Bentley

ACKNOWLEDGEMENTS

AS ALWAYS IN A PROJECT LIKE THIS conducted over a span of years there are many people to thank for their contributions. First and foremost, Caroline Hodgson's family: Rosalie Savage for sharing her grandmother's mementos and stories, and Denis James for the family photographs and documents. Thank you to you both for your unwavering support and generous encouragement of our research and speculations about your family.

While most of the research was conducted in Australia, much of it was done during or between the Covid lockdowns of 2020–21. Many thanks are due to Dr Cornelia Pohlmann for the genealogical research she undertook in Germany during that time.

Luckily many people and organisations were able and willing to answer our questions by email: to the archaeologists Sarah Hayes, Geoff Hewitt and Ramona Angelico, and the musicians Dr Philip Matthias (Director of Music, St Patrick's Cathedral) and Ria Anjelika Polo (organist), thank you.

And then there were the staff of all the libraries and archives who helped us along the way, beginning with the volunteers at the Genealogical Society of Victoria (Linley Hooper, Michael Rumpff, Jenny Redman and Yvonne Izatt). Others included Carly Peters (Southern Metropolitan Cemeteries Trust), Mrs Lesley Edwards (Lancing College Archives), Charlie Farrugia (Public Record Office Victoria), Rachel Naughton (Catholic Archdiocese of Melbourne), Greg Gerrand, Kylie Best and Sarah Matthews (State Library Victoria), Jillian Hiscock (Royal Historical Society of Victoria) and Damian Cole (National Library of Australia).

For help with especially elusive matters, thank you to the staff at the Police Museum (especially Anna Burnett) and Leanne Robinson for their patience in unravelling the mystery of Stud's job at the Melbourne Omnibus Company; to Dr John Waugh and Dr Susanne Davies (on the common law provisions relating to bawdy houses), and Helen Harris (we would never have found those papers at PROV without her).

If it takes a village to raise a child, it takes a city to make a history book. From a Christmas talk to the Public Record Office volunteers in 2018 (thank you, Meg Jenkins) to the AGM of the Friends of St Kilda Cemetery in October 2023 (thank you, Claire Barton, Gabriel Hermes and Geoff Paterson), people have asked questions about Madame Brussels, listened to our stories and suggested answers to our lingering puzzles. It has been a joyful journey as a result, made richer when Alex McDermott finally ended Barbara's hunt for Philip's thesis by introducing us. Thank you, Alex. For the making of this book, thank you to its editor, Kirstie Innes-Will, and a special thank you to Kate Hatch for her magnificent editing of *The Women of Little Lon*, which led directly to *Madame Brussels*. Another special thank you to Liza Dezfouli for all the conversations as well as the sketches, and to Dan Drobik for yet another batch of maps. It was all good fun.

IMAGE CREDITS

The images on the part openers are details of illustrations by Liza Dezfouli. They are reproduced courtesy of the artist.

Eastern portion of the Melbourne Central Business District, showing locations mentioned in the text and sites of general significance (p. viii): Illustration by Dan Drobik. Image reproduced courtesy of the artist.

Madame Brussels' environs: part of the 'Little Lon' district in 1886 (p. x): Illustration by Dan Drobik. Image reproduced courtesy of the artist.

Caroline Lohmar's early life in Europe: map showing location of Beelitz and Potsdam in Germany and major cities she visited (p. 10): Illustration by Dan Drobik. Image reproduced courtesy of the artist.

Caroline Lohmar's childhood homes in Prussia: map showing location of Scheiderhöhe, Katzwinkel, Neuhonrath, Klefhaus, Rothehöhe in Germany (p. 10): Illustration by Dan Drobik. Image reproduced courtesy of the artist.

A photograph of Caroline and Studholme Hodgson taken at the studio of Ghémar Frères in Brussels around the time of their wedding in 1871 (p. 16): Caroline Hodgson Collection, Manuscripts Collection, State Library Victoria. Image reproduced courtesy of the library.

The future King Edward VII and Queen Alexandra by Ghémar Frères, albumen carte-de-visite, 1860s–70s (p. 16): National Portrait Gallery UK. Image reproduced courtesy of National Portrait Gallery UK.

A photograph of Lizzie Jane Hodgson taken at the studio of Ateliers, 217 Bourke St East, Melbourne, [1871–76] (p. 25): Caroline Hodgson Collection, Manuscripts Collection, State Library Victoria. Image reproduced courtesy of the library.

A photograph of Studholme Hodgson taken at the studio of Johnstone, O'Shannessy & Co, Melbourne [early 1870s?] (p. 27): Caroline Hodgson Collection, Manuscripts Collection, State Library Victoria. Image reproduced courtesy of the library.

Caroline Hodgson's boarding house in 'Central-terrace', Peel Street, North Melbourne; number 1 is first on the left (p. 28): Illustration by Liza Dezfouli. Image reproduced courtesy of the artist.

Caroline Hodgson's first brothel, next to 1 Central Terrace, Peel Street, North Melbourne (p. 33): Illustration by Liza Dezfouli. Image reproduced courtesy of the artist.

A photograph of Caroline Hodgson taken at the studio of F Hasler, 96 Elizabeth Street, Melbourne, [1875–80]. The iconography used in this photograph generally means 'in mourning', and it is likely to have been in relation to the death of one of her sister Maria's children in Germany (p. 41): Caroline Hodgson Collection, Manuscripts Collection, State Library Victoria. Image reproduced courtesy of the library.

Mrs Kemp's brothel and residence (1872–95) in Drummond Street, Carlton (p. 52): Illustration by Liza Dezfouli. Image reproduced courtesy of the artist.

Lonsdale Street, looking west from Spring Street and the Star of the East Hotel, Melbourne 1874–75 (D'Orsey set up in 1874), American & Australasian Photographic Company (p. 53): Mitchell Library, State Library New South Wales, ON 4 Box 62, No 500, IE1250285.

The only known photograph showing the location of Madame Brussels' brothels in the 1880s, Paterson Brothers photographers 1875 (p. 54): State Library Victoria. Image reproduced courtesy of the library.

Invitation to a birthday party at Studholme Villa, Lonsdale Street East, 8 August 1885 (p. 56): Caroline Hodgson Collection, Manuscripts Collection, State Library Victoria. Image reproduced courtesy of the library.

Cole's Patent Whipping Machine for Flogging Naughty Boys in School (p. 78): E.W. Cole, *Cole's Funny Picture Book No. 1*, Cole Publications, Melbourne 1991 [Original Edition 1879], p. 41.

Survey of Madame Brussels' rented brothels at numbers 6 and 8 Lonsdale Street, Melbourne, with brick walls outlined with diagonal strokes, wooden walls with strokes square to the walls (p. 89): Public Record Office Victoria VPRS 8600/P1 Survey Field Books, unit 25, book 447, page 46. Image reproduced courtesy of the Public Record Office Victoria.

Survey of the frontage of Caroline Hodgson's properties at 30, 32 and 34 Lonsdale Street, Melbourne (p. 91): Public Record Office Victoria, VPRS 8600/P1 Survey Field Books, unit 25, book 447, page 3. Image reproduced courtesy of the Public Record Office Victoria.

Detail of street-facing portion of Caroline Hodgson's properties from survey of 30, 32 and 34 Lonsdale Street, Melbourne, with brick walls outlined with diagonal strokes, wooden walls with strokes square to the walls and picket fences with two small diagonal strokes (p. 92): Public Record Office Victoria VPRS 8600/P1 Survey

Field Books, unit 25 book 447 page 68. Image reproduced courtesy of the Public Record Office Victoria.

The back section of Caroline Hodgson's private house, Studholme Villa; detail from survey of 34 Lonsdale Street, Melbourne, brick walls outlined with diagonal strokes, wooden walls with strokes square to the walls (p. 93): Public Record Office Victoria VPRS 8600/P1 Survey Field Books, unit 25 book 447 page 68. Image reproduced courtesy of the Public Record Office Victoria.

Detail from survey of 30, 32 and 34 Lonsdale Street, Melbourne, brick walls outlined with diagonal strokes, wooden walls with strokes square to the walls (p. 94): Public Record Office Victoria VPRS 8600/P1 Survey Field Books, unit 25 book 447 page 67. Image reproduced courtesy of the Public Record Office Victoria.

Detail from MMBW plan 1019 [1895] showing the boundary of Caroline Hodgson's establishment in Lonsdale Street after renting the adjoining property on Casselden Lane [misnamed as 'Castletown Place' by the surveyors] in 1887 (p. 96): State Library Victoria. Image reproduced courtesy of the library.

Photograph of Henry Varley, c. 1905 (p. 100): Frontispiece, *Henry Varley's Life-story* by his son, Henry Varley, B.A., London, Alfred Holness, [1913].

Miss Aspasia (to the District Court Bench). – 'Now, Gentlemen, open your eyes and imagine that I am the incarnation of purity and virtue.'
The Bench (in unison; fortissimo). – 'You are, you are, we know you are.' (p. 105): 'Mesmerised', *Melbourne Punch*, 16 May 1889, pp. 8–9.

Alfred Plumpton (p. 116): *The Bulletin*, 8 June 1889, vol. 10 no. 486, p. 3.

A photograph of Caroline Hodgson taken at the studio of Johnstone, O'Shannessy & Co, Melbourne, pre-1876 (p. 120): Caroline Hodgson Collection, Manuscripts Collection, State Library Victoria. Image reproduced courtesy of the library.

'Gnarwin', 39 Beaconsfield Parade, St Kilda, when Caroline Hodgson owned it (p. 128): Illustration by Liza Dezfouli. Image reproduced courtesy of the artist.

A photograph of Charles Studholme Hodgson (1873–1950) (p. 139): Private family collection. Image reproduced courtesy of Denis James.

Front of dance card for event at Caroline Hodgson's private house, Studholme Villa, Lonsdale Street East, 8 August 1885 (p. 140): Caroline Hodgson Collection, Manuscripts Collection, State Library Victoria. Image reproduced courtesy of the library.

Flyleaf of 'Sparks of Light for every day', a gift from Sister Ignatius Murphy (p. 151): Rosalie Savage family collection. Image reproduced courtesy of Rosalie Savage.

Detail of 'cottage' on Casselden Lane – a patchwork of old wooden buildings with gate to main brothel (p. 187): Public Record Office Victoria, VPRS 8600/P1 Unit 25 Survey Field Books, unit 25 book 447 page 69. Image reproduced courtesy of the Public Record Office Victoria.

Detail from land transfer survey showing gate at the rear of 34 Lonsdale Street leading to Gorman Alley and paling fence across the rest of the property (p. 189): Public Record Office Victoria, VPRS 19093/C1 Application Examiner's Notes, Application Number AP037699, 11 November 1908. Image reproduced courtesy of the Public Record Office Victoria.

Sketch of Caroline Hodgson (p. 195): *Truth* (Melbourne), 13 April 1906, p. 5.

Sketch of Martha Burrell (p. 196): *Truth* (Melbourne), 13 April 1906, p. 5.

A photograph of Caroline Hodgson taken at the studio of J. Botterill, Bee-Hive Chambers, Elizabeth Street, Melbourne, [1875–79] (p. 224): Caroline Hodgson Collection, Manuscripts Collection, State Library Victoria. Image reproduced courtesy of the library.

A photograph of Irene Bolger [Irene Hodgson, nee Lily Grelcke] about 1909 (p. 228): Private family collection. Image reproduced courtesy of Rosalie Savage.

NOTES

The following abbreviations have been used in the endotes:

PROV   Public Record Office Victoria
VA   Victorian Agency
VPRS   Victorian Public Record Series

The first mention of a record series gives the full citation (with VA and VPRS descriptors for PROV), but brief citations are provided thereafter.

CHAPTER 1: TELLING CAROLINE HODGSON'S STORY

1   The original Madame Brussels bar closed in July 2021: Dani Valent, 'Iconic Melbourne Rooftop Bar Madame Brussels to Close After 15 years', *The Sydney Morning Herald*, 5 July 2021. It reopened in November 2021: 'Madame Brussels Saved From Permanent Closure by the Double Happiness and New Gold Mountain Owners', *Broadsheet* (Melbourne), 19 October 2021. Madame Brussels Lane runs north from Lonsdale Street between Spring and Exhibition Streets on the site of 34 (167) Lonsdale Street (East).

2   See, for example, Emmett Murphy, *Great Bordellos of the World: An Illustrated History*, London: Quartet, 1983.

3   'Sarah Fraser's Exquisite Decorative Objects', Barbara Minchinton, *The Women of Little Lon: Sex Workers in Nineteenth-Century Melbourne*, Carlton: La Trobe University Press, 2021, pp. 111–36.

4   L.M. Robinson, *Madame Brussels: This Moral Pandemonium*, Carlton: Arcade Publications, 2009; Philip Bentley, 'Hodgson, Caroline (1851–1908)', *Australian Dictionary of Biography*, Supplementary Volume, Carlton: Melbourne University Press, 2005.

5   Sarah Hayes and Barbara Minchinton, 'Sex and the Sisterhood: How Prostitution Worked for Women in 19th-Century Melbourne', *The Conversation*, 14 February 2018.

6   Caroline Hodgson collection, State Library Victoria, MS Box 4985.

7   'Wayward Women?', exhibition, Old Treasury Building, Melbourne, 24 June 2019 – 20 June 2021.

8   *The Daily News* (Perth), 24 May 1889, p. 3, quoting the *Daily Telegraph*.

9   *Sex Work Decriminalisation Act* 2022 (Vic).

CHAPTER 2: A WEDDING IN LONDON

1   Many years ago her name was transcribed incorrectly as 'Lohman' in an index of original documents, and as a result many writers, including ourselves, have repeated the mistake; marriage registration: Caroline Lohmar, father John Lohmar, married Studholme George Hodgson on 18 February 1871 at St George Hanover Square, Westminster, London, certificate No. 191, 1871.

2   'London, England, Crisp's Marriage Licence Index, 1713-1892', Ancestry.com, accessed 16 May 2021.

3   Bernd Schumalski, 'Lohmar, Johann Baptist', *Familienbuch der katholischen Kirchengemeinde Scheiderhöhe* (Family Index of the Catholic Parish Scheiderhöhe), n.p., 1866–1900, p. 120.

4   1871 England Census St George Hanover Square, Belgrave, ED 32, household schedule 318, Piece 111, Folio 109 p. 48, living at 73 Charlwood St W: Ellen Chappell, wife age twenty-six, and Susannah Lintott, servant / nurse domestic, age twenty-one.

5   Research done in Germany by Dr Cornelia Pohlmann from 21 December 2019 to 6 January 2021, genealogy.corneliapohlmann.de; Johanna Charlotta Friederica Schulz, birth registration Beelitz, October 1817, No. 36, p. 94.

6   Schumalski, 'Lohmar, Johann Baptist', p. 120; Johanna Charlotta Friederica Schulz, birth registration Beelitz, October 1817 No. 36 p. 94; Maria Lohmar was born 27 September 1844: Bernd Schumalski, 'Baum, Peter', *Familienbuch der katholischen Kirchengemeinde Scheiderhöhe*, 1866–1900, p. 17.

7   Re flyleaf, personal communication, Rosalie Savage, 10 August 2022; Maria was born 27 September 1844, and another baby was born 1849 (no date given), so with Caroline's birthday on 8 August it is most likely she was born either in 1846 or 1847, but 1845 and 1848 are both possible.

8   Caroline Hodgson gave her father's name as 'John Lohmar' on her marriage registrations; Schumalski, 'Baum, Peter', p. 17.

9   On mixed marriages in Prussia in the nineteenth century, see M. Ott, 'Clemens August von Droste-Vischering', *The Catholic Encyclopedia*, New York: Robert Appleton Company, 1909.

10   This and following details from Schumalski, 'Lohmar, Johann Baptist', p. 120.

11   Maria Lohmar married Peter Baum in 1874 and they had seven children between 1876 and 1887; by 1895, only two were still living: Schumalski, 'Baum, Peter', p. 17.

12   See Appendix 3 for details.

13   There are conflicting claims regarding Field Marshall Studholme Hodgson's year of birth. The *Dictionary of National Biography* (London, Oxford University Press, Vol. 9, p. 966) claims he was born in 1708, while Marthan Klein claims on a family tree on Geneanet.org that he was christened 27 November 1705.

14   Studholme Hodgson married Catherine Howard (1734–98) in 1756; she was the daughter of Lieutenant-General Thomas Howard and sister of Field Marshall Sir George Howard; Governor of Fort George and Fort Augustus: Henry Manners Chichester, 'Hodgson, Studholme', *Dictionary of National Biography*, p. 964.

15   'General Studholme John Hodgson', military.wikia.org; George Clinch, 'John Studholme Hodgson', *Dictionary of National Biography, 1885–1900*, Vol. 27.

16   Some records spell her name 'Selina' and others 'Selena'. It is standardised here as it was spelled in George Duke's will: 'Selena'; Will of George Duke, January 1833, PROB 11: Will Registers Piece 1838: Teignmouth, Quire Numbers 601–40 [Ancestry.com]; Bank of England Wills Extracts 1717–1845 [findmypast.com].

CHAPTER 3: A PHOTOGRAPH IN BRUSSELS

1   See, for example, *Félicien Rops*, photograph, 1860s–70s, The Metropolitan Museum of Art, and *George Wilfred Keane*, photograph, 1860s–70s, National Portrait Gallery, UK; also *Victor Hugo*, photograph, 1860–75, National Science and Media Museum, UK.

2   Cartes-de-visite ('visiting cards') bearing a person's image were popular in the nineteenth century, both as calling cards and as mementos for family and friends, but also as souvenirs of important events.

3   'Paterfamilias', meaning the male head of the family, the responsible male figure who leads the household: 'False Photographs', *Aberdeen Journal*, issue 6012, 1 April 1863, p. 6, reprinted from *London Review*.

4   The Lancing College register of students misspells the family name as 'Hodson', including listing the boys' father as 'R.S. Hodson, of Appleshall, Andover', but gives Stud's correct birth date. The register shows John Studholme Hodson attending from July/August 1850 to October 1851, and Studholme George Hodson from October 1850, 'Left March 1851 for St George's School, Leyton': *The Lancing Register*, p. 11, obtained from Mrs Lesley Edwards, Archivist, Lancing College Archives, pers. comm. 14 June 2021. The 1851 census (taken

on 30 March 1851) reports Stud at Leyton, Essex, and his younger brother John Studholme Hodgson at New Shoreham; both were Nathaniel Woodard schools, which formed the basis of today's Lancing College; Studholme G Hodgson, fifteen, Scholar at Home b. Hampshire Appleshaw: 1851 England Census Leyton, Essex, West ham, ED 2a, Household 84, Piece 1769, Folio 87, p. 22, Leyton Street; John S Hodson, 12, Student, St N College, b. Appleshaw nr Andover: 1851 England Census Sussex, New Shoreham, Church St Class HO107, Piece 1647, Folio 280, p.72, GSU roll 193552, Enumeration District 10a.

5 John had reached the rank of second mate by 1861: John Studholme Hodgson, Certificate of Competency as Second Mate, 10 September 1861, issued at Dublin, UK and Ireland, Masters and Mates Certificates, 1850–1927, No. 24226, Master's Certificates. Greenwich, London, UK, National Maritime Museum.

6 'Soudholme' Hodgson First Cabin passenger on the *Europa*, *The Sydney Morning Herald*, 24 May 1855, p. 4; the family friends were the Everetts, see Margaret Eleanor Rodwell (ed.), *The Ollera Papers 1838–1857: The Family Letters of George, John and Edwin Everett*, Armidale: School of Humanities, University of New England, 2017.

7 See photograph of brothers in Sydney, Caroline Hodgson collection, State Library Victoria, MS Box 4985.

8 S.Y.Hodgson [*sic*] on *Flying Cloud* from Sydney, *The Sydney Morning Herald*, 30 May 1868, p. 6.

CHAPTER 4: ARRIVING IN MELBOURNE

1 'The Opera', *The Argus*, 24 June 1871, p. 5.

2 *The Argus*, 24 June 1871, p. 8.

3 *The Argus*, 24 June 1871, p. 1.

4 'Steam Navigation Board' and 'Floods in Gipps Land', *The Argus*, 24 June 1871, p. 6.

5 *The Land Act* 1869, 33 VICTORIAE No. 360.

6 *An Act to Provide for Reimbursing Members of the Legislative Council and of the Legislative Assembly Their Expenses in Relation to Their Attendance in Parliament* 1870, 34 VICTORIAE No. 383.

7 John Studholme Hodgson, Certificate of Competency as Second Mate, 10 September 1861.

8 John S. Hodgson married Elizabeth J. O'Brien twice, (a situation that may have been related to their different religious affiliations), first in Newtown, New South Wales, Registry of Births, Deaths & Marriages NSW, registration No. 1083/1866; locations from PROV, VPRS 586/Po Port Melbourne (Borough of Sandridge) Rate Books 1867–1876; John Studholme Hodgson gave 'Steam

Ship Penola' as his 'usual' address when he married Elizabeth Jane O'Brien for the second time, on 9 May 1869 in Melbourne, Births, Deaths and Marriages Victoria, registration No. 2329/1869; marriage certificate State Library Victoria, Caroline Hodgson Collection, MS Box 4985; Selina Mary Hodgson born 9 May 1869, Births, Deaths and Marriages Victoria, registration No. 11449/1869; Studholme Robert Hodgson born 21 April 1871, Births, Deaths and Marriages Victoria, registration No. 12065/1871.

9   PROV, VA 859 Port Melbourne (Borough of Sandridge), VPRS 586/P0 Rate Books 1869–70, No. 915, https://prov.vic.gov.au/archive/62CD6E41-F3D3-11E9-AE98-17C5A23A60C4?image=37; John Studholme Hodgson, Mariner, lived at Lot 16 Stokes St (one of three houses on 66 x 165 frontage to Stokes Street built since 1868–69 rates); John and family lived there until at least December 1875.

10   Elizabeth Jane Hodgson was born about 1840, death certificate 40, NSW register No. 719, State Library Victoria, Caroline Hodgson Collection, MS Box 4985.

11   Studholme Hodgson Oath Sheet: Victoria Police Archives, Book 38, 1892; Public Record Office Victoria, Inward Overseas Passenger Lists, prov.vic.gov. au/archive/3B401423-F96C-11E9-AE98-4F6784238BE1?image=87, accessed 18 April 2023.

CHAPTER 5: A SINGLE WOMAN'S BUSINESS

1   Robert Haldane, *The People's Force: A History of Victoria Police*, 3rd edn, Carlton: Melbourne University Press, 2017, p. 69; *The Advocate*, 13 September 1873, p. 11.

2   Victoria Police, Record of Conduct and Service, Studholm [*sic*] Hodgson, register No 2498, Book 38, 1892; his actual date of birth was 22 September 1835: *Salisbury & Winchester Journal*, 28 September 1835 p. 4; details of Studholme Hodgson's time as a policeman are drawn from this source unless otherwise referenced.

3   See, for example, *The Age*, 22 October 1874, p. 3; 'Rape', *Kerang Times and Swan Hill Gazette*, 31 October 1879, p. 3; 'Extraordinary Poisoning Case', *The Portland Guardian*, 13 March 1883, p. 2.

4   Charles Studholme Hodgson, born 16 March 1873 at Sandridge, Births, Deaths and Marriages Victoria, registration No. 12589/1873.

5   *The Record and Emerald Hill and Sandridge Advertiser*, 21 August 1873, p. 3.

6   PROV, VA 511 Melbourne (Town 1842–47; City 1847-ct), VPRS 5707/P0 Rate Books (Hotham/North Melbourne) 1873–1874, No. 356, 'Sturdod Hudson, Trooper', https://prov.vic.gov.au/archive/6D3988DA-F4D1-11E9-AE98-D986C93AC9D6?image=11#.

7   'Studholme Hodgson' was recorded at 1 Central Terrace, Peel Street Hotham when he was actually in Woods Point: *Sands & McDougall's Melbourne and Suburban Directory for 1874*, Melbourne, Sands and McDougall, 1874, p. 227.

8   Shurlee Swain, 'Sex Ratio', Encyclopedia of Melbourne, emelbourne.net.au/
     biogs/EM01361b.htm, accessed 18 September 2018.

9   'Boarding and Lodging Houses', Encyclopedia of Melbourne, emelbourne.net.
     au/biogs/EM00206b.htm, accessed 16 September 2018, republished from
     Seamus O'Hanlon, *Together Apart: Boarding House, Hostel and Flat Life in
     Pre-War Melbourne*, Melbourne: Australian Scholarly Publishing, 2002.

10   *The Argus*, 27 May 1874, p. 8.

11   *The Argus*, 4 April 1872, p. 8.

12   *The Argus*, 6 March 1874, p. 8.

13   Mary Jane Wickham's husband, John Wickham, died in 1873; for more of her
     story, see PROV, VA 2620 Registrar of Probates, Supreme Court, VPRS 28/P0
     Probate and Administration Files 70/053, John Wickham.

14   *The Argus*, 13 July 1874, p. 1.

15   For example, *The Argus*, 17 April 1874, p. 8; 18 April 1874, p. 12; 24 April 1874,
     p. 8.

16   *The Argus*, 3 October 1874, p. 8.

17   Mary Jane Wickham married Michael Power, Births, Deaths and Marriages
     Victoria, registration No. 4231/1875; *Sands & McDougall's Melbourne and
     Suburban Directory for 1875*, Melbourne: Sands and McDougall, 1875, p. 237
     shows her still at 2 Central Terrace, but there is often a delay involved in
     recording information about occupants.

18   *The Argus*, 28 August 1873, p. 1; 9 June 1874, p. 1; 21 & 26 August 1874, p. 1.

19   *The Argus*, 30 September 1874, p. 1.

20   The 'Mr Hodson' of Peel Street, Hotham, urgently requiring William Cook
     to call upon him, was probably Caroline Hodgson. *The Argus* might have
     misheard her 'Mrs' as 'Mr' when she placed her advertisement, but it is more
     likely that she deliberately used 'Mr', knowing that William Cook would
     understand its meaning.

21   'Penola', *The Argus*, 28 May 1869, p. 4.

22   *The Adelaide Observer*, 23 November 1867, p. 5.

23   Sex workers who were renting Melbourne houses in the nineteenth century
     tended to give their occupation as 'Boarding House Keeper'; see listing for no.
     364 on p. 12 of PROV, VPRS 5707/P0000, 1874–1875 (https://prov.vic.gov.au/
     archive/6D3BF9DC-F4D1-11E9-AE98-0B090A60938F?image=12#), 'as at
     December 1874', occupant Caroline Hodson owner McGeorge, brick dwelling,
     six rooms; *Sands & McDougall's Melbourne and Suburban Directory for 1875*,
     Melbourne, Sands and McDougall, 1875, p. 237 lists 'George Hodson' at 27 Peel

Street, probably a mix of 'Caroline Hodson' (as spelt in the Rate Books) and 'McGeorge', the owner.

24   See entries for nos 357 and 358 on p. 16 of PROV, VPRS 5707/P0000, 1873–1874 (https://prov.vic.gov.au/archive/6D3AE86B-F4D1-11E9-AE98-914FD9415 BB3?image=16), no. 364 on p. 12 of PROV, VPRS 5707/P0000, 1874–1875 (https://prov.vic.gov.au/archive/6D3BF9DC-F4D1-11E9-AE98-0B090A6 0938F?image=12#) and no. 364 on p. 12 of PROV, VPRS 5707/P0000, 1875–1876 (https://prov.vic.gov.au/ archive/6D3D596D-F4D1-11E9-AE98-CF71629E134B?image=12#).

25   *The Bendigo Advertiser*, 18 June 1877, p. 3.

CHAPTER 6: THE MOVE TO LONSDALE STREET

1   Courtesans in ancient Greece: 'Thaïs', Wikipedia, en.wikipedia.org/wiki/Thais; 'Lais of Hyccara', Wikipedia, en.wikipedia.org/wiki/Lais_of_Hyccara; 'Phryne', Wikipedia, en.wikipedia.org/wiki/Phryne, all accessed 1 October 2022; John Lee, licensee of the Earl of Zetland Hotel, died in February 1876; his wife Sarah Lee took over the licence, 'Quarterly Licensing Meeting', *The Age*, 6 September 1876, p. 3; ten out of twenty-two licences granted were to women.

2   'Coulisse' is a side scene of a stage; 'omnium gatherum' is a miscellaneous collection (as of things or persons).

3   George Dick Meudell, *The Pleasant Career of a Spendthrift*, London: George Routledge & Sons, Ltd, 1929[?], pp. 273–4; 'proscribed book', 'sold out': 'Lure of the Forbidden', *The Advocate* (Burnie), 31 December 1929, p. 8; 'boycotted book': *Smith's Weekly* (Sydney), 7 December 1929, p. 21; 'Boycotted', *The Age*, 27 November 1929, p. 1; 'These people persuaded Robertson & Mullens to cancel its contract as agent for this book, and the bookselling trade followed suit, and banned the book amongst book buyers. The author has sold the books thrown on his hands, and obtained a further supply from London': *Labor Call*, 6 Feb 1930, p. 7; '2nd edition' April 1936.

4   George Dick Meudell [incorrectly indexed as 'Mendell'] born 29 January 1860, Sandhurst [Bendigo] Births, Deaths and Marriages Victoria, registration No. 4955/1860.

5   William Meudell, 'County Court', *The Bendigo Advertiser*, 26 August 1875, p. 3; Bendigo was called 'Sandhurst' at that time.

6   Julian Thomas, *The Vagabond Papers: Sketches of Melbourne Life, in Light and Shade*, Melbourne: George Robertson, 1877, p. 202.

7   Lizzie Jane's husband, John, was captaining merchant ships in and out of New Zealand; the family moved to Lyttleton near Christchurch in 1877, leaving Caroline without family in Victoria. See *New Zealand Herald*, 22 July 1876, Vol.

XIII, Issue 4583, Captain Hodgson on the *Tower Hill* to Hokianga from Dunedin.

8   Stud G. Hodgson, Statutory Declaration 23 September 1876, PROV, VA 862 Office of the Registrar-General and the Office of Titles, VPRS 460/P0 Applications for Certificates of Title, unit 833 file 9740 re 169 Lonsdale Street East.

9   *Married Women's Property Act* 1870, 34 VICTORIAE no. 384 s.3 and s.12.

10   'Memories of Brussels', *Truth* (Melbourne), 31 March 1906, p. 6.

11   Victoria Certificate of Title Vol. 911 Folio 182193; Victoria, Registrar-General's Office, Old Law Memorial Book 299 No. 696; PROV, VPRS 460/P0, unit 833 file 9740.

12   Minchinton, *The Women of Little Lon*, pp. 111–36 and pp. 161–74.

13   Her education would have had an emphasis on moral earnestness, humility, self-sacrifice and obedience to authority. See Ellwood P. Cubberley, *The History of Education: Educational Practice and Progress Considered as a Phase of the Development and Spread of Western Civilization*, Boston: New York, Chicago,:Houghton Mifflin Company, 1920, p. 572.

14   *The Sydney Morning Herald*, 10 December 1842, p. 3; *The Australian*, 3 May 1845, p. 3; *Bell's Life in Sydney and Sporting Reviewer*, 10 November 1849, p. 2; *Bell's Life in Sydney and Sporting Reviewer*, 10 August 1850, p. 2.

15   See, for example, 'Unpleasant Neighbours', *Weekly Times*, 29 April 1871, p. 11.

16   PROV, VA 511 Melbourne (Town 1842–47; City 1847-ct), VPRS 5708/P0 Rate Books (Gipps Ward) 1878, No. 1972, https://prov.vic.gov.au/archive/762AA811-F4D1-11E9-AE98-B99DB69950EB?image=107, Mrs West owner, Mrs Hudson tenant, 122 Stephen St, Brick house 7 rooms; *The Age* incorrectly reported the house as being in Flinders Street, 10 September 1878, p. 2.

17   See entry no. 948 in PROV, VPRS 5708/P0000, 1878, p. 56, Mrs Hodgson owner and occupier 169 Lonsdale St Brick house 5 rooms.

18   For details of the case, see *The Age*, 10 September 1878, p. 2, *The Australasian*, 14 September 1878, p. 22 and *The Argus*, 10 September 1878, p. 5: both of the latter report 'Caroline Hudson' as the defendant.

19   *The Argus*, 10 September 1878, p. 5.

20   *An Act for the More Easy Recovery of Certain Debts and Demands* 1857, 21 VICTORIAE no. 29 s.35.

21   Ibid.

22   In 1878 Mrs West owned 179 and 181, and Caroline owned 169; the following year Caroline also rented 183/185, and 187/189 Lonsdale Street East. It should be noted that these numbers are taken from the rate books, which are more accurate that those reported in the directories – the two sources often disagree.

23   Catherine West died 22 November 1879, age seventy-two years, at 181 Lonsdale St. East, Births, Deaths and Marriages Victoria, registration No. 11205/1879.

24   Sarah Fraser, boarding house keeper, died 22 March 1880, Births, Deaths and Marriages Victoria, registration No. 2098/1880.

CHAPTER 7: WHAT'S IN A NAME?

1   'House of Ill Fame in Little LaTrobe Street', 11 November 1879, PROV, VA 724 Victoria Police (including Office of the Chief Commissioner of Police), VPRS 937/P0 Inward Registered Correspondence, Melbourne District unit 301, 'one resident gone to Madame Brussels in Lonsdale st'.

2   Cecilia Scarlet was an alias of Elizabeth Cole, PROV, VA 2549 Supreme Court of Victoria, VPRS 516/P0 Central Register of Female Prisoners, https://prov.vic. gov.au/archive/2775E148-F3A9-11E9-AE98-5F8C00C39BB6?image=33; May Blanch worked at Bon Accord house, 'Assault on a Bailiff', *The Herald*, 17 December 1892, p. 6.

3   'Big Jane' was Jane Mill through most of her years in Melbourne, and 'Scotch Maud(e)' was Maud Miller. For a 'scotch maud' see theclothshed.blogspot. com/2012/04/shepherds-plaid.html, accessed 25 July 2021.

4   Jean-Michel Chaumont, 'The White Slave Trade Affair (1880–1881): A Scandal Specific to Brussels?', *Brussels Studies*, 2011, No. 46, p. 3, journals.openedition. org/brussels/838, accessed 6 April 2020.

5   Unless otherwise referenced, this and following details about the sex industry in Brussels in the nineteenth century have been drawn from Sophie de Schaepdrijver, 'Regulated Prostitution in Brussels, 1844–77. A policy and its implementation', *Crime and Criminal Justice History*, no. 37, January 1986, pp. 89–108, jstor.org/stable/20755019, accessed 11 August 2020; and Maja Mechant, 'Selling Sex in a Provincial Town: Prostitution in Bruges' in Magaly Rodriguez Garcia, Lex Heerma van Voss, Elise van Nederveen Meerkerk (eds), *Selling Sex in the City: A Global History of Prostitution, 1600s–2000s*, Leiden and Boston: Brill, 2017, pp. 60–84.

6   William W. Sanger, *The History of Prostitution: Its Extent, Causes, and Effects Throughout the World*, New York: Harper & Brothers, 1858, p. 188.

7   de Schaepdrijver, p. 91.

8   See Maja Mechant, 'The Social Profile of Prostitutes' and Susan P. Conner 'The Paradoxes and Contradictions of Prostitution in Paris' in *Selling Sex in the City*, pp. 833–58 and 171–200.

9   Deborah Gorham, 'The "Maiden Tribute of Modern Babylon" Re-Examined: Child Prostitution and the Idea of Childhood in Late-Victorian England',

Victorian Studies, Vol. 21, No. 3, 1978, p. 358: In Belgium 'a system of debt was used against women who wished to leave, and in some of the brothels the inmates were physically restrained by such measures as the use of doors that could only be opened from the outside.'; see also Mechant, 'Selling Sex in a Provincial Town', p. 77, on 'debt bondage'.

10   Céleste de Chabrillan, *The French Consul's Wife: Memoirs of Céleste De Chabrillan in Gold-Rush Australia*, translated by Patricia Clancy and Jeanne Allen, Melbourne: Miegunyah Press, 1998.

11   Céleste Mogador, 'Translator's Introduction', translated by Monique Fleury Nagem, in *Memoirs of a Courtesan in Nineteenth-Century Paris*, Lincoln: University of Nebraska Press, 2001, p. xv.

12   Regarding Belgium, 'Many of the records have been destroyed including all registers of "public women". What remains is in a "chaotic state" but does include the *tolérance* papers from 1844–77. These provide details of the permit holders (some 250) and by crosschecking with rate books and census returns the identities of some of the sex workers can be ascertained', Sophie de Schaepdrijver, 'Regulated Prostitution in Brussels, 1844–77. A policy and its implementation', *Crime and Criminal Justice History*, No. 37, January 1986, jstor.org/stable/20755019, p. 94.

13   Quote from 'Brussells [*sic*] in Melbourne', *Truth* (Melbourne), 31 October 1903, p. 5.

14   1871 England Census was taken on the night of 2 April 1871; 1871 England census 26 South Molton Street, The National Archives; Kew, London, England, RG10, Piece 93, Folio 8, p. 9, GSU roll 824587, Enumeration District 4.

15   1881 England census 26 South Molton Street, The National Archives, Kew, London, England, RG11, Piece 91, Folio 51, p. 8, GSU roll 1341020.

16   Martha Ann Scott, born Durham, married Arthur N. Coates 1876: 1881 England Census, RG11, Piece 1487; Folio 85, p. 3, Enumeration District 7.

17   Arthur Nance Coates and Martha Ann Scott, living at 51 Church Row, Parish of St Anne Limehouse: London Metropolitan Archives; London, England; London Church of England Parish Registers; Reference Number: P93/ANN/039, 1876.

18   Charles Meredith died 25 June 1868 at 26 South Molton St. Grosvenor Square, England and Wales National Probate Calendar (Index of Wills and Administrations) 1868, p. 151.

19   Andreas Furtwängler married Maria Meredith 5 February 1853, City of Westminster Archives Centre, London, England, Westminster Church of

England Parish Registers, STG/PR/7/41; The National Archives, London, England, HO 2, Piece 180, England Alien Arrivals Certificate Number 3663.

20   Alice Furtwängler, born 16 May 1860, baptised 8 July 1860, Saint Mary Le Strand, Westminster, London, FHL film number 572509.

21   Andreas Furtwängler, The National Archives, Kew, Surrey, England, Duplicate Certificates of Naturalisation, Declarations of British Nationality, and Declarations of Alienage, HO 334, Piece 8; for chain migration, see for example John and Andreas Furtwängler, 1851 England Census, HO107, Piece 1511, Folio 260, Page 16, GSU roll 87845, Enumeration District 4d, and Ferdinand Furtwängler living with his brother Acmilian, his brother-in-law Joseph Rombach, and Martin Winterhalden, a widowed clockmaker, 1881 England Census, RG11, Piece 150, Folio 15, p. 24, Enumeration District 14a.

22   Ferdinand Furtwängler arrived in England in 1844: The National Archives, London, England, HO 2, Piece 180, England Alien Arrivals Certificate Number 2172; he died in Drury Lane in 1849: The National Archives, Kew, Surrey, England, Records of the Prerogative Court of Canterbury, PROB 11, Piece 2101, Vol 16 (1849); John Furtwängler went to US: 1870 United States Federal Census, Township 2 Range 1, Clinton, Illinois, Roll M593_196, p. 224A.

23   Andreas Furtwängler arrived from 'Belge': The National Archives, London, England, HO 2, Piece 180, England Alien Arrivals Certificate Number 3663, and Ferdinand from Belgium: The National Archives, London, England, HO 2, Piece 180, England Alien Arrivals Certificate Number 2172.

24   Ian Gibson, *The Erotomaniac: The Secret Life of Henry Spencer Ashbee*, Cambridge, MA.: De Capo, 2001; also contemporary comments, 'In Belgium the trade is at its zenith; and it would seem as if the production of French immoral books had centered itself in Brussels. Not only however are French books there published, but English ones also, and the Belgians even print at present books in English for London booksellers', and 'the depravity of Brussels, considering its size, is undoubtedly one of the most vicious capitals in Europe', Pisanus Fraxi [Henry Spencer Ashbee], *Index Librorum Prohibitorum: Being notes Bio Biblio Icono graphical and Critical on Curious and Uncommon Books*, London: Privately Printed, 1877, p. xxxii and p. 146.

25   For a tracing of this idea of sophistication offered by a connection to France, see Alexis Bergantz, *French Connection: Australia's Cosmopolitan Ambitions*, Sydney: NewSouth, 2021.

CHAPTER 8: THE SHAPE OF A 'FLASH BROTHEL'

1   Quoted by John Norton from Robert Southey, 'The Devil's Walk': '*He passed a cottage with a double coach-house, // A cottage of gentility; //And he owned with a grin // That his favourite sin // Is pride that apes humility.*'

2   Victorian Parliament, 'Royal Commission on Police: Proceedings of the Commission, Minutes of Evidence', 'Parliamentary Paper' no. 21, 1883, quotes from Patrick Weldon questions 6811 and 6845.

3   Mary Jane Carboni married George Stephen Kemp, Births, Deaths and Marriages Victoria, registration No. 523/1857; Pauline Elizabeth Kemp born 1858, Births, Deaths and Marriages Victoria, registration No. 6723/1858; Esther Annie Kemp born 1860, Births, Deaths and Marriages Victoria, registration No. 2302/1860; her husband repudiated her debts the same year: *The Star* (Ballarat), 7 [8, 9, 10 & 12] November 1860, p. 3.

4   Leah Abrahams, for example, built 'Benvenuta' – now Medley Hall, a college of the University of Melbourne – across the road. She was a pawnbroker who provided Caroline Pohl (Hodgson) with a loan in 1907: see PROV, VPRS 28/P0002, 108/351, p. 8 (https://prov.vic.gov.au/archive/ D451F4BE-F1EB-11E9-AE98-F354BA74AE94?image=8).

5   Victorian Parliament, 'Royal Commission on Police', 1883, quotes from James Dalton, questions 884 and 961.

6   *Mercury and Weekly Courier*, 20 July 1878, p. 3.

7   Geo. Stephen Kemp died in Prahran, Births, Deaths and Marriages Victoria, registration No. 4264/1889; Mary Jane Kemp died 21 October 1895, Births, Deaths and Marriages Victoria, registration No. 12468/1895.

8   The photograph is catalogued by the Mitchell Library as 1870–75, but since D'Orsey only set up business there in 1874, it is more likely 1874 or '75.

9   'Belvew House next to the South Australia hotel' in 'Re Brothels anonymous letter', 28 January 1889, See PROV, VPRS 937/P0006, Box 7 (https://prov.vic. gov.au/archive/RG937-P0006/boxes/7).

10   'To Bricklayers and Carpenters', *The Argus*, 22 January 1852, p. 3; 'To Stonemasons and Bricklayers', *The Argus*, 28 January 1853, p. 8.

11   PROV, VA 511 Melbourne (Town 1842-1847; City 1847-ct), VPRS 9288/P1 Notices of Intention to Build No. 113, 21 February 1860, 'owner' (tenant) Mrs E Wilson, 'to build an addition to a house, at the back'.

12   PROV, VPRS 5708/P0000, 1880, 1880-01-01 - 1880-12-31 Open, Physical, North Melbourne, Online, Image 56 (https://prov.vic.gov.au/ archive/762D4023-F4D1-11E9-AE98-1BCE31DE64ED?image=56).

13   Bought 8 February 1882, PROV, VA 914 Supreme Court of N.S.W. for the District of Port Phillip, VPRS 18873 Memorial Books, 299 p. 696.

14   Peter Lerner was in residence in 1882 and 1883: PROV, VPRS 5708/P0000, 1882, Image 54, entry for no. 958 (https://prov.vic.gov.au/archive/7630C296- F4D1-11E9-AE98-B122539F03B4?image=54) and PROV, VPRS 5708/P0000,

1883, p. 54, entry for no. 950 (https://prov.vic.gov.au/
archive/7631FB17-F4D1-11E9-AE98-3FE87DBE5A69?image=54).

15 York St [originally Park Road] South Melbourne, purchased 30 October 1884,
Crown allotment five section five, 100' X 156' Victoria Certificate of Title
Volume 1625 Folio 324819.

16 Geoffrey Serle, 'Gaunson, David (1846–1909)', *Australian Dictionary of
Biography*, National Centre of Biography, Australian National University, adb.
anu.edu.au/biography/gaunson-david-3599/text5581, accessed 24 April 2022.

17 Bought 10 March 1885, Victoria Certificate of Title Vol. 1668 Folio 333434.

18 Confirmed by Senior Constable Lawrence Gleeson in 1889: 'She also has a
private residence close by called Studholme Villa in which she spends most of
her time', 'Brothels in Lonsdale Street Prosecution of "Madame Brussels"',
10 May 1889, Brief of case 1889, PROV, VPRS 937/P0, unit 327; in 1886
builders turned one room into a kitchen before enlarging the back verandah
and bathroom, Victoria Certificate of Title Vol. 1668 Folio 333434; PROV,
VPRS 9288/P1, (1) No. 2438/1886 and (2) 2462/1886.

19 State Library Victoria, Caroline Hodgson Collection, MS Box 4985, party
invitation.

CHAPTER 9: A DAY IN THE LIFE OF A 'FLASH MADAM'

1 'Immoral Houses in Melbourne', *The Age*, 9 May 1889, p. 5.

2 See, for example, Sarah Hayes and Barbara Minchinton, 'Diversity and
Change in Little Lon: Ongoing Historical and Archaeological Research', in
Tim Murray et al. (eds), *The Commonwealth Block, Melbourne: A Historical
Archaeology*, Studies in Australasian Historical Archaeology series, Sydney:
Sydney University Press, 2019, pp. 106–07.

3 'Prosecution Under the Licensing Statute', 1 June 1882, *The Herald*, p. 3
and *The Argus*, 2 June 1882, p. 3.

4 'Memories of Brussels', *Truth* (Melbourne), 31 March 1906, p. 6.

5 *The Herald*, 9 June 1884, p. 2.

6 'Madam Brussells' Denial', *The Herald*, 11 June 1884, p. 2.

CHAPTER 10: THE LEGAL SETTING

1 Victoria's regulation of prostitution came initially through English law
(received in Victoria from New South Wales via the *Australian Courts Act* of
1828): *An Act for the Punishment of idle and disorderly Persons, and Rogues
and Vagabonds, in that Part of Great Britain called England* [Vagrancy Act]
1824, 5 GEORGE IV c 83 s.3, wherein 'every Common Prostitute wandering in

the public Streets or public Highways, or in any Place of public resort, and behaving in a riotous or indecent Manner … shall be deemed an idle and disorderly Person'. The illegality consisted of the 'riotous and indecent' behaviour. Under English common law a brothel was defined as a public nuisance and brothel-keeping could be prosecuted as a misdemeanour, but that required Supreme Court action and was rarely undertaken in Victoria; three cases appear to have been prosecuted in Ballarat and none elsewhere. The first was in 1855 (against Rosamond Butler: *Geelong Advertiser and Intelligencer*, 26 April 1855, p. 2), the second in 1858 (against Mary Johnson: *The Star* (Ballarat), 11 February 1858, p. 2), and the last against Thomas Lee Kow and his wife Anne Jane Lee Kow ('Chinese Disorderly Houses Conviction of Loo Kow & wife (Police Employ Barrister)', 1866, PROV VPRS 937/P0, unit 16). The Victorian law was *An Act for the better prevention of Vagrancy and other Offences* 1852, 16 VICTORIAE No 22; the women's activities were not illegal, but their earnings were unlawful, the difference being that 'illegal' activities are criminal, but 'unlawful' activities are immoral or contrary to public policy – that is, there is no specific law against them. For a full history of Victoria's vagrancy laws, see Susanne Davies, 'Vagrancy and the Victorians: The Social Construction of the Vagrant in Melbourne, 1880–1907', PhD, University of Melbourne, 1990.

2 *Town and Country Police Act* 1854 18 VICTORIAE No. 14.

3 *The Neglected and Criminal Children's Act* 1864, 27 VICTORIAE No. 216 s.13 (3).

4 *The Criminal Law and Practice Statute* 1864, 27 VICTORIAE No. 233 Part I (6) s.44; s.48 of the same act raised the age of consent for girls to 12.

5 *The Age*, 21 December 1872, p. 7.

6 'How Girls Are Entrapped', *The Age*, 17 December 1872, p. 3; 'Madame de Beaumont's Disorderly House', PROV VPRS 937/P0, unit 293.

7 For a sample of the ridicule faced by people of 'new money', see Marcus Clarke, 'The Wicked World, No. V., Nasturtium Villas', *Weekly Times*, 14 February 1874, p. 9; for an analysis of how this dynamic worked in Victoria, see Sarah Hayes, *Flashy, Fun and Functional: How Things Helped to Invent Melbourne's Gold Rush Mayor*, Studies in Australian Historical Archaeology 6, Sydney: Sydney University Press in association with the Australasian Society of Historical Archaeology, 2018.

8 See, for example, 'Brussells [*sic*] in Melbourne', *Truth* (Melbourne), 31 October 1903, p. 5.

9 See, for example, letter from 'Anxious Mother', *The Argus*, 29 September 1881, p. 9; 'Loose Women in the Streets', *The Argus*, 30 September 1881, p. 7; letter from 'Eradicator', *The Argus*, 3 October 1881, p. 7.

10 For example, Inspector Kabat, 'Unpleasant Neighbours', *Weekly Times*, 29 April 1871, p. 11; 'Dr Rowan re Prostitutes in Collins St', Constable Holland 11 September 1882, PROV VPRS 937/0, unit 307; 'Prostitutes in Lonsdale St', report Inspector Pewtress 20 November 1883, PROV VPRS 937/0, unit 310.

11 'Tasmania Hotel', Inspector Sadlier 19 August 1874, PROV VPRS 937/0, unit 296; 'Prostitutes in Lonsdale St', report Inspector Pewtress 20 November 1883, PROV VPRS 937/0, unit 310.

12 'Prostitutes in Lonsdale Street East', Letter from Chief Commissioner of Police, 30 October 1880, PROV VPRS 937/0, unit 303.

13 The story of Samuel Nathan's case is drawn from the following: *The Herald*, 8 December 1883, p. 4; 'Aspasia and her Abettors', *The Herald*, 12 December 1883, p. 3; 'Aspasia and her Abettors', *The Herald*, 15 December 1883, p. 3; 'The Suppression of Disorderly Houses', *The Argus*, 17 December 1883, p. 4; 'Aspasia and her Abettors', *The Herald*, 19 December 1883, p. 3; 'Aspasia and her Abettors', *The Herald*, 8 February 1884, p. 3; 'Melbourne General Sessions', *The Argus*, 9 February 1884, p. 7; 'The Nathan Case', *The Argus*, 8 March 1884, p. 5; 'Re Nathan', *The Argus*, 10 March 1884, p. 6; 'A Salutary Lesson', *The Ovens and Murray Advertiser*, 15 March 1884, p. 8; 'Minnie Fitzgerald Gone to San Francisco', PROV VPRS 937/0, unit 311.

14 Joseph Panton was one of the magistrates complained of by the police for being lenient towards sex workers in this period, see Report of Constable Kissane, 8 September 1882, 'Dr Rowan re Prostitutes in Collins st', PROV VPRS 937/Po, unit 307.

15 Judge John McFarland and Police Magistrate Arthur Akehurst; lack of Police Magistrate's legal training, David Dunstan, 'Akehurst, Arthur Purssell (1836–1902)', *Australian Dictionary of Biography*, National Centre of Biography, Australian National University, adb.anu.edu.au/biography/akehurst-arthur-purssell-12769/text23033, accessed online 1 September 2021.

16 Victoria, Certificate of Title Vol. 1388 Folio 277447, transfer Samuel Nathan to Caroline Hodgson, 10 March 1885.

17 Victoria, *Parliamentary Debates*, Legislative Council, 15 December 1885, p. 2407; *The Age*, 16 December 1885, p. 5.

18 'Lapsed in the Assembly': *The Argus*, 19 December 1885, p. 13; 'Deputation': *The Argus*, 11 June 1886, p. 4; 'postponed': *The Argus*, 15 June 1886, p. 5.

19 Report of Constable Stokes re. 'Mary Lawrence & Nellie Golding arrested in a brothel in Lonsdale Street east kept by Madam Brussell' 17 March 1889, 'Brothels in Lonsdale Street Prosecution of "Madame Brussells"', 10 May 1889, PROV VPRS 937/Po unit 327.

20 Philip Bentley, '"Edifices of Venereal Renown and Gilded Palaces of Sin": Madame Brussels: A Life on the Margins in Mid-to-Late-Nineteenth-Century Melbourne', BA (Honours) thesis, Monash University, 1993, p. 15.

21 'Prostitutes & Collins St East', 1 April 1887, PROV, VPRS 937/P0006, Box 4 (https://prov.vic.gov.au/archive/RG937-P0006/boxes/4).

22 Barbara Minchinton and Sarah Hayes, 'Brothels and Sex Workers: Variety, Complexity and Change in Nineteenth-Century Little Lon, Melbourne', *Australian Historical Studies*, Vol. 51, No. 2, 2020, pp. 165–83.

CHAPTER 11: A CURIOUS GENTLEMEN'S CLUB

1 Penny Russell, *'A Wish of Distinction': Colonial Gentility and Femininity*, Melbourne: Melbourne University Press, 1994; Penny Russell, *Savage or Civilised? Manners in Colonial Australia*, Sydney: University of New South Wales Press, 2010.

2 Britain introduced contagious diseases acts in 1864, 1866 and 1869 which required sex workers in designated 'garrison towns' to be registered and have regular medical checks for sexually transmitted infections; if they were found to be infected they were confined in lock hospitals until 'cured'; the laws were suspended in 1883 and repealed in 1886; for Victoria's attempt at similar legislation see Minchinton, *The Women of Little Lon*, p. 206.

3 Michel Foucault, *The History of Sexuality: Vol. 1 part II: The Repressive Hypothesis*, London, Allen Lane 1979; Michael Mason, *The Making of Victorian Sexuality*, Oxford: Oxford University Press, 1994.

4 'The Dictionary of Victorian London', victorianlondon.org/districts/holywellstreet.htm, accessed 13 February 2022; Gibson, *The Erotomaniac*, p. xi.

5 Gibson, *The Erotomaniac*, p. xii; Peter Mendes, *Clandestine Erotic Fiction in English, 1800–1930: A Bibliographical Study*, Aldershot, UK: Scolar Press, c.1993, p. 28.

6 *An Act for the General Regulation of the Customs in the Colony of Victoria* 1852, 15 VICTORIAE No. 23, s. 29: 'That if any indecent or obscene Print Painting Book Card Lithographic or other Engraving or any other indecent or obscene article shall be imported into the said Colony the same shall be forfeited and shall and may be seized by any officer of Customs and destroyed as the Collector of Customs shall direct; *An Act to Consolidate and Amend the Laws Relating to the Customs* 1857, 21 VICTORIAE no. 13, s. 34 A Table of Prohibitions Inwards: Goods absolutely prohibited to be imported: … Blasphemous indecent or obscene prints paintings books cards lithographic or other engravings or other blasphemous indecent or obscene articles.'

7 *The Ballarat Star*, 29 October 1875, p. 3.

8   *Geelong Advertiser*, 29 October 1875, p. 2.

9   *The Leader* (Melbourne), 24 December 1875, p. 16.

10 *Geelong Advertiser*, 10 October 1876, p. 3; *The Age*, 11 October 1876, p. 2.

11 *An Act for More Effectually Preventing the Sale of Obscene Books, Pictures, Prints, and Other Articles* 1876, 40 VICT no 544 s. 2: 'liable on conviction for a first offence to a penalty not exceeding Twenty pounds or imprisonment not exceeding six months, and for any second or subsequent offence to a penalty not exceeding Fifty pounds or to imprisonment not exceeding twelve months; *Leader* (Melbourne), 14 October 1876, p. 20; Richard Egan Lee seems to have seen the writing on the wall (and the imminent cost of a hefty fine) and shut down his press, at least for the time being.'

12 *The Fruits of Philosophy*, by the American doctor, Charles Knowlton, was first published in 1832 in Massachusetts; Bradlaugh and Besant deliberately published it in 1877 to test the obscenity laws; they published a revised edition after their conviction was quashed: Caroline Meek and Claudia Nunez-Eddy, 'The Fruits of Philosophy (1832), by Charles Knowlton', *Embryo Project Encyclopedia*, 5 October 2017, embryo.asu.edu/pages/fruits-philosophy-1832-charles-knowlton. Annie Besant was a social reformer and leading theosophist and came to Melbourne several times, for example, *The Age*, 4 September 1894, p. 6.

13 H.K. Rusden, 'Mr Bradlaugh's Conviction for Free Printing on the Population Question', Melbourne: E. Purton & Co., 1877; around the time of the trial in 1877 a series of advertisements was placed in Adelaide newspapers by a person wanting to purchase a copy of *The Fruits of Philosophy*, but none seem to have appeared in Melbourne papers, *The South Australian Advertiser* (Adelaide), 12 July 1877, p. 7; *The Express and Telegraph* (Adelaide); 12 and 14 July 1877 p. 4; 6 September 1877, p. 2; 10 September 1877, p. 3.

14 For example, Lisa Z. Sigel, *Governing Pleasures: Pornography and Social Change in England, 1815–1914*, New Brunswick, New Jersey and London: Rutgers University Press, 2002; Dane Kennedy, *The Highly Civilized Man: Richard Burton and the Victorian World*, Cambridge, M.A.: Harvard University Press, 2005; Deborah Lutz, *Pleasure Bound: Victorian Sex Rebels and the New Eroticism*, New York: W.W. Norton & Co., 2011.

15 Kennedy, *The Highly Civilized Man*, p. 134.

16 It should be noted that the Anthropological Society of London became in time 'the leading forum for scientific racism in Britain': Kennedy, *The Highly Civilized Man*, p. 134.

17 Lutz, *Pleasure Bound*, p. 149; Kennedy, *The Highly Civilized Man*, p. 168.

18 Sigel, *Governing Pleasures*, p. 51.

19   Gibson, *The Erotomaniac*, p. 66.

20   Mendes, *Clandestine Erotic Fiction in English 1800–1930*, p. 12.

21   'Kama Shastra Society of London and Benares': Kennedy, *The Highly Civilized Man*, p. 217; for example, publisher James Henry Gaball: Ian Gibson, *The Erotomaniac*, p. 37.

22   Joseph Delpierre, the Belgium Consul, was one of their number: Gibson, *The Erotomaniac*, pp. xii and 20–30.

23   Sigel, *Governing Pleasures*, p. 50.

24   Ibid., p. 77.

25   The term 'boarding school syndrome' was coined by Professor Joy Schaverian for the psychological effects; for the link with flagellation see Lutz, *Pleasure Bound*, Part II: Men Together, pp. 115–204: 'around 50 percent of all pornography produced from 1840 to 1880 centered [*sic*] on flogging. It also is the richest in terms of variety of genre. There are novels; poems; plays; lectures (such as the 'Experimental Lecture by Colonel Spanker on the exciting and voluptuous pleasures to be derived from crushing and humiliating the spirit of a beautiful and modest young lady …)', p. 124; re: the connection between boarding schools and flagellation see p. 142.

26   'Country News', *The Age*, 22 October 1874, p. 3; 'Rape', *Kerang Times and Swan Hill Gazette*, 31 October 1879, p. 3.

27   Charles Terrot, *Maiden Tribute: A Study of White Slave Traffic of the Nineteenth Century*, London: Muller, 1959, pp. 54, 91.

28   'Extraordinary Revelations of Alleged High-Life', *Reynolds's Newspaper* (London), 31 May 1885, Issue 1816; Claire Cunnington, 'Josephine Butler "a non-repressive Puritan" and Mary Jeffries the "Empress of Vice"', June 2018, researchgate.net/publication/325576123, accessed 4 August 2020.

29   Michael Pearson, *The Age of Consent: Victorian Prostitution and its Enemies*, Newton Abbot: David & Charles, 1972, pp. 105 and 138.

30   In 1885 she was also required to find sureties of £400 'to be of good behaviour for two years', *The Pall Mall Gazette* (London), 6 May 1885, Issue 6285; for conviction in 1887, Pearson, *The Age of Consent*, p. 214.

31   The age of consent for girls was only raised from twelve to thirteen in England in 1861.

32   Pearson, *The Age of Consent*, pp. 150–52.

33   'The Maiden Tribute of Modern Babylon', *The Pall Mall Gazette*, 6, 7, 8 and 10 July 1885, Issues 6336–39.

34   *An Act to Make Further Provision for the Protection of Women and Girls,*

the Suppression of Brothels, and Other Purposes [Criminal Law Amendment Act 1885] UK, 48 & 49 VICTORIAE c.69.

35 Janet McCalman, *Vandemonians: The Repressed History of Colonial Victoria*, Melbourne: Miegunyah Press, 2021, p. 127.

36 Victorian Parliament, 'Report from the Select Committee upon a Bill for the prevention of Contagious Diseases', Parliamentary Paper no. 14, 1878; the purpose of the committee was to collect evidence on the prevalence of sexually transmitted infections in Victoria and recommend whether or not sex workers should be forcibly examined and detained if they were found to be infected; witnesses included the Chief Commissioner of Police, the Chief Medical Officer, an ex-Police Magistrate and numerous other police and doctors but no women.

37 Ibid., David Boswell Reid question 584 and William Thomson question 786, George Brown Hill made the claim in questions 197 and 198. Dr John Singleton (who interviewed hundreds of young women in his Home for Fallen Women) reported nothing about the trafficking of virgins, either to the parliamentary committee or to the readers of his memoirs. The Chief Commissioner of Police explicitly said that he did not believe there was such a system in Melbourne (question 50), and the Superintendent of Police in the Melbourne District said there had been cases of young girls induced into prostitution, but he did not think it was frequent (question 1033).

38 Chaumont, 'The White Slave Trade Affair'.

39 See, for example, 'Brothels Union Place, Girl Daggerstine', PROV VPRS 937/Po, unit 316; 'Vict Coffee Palace used as House of Assignation', PROV VPRS 937/Po, unit 334; for newspapers see 'Keeping a Disorderly House', *The Argus*, 2 February 1864, p. 5; 'Mother and Daughter, Disgusting Allegations', *Independent* (Footscray), 9 August 1902, p. 2.

40 *The Age*, 12 November 1885, p. 4; *The Herald*, 1 December 1885, p. 3; *The Argus*, 8 December 1885, p. 4.

41 The articles were also published in *The Argus*. For example, 'The Land of the Golden Fleece. VII. – Marvellous Melbourne', *The Argus*, 8 August 1885, p. 5; they were gathered together and reprinted in George Augustus Sala, *The Land of the Golden Fleece: George Augustus Sala in Australia and New Zealand in 1885*, Robert Dingely (ed.), Canberra, Mulini Press, 1995.

42 Sala, *The Land of the Golden Fleece*, p. v; Lutz, *Pleasure Bound*, p. 124; Etonensis, *The Mysteries of Verbena House; or, Miss Bellasis Birched for Thieving*, 1881–82, edited by Mark McDougal and republished by Birchgrove Press, Fitzroy North, 2011.

43 Sala, *The Land of the Golden Fleece*, p. 64.

44 Ibid., p. 67.

45   Ibid., pp. 228–31; Sigel, *Governing Pleasures*, p. 55.

46   His wife joined him in Melbourne: Sala, *The Land of the Golden Fleece*, p. xii.

47   'Sarah Fraser's Exquisite Decorative Objects', Minchinton, *The Women of Little Lon*, pp. 111–36.

48   *Western Daily Press* (Yeovil), 8 September 1868, Vol. XXI, Issue 3263, p. 3; Lieutenant General Studholme Hodgson, Visitor, 1871 England Census, The National Archives, Kew, London, England, RG10, Piece 1106, Folio 127, p. 43, GSU roll 827511, Enumeration District 5h.

CHAPTER 12: AN ADOPTION

1   *The Wines Beer and Spirits Sale Statute* 1864, 27 VICTORIAE No. 227 s.8; *The Licensing Act* 1876, 40 VICTORIAE No. 566 s.9.

2   'Perry' is pear cider, from the French 'poiré'.

3   This and following quotes from 'Sunday Trading', *Herald*, 23 March 1886, p. 3.

4   A sovereign was a gold coin worth one pound (twenty shillings), and at that time a girl doing domestic service would have been earning no more than eight shillings a week.

5   *The Age*, 9 August 1887, p. 6.

6   Ibid.

7   'Brussells [*sic*] in Melbourne', *Truth* (Melbourne), 31 October 1903, p. 5.

8   *The Age*, 22 September 1888, p. 7.

9   'Emilie' is sometimes written 'Amelia', as it would have been pronounced by a German speaker, and her family name varies in spelling in Victorian records; arrived Melbourne 12 January 1885 on *Marsala* from Hamburg: A. Grelcke, single man, Foreigner; E Zweikowitz, single female '(bride)' [presumably meaning that Emilie and Adolphe were partners if not actually married], Foreigner, A Zweikowitz, infant male [Amandus] age '1/2', Foreigner, PROV, VA 606 Department of Trade and Customs, VPRS 947/Po Inward Overseas Passenger Lists, https://prov.vic.gov.au/archive/3B7220C8-F96C-11E9-AE98-5962227293B5?image=25.

10   Alice Charlotte Grelcke, born 19 June 1885, Births, Deaths and Marriages Victoria, registration No. 20713/1885.

11   Elise [Alice] Greleke [*sic*], died 16 January 1887, Births, Deaths and Marriages Victoria, registration No. 3818/1887.

12   Lily Grelcke, born 24 October 1887, Births, Deaths and Marriages Victoria, registration No. 26651/1887.

13   'Amandus 3' appears on Lily's birth registration, but no further evidence of

him has been found: it is likely that he – like baby Alice – died young; Emilie's story, and that of her daughter Lily, is currently being written by one of Emilie's descendants: personal communication, Rosalie Savage 24 October 2022.

14   Purchased York St/Park Rd South Melbourne on 30 October 1884, Victoria Certificate of Title, Volume 1625, Folio 324819; purchased 75 Carter St, 27 April 1887, Victoria Certificate of Title, Volume 1972, Folio 394211 and 77 Carter St, 19 November 1887, Victoria Certificate of Title, Volume 1912, Folio 382230.

15   PROV, VA 748 City of South Melbourne, VPRS 8264 Rate Books, Section 43I No. 5790, 'Charlotte Rieman'.

16   Christian Niemann, died at 58 Cromwell Street, Collingwood, in 1885, Births, Deaths and Marriages Victoria, registration No. 11701/1885; John Ernest Christian Niemann age 13, born Victoria 1872, Births, Deaths and Marriages Victoria, registration No. 26741/1872; Eleanor [Ilma] Victoria Margaretta Niemann age 11, born Victoria 1874, Births, Deaths and Marriages Victoria, registration No. 24113/1874.

17   Charlotte Mary Niemann and Martha Lamb Burrell were born to Richard Napoleon Jenkinson and Sarah Ann Faulk Lamb in Tasmania, but there are no birth registrations: Martha born c.1842, Charlotte born 1845; Richard Jenkinson married Sarah Ann Faulk Lamb on 30 September 1844 at Hobart, Libraries Tasmania, Richard Jenkinson RGD37/1/4 no 1399.

18   Martha Lamb Jenkinson married Peter Burrell, Births, Deaths and Marriages Victoria, registration No. 2737/1857; Peter Frederick Burrell born Victoria, Births, Deaths and Marriages Victoria, registration No. 4661/1859 and died age one, 5 May 1860, Births, Deaths and Marriages Victoria, registration No. 6669/1869; Charlotte Mary Jenkinson married Christian Niemann, Births, Deaths and Marriages Victoria, registration No. 4161/1861 and *The Age*, 24 December 1861, p. 7; Christian Niemann born Victoria, Births, Deaths and Marriages Victoria, registration No. 4161/1861, no registered death; *The South Australian Register*, 31 October 1846, p. 3: Passengers on *Herjeebhoy Rustomjee Patel* from Bremen: 'Niemann, wife and five children'.

19   Martha Burrell married George Goodall, NZ 1870/5331; Julia Goodall, born NZ 1873/29707, died NZ 1873/10727; George William Goodall, born NZ 1870/17900, died Victoria 1874, Births, Deaths and Marriages Victoria, registration No. 7497/1874; Henry Lamb Burrell, born 1870, no birth registration, see 'Victorian Humane Society', *The Argus*, 23 July 1881 p. 10.

20   Rosalind House was at 124 Stephen Street: *The Argus*, 12 July 1879, p. 5; *The Argus*, 10 September 1878, p. 5.

21 William and Martha Burrell born Melbourne, Births, Deaths and Marriages Victoria, registration numbers 10141/1880 and 10142/1880; it was common for twins not to survive in that era, but there is usually a death registration.

22 Carrie Niemann, born 25 January 1883 in Richmond, Births, Deaths and Marriages Victoria, registration No. 4868/1883, mother Sarah Annie Niemann; the familiar name 'Carrie Brussels' first appears in the newspapers in 'Insulting Behaviour', *The Age*, 9 August 1887, p. 6, but appears to have been in use for some time.

23 Ruby Niemann born and died at two days, Collingwood, Births, Deaths and Marriages Victoria, registration nos 10348r/1888 and 5299r/1888.

24 Emilie was probably never married to Adolphe Grelcke; she married Wilhelm Gustav Carl Essmann in Toongabbie in 1889, Births, Deaths and Marriages Victoria, registration No. 5240/1889, and returned to Hamburg with him before 1892.

CHAPTER 13: WHAT KIND OF BROTHEL?

1 'Melbourne's Maiden Tribute', *Newcastle Morning Herald and Miners' Advocate* (NSW), 16 April 1889, p. 5.

2 See letter Caroline Hodgson to Charles Hodgson, State Library Victoria, Caroline Hodgson Collection, MS Box 4985.

3 A.E. Dingle, *Vital Connections: Melbourne and its Board of Works 1891–1991*, Melbourne: McPhee Gribble, 1991.

4 PROV, VA 1007 Melbourne and Metropolitan Board of Works, VPRS 8600/P1 Survey Field Books, unit 25 book 447, pp. 3, 4, 67, 68, 69.

5 'Report of the Police Commission', *The Argus*, 16 October 1882, p. 9.

6 *The Argus*, 2 June 1882, p. 3.

7 *The Herald*, 1 June 1882, p. 3.

8 'The Infamous Madame Brussels', *Truth* (Melbourne), 13 April 1907, p. 5.

9 'Brussells [*sic*] in Melbourne', *Truth* (Melbourne), 31 October 1903, p. 5.

10 'Fifty Years a Coroner', *The Argus*, 1 January 1908, p. 4.

11 Curtis Candler, 'Notes about Melbourne, and Diaries, 1848–[19--]', MS Box 4346/5, p. 142, State Library Victoria.

12 Meals were served at Bellevue House in the 1880s: 'Police Intelligence', *Fitzroy City Press*, 21 June 1889, p. 2; Martha Burrell was listed as 'cook' at 32 Lonsdale St on the 1903 Electoral roll: The Commonwealth of Australia, Electoral Roll, State of Victoria, Division of Melbourne, Gipps Polling Place 1903.

13 PROV, VPRS 9288/P1 No. 2438, 27 September 1886; Report of Constable

Stokes re 'Mary Lawrence & Nellie Golding arrested in a brothel in Lonsdale Street East kept by Madam Brussell', 17 March 1889, 'Brothels in Lonsdale Street Prosecution of "Madame Brussells"', 10 May 1889, PROV VPRS 937/P0 unit 327.

14   Cyril Pearl, *Wild Men of Sydney*, London, W.H. Allen, 1958, p. 203.

15   'The Case of Madame Brussels', *Weekly Times*, 11 May 1889, p. 12.

16   The street was known as 'Casselden Street', 'Casselden Lane' and 'Casselden Place' at various times, but has been standardised to 'Casselden Lane'; Caroline Pohl purchased the property 14 March 1906: Victoria Certificate of Title Volume 3099 Folio 619720.

17   David Cunningham died 23 January 1879, leaving his wife Anne Cunningham executrix, PROV, VA 2620 Registrar of Probates, Supreme Court, VPRS 7591/P2 Wills, 19/418.

18   Details are from Raymond Wright, *Who Stole the Mace?*, Melbourne: Victorian Parliamentary Library, 2001, pp. 12–18.

19   The Melbourne City Council rate books show the cottage in Casselden Lane untenanted in 1891 (PROV, VPRS 5708/P0000, 1891, p. 29, entry for no. 896: https://prov.vic.gov.au/archive/763CA980-F4D1-11E9-AE98-D7CC934D216D?image=29 No. 896) and and 1892 (PROV, VPRS 5708/P0000, 1892, p. 25, entry for no. 883: https://prov.vic.gov.au/archive/763E0911-F4D1-11E9-AE98-3164095C2D2C?image=25 No 883), but Annie Wilson is listed in Casselden Lane in the 1891 and 1892 post office directories, *Sands & McDougall's Melbourne and Suburban Directory for 1891*, Melbourne, Sands & McDougall, 1891, p. 46 and for 1892, p. 47; there is no 1893 rate book, the entries for nos 857–59 in PROV, VPRS 5708/P0000, 1894, p. 24 (but https://prov.vic.gov.au/archive/763F1A82-F4D1-11E9-AE98-D5DB4EA3BD81?-image=24 nos. 857–59) show Annie Wilson at Boccaccio House.

CHAPTER 14: THE BUSINESS BROUGHT TO TRIAL

1   Minchinton and Hayes, 'Brothels and Sex Workers', pp. 165–83.

2   In 1890 the Salvation Army headquarters were located in Mrs West's old brothel at 122 Stephen [Exhibition] Street, *Sands & McDougall's Melbourne and Suburban Directory for 1890*, Melbourne, Sands & McDougall, 1890, p. 47; the Little Sisters of the Poor began in two terrace houses on the site of what became St Vincent's Hospital, littlesistersofthe-poor.org.au/Melbourne, accessed 8 October 2022; the Mission to the Streets and Lanes began in Little Lonsdale Street and moved to Spring Street in 1895, findandconnect.gov.au/ref/vic/biogs/E000097b.htm, accessed 8 October 2022.

3   Henry Varley [son], *Henry Varley's Life-Story*, London, Alfred Holness, 1913.

4   Ibid., p. 62.

5   Bridget O'Donnell, *Inspector Minahan Makes a Stand*, London: Picador, 2012, p. 240.

6   Ibid., p. 241; Henry Varley, *The War Between Heaven & Hell in Melbourne: Being a Graphic and Interesting Sketch of the Recent Crusade Against Sin and Social Wickedness in the City, October to December 1890*, Melbourne: Pegg, Chapman and Co., 1891; 'Mr Varley is evidently an uncompromising opponent of the allurements of theatres and such-like places of amusement, particularly skating rinks,' *Geelong Advertiser*, 5 March 1889, p. 3.

7   'Mr Varley, the Revivalist', *Illustrated Australian News*, 3 October 1877, p. 154.

8   *The Argus*, 11 December 1877, p. 4; 'Mr Henry Varley', *The Tasmanian* (Launceston), 23 March 1878, p. 8.

9   'The Late Prosecution of Madame Brussels', *The Daily Telegraph*, 24 May 1889, p. 7; see also *The Daily Telegraph*, 21 May 1889, quoting an offer of £5,000 from someone of the initials 'R A S'.

10 'City Dangers', *The Herald*, 19 March 1889, p. 3; 'Melbourne's Maiden Tribute', *Newcastle Morning Herald and Miners' Advocate* (NSW), 16 April 1889, p. 5.

11 W.T. Stead's term 'maiden tribute' became shorthand for paedophilia and procuring young girls for brothels.

12 *Newcastle Morning Herald and Miners' Advocate* (NSW), 22 April 1889, p. 2.

13 Dr John Madden, barrister, advised the Chief Commissioner of Police that under Victorian common law it was possible for Caroline Hodgson to be indicted as 'the keeper of a bawdy house', an offence carrying the possibility of prison and a fine, but it is not clear why the police did not choose to take this path, 'Brothels in Lonsdale Street Prosecution of "Madame Brussels"', 10 May 1889, John Madden file note [no date], PROV VPRS 937/P0, unit 327; Madden also offered 'to give his professional services at the prosecution, without expense to the Government', 'Brothels in Lonsdale Street Prosecution of "Madame Brussels"', 10 May 1889, H.M. Chomley file note 30 April 1889, PROV VPRS 937/P0, unit 327; 'The Proposed Crusade Against Disorderly Houses', *The Herald*, 9 April 1889, p. 4.

14 'Brothels in Lonsdale Street Prosecution of "Madame Brussells"', 10 May 1889, Crown Solicitor file note 23 April 1889, PROV VPRS 937/P0, unit 327.

15 See, for example, the women forming a deputation to the Chief Secretary, 'Disorderly Houses', *The Herald*, 30 April 1889, p. 2.

16 *The Herald*, 19 March 1889, p. 3; 'The Proposed Crusade Against Disorderly Houses', 9 April 1889, p. 4.

17   Solicitor Mr Maddock [of the firm 'Maddock & Johnson of 70 Queen Street'], and barrister Dr John Madden, 'Brothels in Lonsdale Street Prosecution of "Madame Brussells"', 10 May 1889, H.M. Chomley memos to Superintendent Sadlier 30 March 1889 and 6 April 1889, PROV VPRS 937/P0, unit 327.

18   Newspaper reports about the case include *The Age*, 29 April 1889, p. 4; 'Disorderly Houses', *The Herald*, 30 April 1889, p. 2; 'The Case Against "Madame Brussels", an adjournment agreed to', *The Herald*, 3 May 1889, p. 3; 'The Suppression of Disorderly Houses, Madame Brussels at the District Court, the Charge Dismissed', *The Herald*, 8 May 1889, p. 3; 'Immoral Houses in Melbourne', *The Age*, 9 May 1889, p. 5; 'The Case of Madame Brussels', *Weekly Times*, 11 May 1889, p. 12.

19   Quotes from 'Brothels in Lonsdale Street Prosecution of "Madame Brussells"', 10 May 1889, PROV VPRS 937/P0, unit 327.

20   'Re Madame Brussels', John Madden [no date], 'Brothels in Lonsdale Street Prosecution of "Madame Brussells"', 10 May 1889, PROV VPRS 937/P0, unit 327.

21   'Aspasia and her Abbettors', *The Herald*, 8 February 1884, p. 3.

22   'Re Madame Brussels', John Madden [no date], 'Brothels in Lonsdale Street Prosecution of "Madame Brussells"', 10 May 1889, PROV VPRS 937/P0, unit 327.

23   The police knew that hers was not the only 'flash brothel' in Melbourne, since Senior Constable Lawrence Gleeson had pointed out another in Young Street, Fitzroy, as part of his report relating to the prosecution: 'Brothels in Lonsdale Street Prosecution of "Madame Brussells"', 10 May 1889, Report L. Gleeson 4 April 1889, PROV VPRS 937/P0, unit 327.

24   See Chapter 21, 'Influence or Corruption?'

25   'The Suppression of Disorderly Houses, Madame Brussels at the District Court, the Charge Dismissed', *The Herald*, 8 May 1889, p. 3.

26   As reported in *The Inquirer and Commercial News* (Perth), 24 May 1889, p. 5; 'Mesmerised', *Melbourne Punch*, 16 May 1889, pp. 8–9.

CHAPTER 15: A WIN FOR THE MORALISTS

1   Pauline François married Louis Wien at Balmain, New South Wales, in 1876, Births, Death and Marriages NSW registration No. 1289/1876; the spelling in the records varies between 'Wien' and 'Wein', but the pronunciation 'Vine' suggests that it was 'Wein'. The newspapers generally called her 'Madame Vine'.

2   'Baden Baden Café', *The Age*, 23 February 1888, p. 6.

3   'Notice of Intention to Apply', *The Herald*, 16 April 1888, p. 4; this and following details in 'Madame Vine's Insolvency Estate', *The Herald*, 1 October 1889, p. 3; 'Sly-Grog Selling at Fitzroy', *Weekly Times*, 30 March 1889, p. 6.

4   'Suppression of Disorderly Houses, the Case of Madame Vine', *The Herald*, 1 July 1889, p. 3.

5   For a history of her shonky deals, see 'Madame Vine's Insolvency Estate', *The Herald*, 1 October 1889, p. 3.

6   *Melbourne Punch*, 16 May 1889, p. 1.

7   'Suppression of Disorderly Houses, the Case of Madame Vine', *The Herald*, 1 July 1889, p. 3.

8   *The Herald*, 31 Jul 1890, p. 4; the man who came 'off the bench' was Mr William Ievers, sen.

9   'Suppression of Disorderly Houses', *The Argus*, 9 July 1889, p. 6.

10 'New Insolvents', *The Argus*, 8 August 1889, p. 7.

11 *South Australian Police Gazette*, 21 August 1889, p. 135; 'A Probable Arrest', *The Australian Star* (Sydney), 23 August 1889, p. 6; 'Arrest of Woman Vine', *The Argus*, 28 August 1889, p. 8.

12 *The Argus*, 28 February 1890, p. 4.

13 Mary Jane Kemp died age sixty-six, Births, Deaths and Marriages Victoria, registration No. 12468/1895.

14 'Mr Varley's Crusade', *The Herald*, 27 May 1889, p. 4.

15 *The Age*, 24 May 1889, p. 4.

16 'Mr Varley's Crusade', *The Herald*, 27 May 1889, p. 4; 'Immorality in Melbourne', *The Argus*, 25 June 1889, p. 9.

17 See, for example, 'Society for the Promotion of Morality', *The Argus*, 26 August 1885, p. 7; Victoria, *Parliamentary Debates*, Legislative Council, 2 December 1885, p. 2142.

18 Victoria, *Parliamentary Debates*, Legislative Council, 15 December 1885, p. 2407; Victoria, *Parliamentary Debates*, Legislative Assembly, 17 December 1885, p. 2536; action on the bill 'postponed': *The Argus*, 15 June 1886, p. 5.

19 *Weekly Times*, 29 June 1889, p. 11.

20 *Police Offences Act* 1891, 55 VICTORIAE No. 1241.

21 *Crimes Act* 1891, 55 VICTORIAE No. 1231.

22 Mr Duffy, 'Crimes Act Amendment Bill', Victoria, *Parliamentary Debates*, Legislative Assembly, 16 December 1891, p. 3124.

23 Captain Taylor, 'Crimes Act Amendment Bill', Victoria, *Parliamentary Debates*, Legislative Assembly, 16 December 1891, p. 3126.

24 Michael Cannon, *The Land Boomers*, Melbourne University Press, 1966, p. 213.

CHAPTER 16: A LOVER PERHAPS

1 'The Social Evil', *The Herald*, 14 May 1889, p. 4, reprinted in *Christian Colonist* (South Australia), 24 May 1889, p. 5.

2 Louisa Clarke Wells nee Louisa Christina Elrington, see webarchive.nla.gov. au/awa/20040712085956/http://www.zip.com.au/~viv/louisa.htm, accessed 10 September 2021.

3 This and following quote from *Christian Colonist* (South Australia), 24 May 1889, p. 5, reprinted from *The Herald* (Melbourne), 14 May 1889, p. 4.

4 Britain's contagious diseases acts were repealed in 1886 after Josephine Butler campaigned against them for over 15 years; there is no record of Mrs Clarke Wells directly approaching parliamentarians.

5 'Mrs Clarke Wells Obstructs Footpath', Constable Wardley 19 May 1889, PROV VPRS 937/Po, unit 327.

6 'The Move on Bye-Law', *The Herald,* 27 May 1889, p. 2.

7 A copy of her pamphlet 'Social Purity' can be found attached to Constable Wardley's report, 19 May 1889, 'Mrs Clarke Wells Obstructs Footpath', PROV VPRS 937/Po, unit 327.

8 'The Social Evil', *The Herald*, 14 May 1889, p. 4, reprinted in *Christian Colonist* (South Australia), 24 May 1889, p. 5.

9 *Bendigo Advertiser*, 29 April 1889, p. 2.

10 O'Donnell, *Inspector Minahan Makes a Stand*, p. 242.

11 See, for example, *The Bulletin*, 8 June 1889, p. 12 and 'Brussells [*sic*] in Melbourne', *Truth* (Melbourne), 31 October 1903, p. 5; *Truth* claimed that Plumpton and others were named by Varley, and implied that the names were printed in *The Daily Telegraph,* but no names appear in this period.

12 The name has been cut out of the document: 'Brothels in Lonsdale Street Prosecution of "Madame Brussells [*sic*]"', 10 May 1889, Report of Constable Stokes re. 'Mary Lawrence & Nellie Golding arrested in a brothel in Lonsdale Street east kept by Madam Brussell [*sic*]', 17 March 1889, PROV VPRS 937/Po, unit 327; Constable Munro attended one of Varley's lectures, and his report of 27 May 1889 repeated Varley's assertion that 'one of the magistrates that tried the case was seen in Collins St less than an hour after the case was dismissed

arm in arm with a notorious supporter of Madame Brussells [*sic*] who makes it his business to introduce gentlemen to this degraded woman's houses', but he did not name anyone, 'Varley's Crusade Against Vice', PROV VPRS 937/P0, unit 327.

13   'Our Melbourne Letter', *The Ovens and Murray Advertiser* (Beechworth), 1 June 1889, p. 13; 'Welcome to Mr Charles Santley Breakfast at Menzies Hotel', *The Herald*, 15 May 1889, p. 3.

14   See, for example, 'Varley's Crusade Against Vice', Report of Constable Munro, 27 May 1889, PROV VPRS 927/P0, unit 327.

15   'Brussells [*sic*] in Melbourne', *Truth* (Melbourne), 31 October 1903, p. 5.

16   Caroline Pohl, Will PROV VPRS 7591/P2, 108/351.

17   London Metropolitan Archives, *Admission and Discharge Register for Girls*.

18   *Table Talk*, 9 May 1890, p. 15.

19   London Metropolitan Archives, Register: *Admission and Discharge Register for Girls*.

20   'Australians Abroad', *The Australasian*, 10 May 1902, p. 45.

21   Charlotte Elizabeth Ann Tasker born Durham, Gateshead, July quarter 1841 Vol. 24, p. 134, FreeBMD. *England & Wales, Civil Registration Birth Index, 1837–1915*; marriage London Metropolitan Archives, London, England, London Church of England Parish Registers, P83/PAU1/013 1862.

22   1861 England Census Middlesex, St Pancras, Kentish Town, District 21, 2 Grafton Terrace, RG 9, Piece 123, Folio 64, p. 28, GSU roll 542577, Enumeration District 21 (incorrectly indexed as 'age 48' etc); 1861 England Census Middlesex, St Pancras, Grays Inn Road, District 12, 30 Swinton Street, RG 9, Piece 107, Folio 70, p. 47, GSU roll 542574, Enumeration District 12; 'Professor of Singing' in the nineteenth century census records means 'singing teacher' rather than university professor.

23   *Queenscliff Sentinel Drysdale Portarlington and Sorrento Advertiser*, 19 October 1889, p. 3.

24   'Miss Lizzie Wilson's Concert', *Islington Gazette* (London), 21 May 1864, issue 401, [n.p.].

25   Alfred Ernest Plumpton born 15 June 1871 Registered Marylebone, All Souls, Middlesex, no 436; father is given as Alfred William Edward Plumpton, Professor of Music, mother Eliza Ellerby Plumpton formerly Capner, 2 High St Hornsey.

26   Alfred Ernest Plumpton baptised 17 January 1875 at St Mary's Hulme, Lancaster, No. 2881.

27 'Mr Lindsay Sloper's Matinee', *Morning Post* (London), 4 July 1871, p. 1; *The Standard* (London, England), 19 June 1872, Issue 14941, p. 3; *The Sydney Morning Herald*, 5 December 1871, p. 8.

28 *The Standard* (London), 8 June 1872, Issue 14932; Madame Tasca at the Crystal Palace, *Morning Post* (London), 22 May 1873, Issue 31479, p. 1.

29 *The Argus*, 22 June 1878, p. 7.

30 *The Age*, 5 July 1878, pp. 2 and 8.

31 'Madame Tasca's Farewell Performance', *The Argus*, 12 August 1878, p. 9.

32 *Geelong Advertiser*, 27 September 1878, p. 2; *The Telegraph, St Kilda Prahran and South Yarra Guardian*, 19 July 1879, p. 3.

33 Henry Varley, *The War Between Heaven & Hell in Melbourne*, p. 9.

34 Frederick Standish, Diary, 7-8 November 1857, http://handle.slv.vic.gov.au/10381/264612, accessed 13 September 2021.

35 *The Argus*, 6 August 1878, p. 3; 'Alfred the Great', *The Argus*, 23 December 1878, p. 6.

36 J.S. Legge, 'Standish, Frederick Charles (1824–1883)', *Australian Dictionary of Biography*, National Centre of Biography, Australian National University, https://adb.anu.edu.au/biography/standish-frederick-charles-4632/text7631 published first in hardcopy in 1976, accessed online 15 September 2021.

37 London Metropolitan Archives, *Admission and Discharge Register for Girls*.

38 *The Herald*, 1 June 1882, p. 3; 'Report of the Police', *The Argus*, 16 October 1882, p. 9.

39 'The Melbourne Musical Festival', *The Argus*, 21 December 1882, p. 8.

40 Ibid.

41 Personal communication, Ria Anjelika Polo including video, 7 October 2021.

42 *The Mercury*, 27 September 1878, p. 2.

43 'The Alexandra College Hamilton', *Hamilton Spectator*, 1 April 1882, p. 4.

44 *The Age*, 23 November 1882, p. 4.

45 *Hamilton Spectator*, 23 November 1882, p. 2.

46 *The Australasian*, 2 December 1882, p. 18.

47 *The Herald*, 27 November 1882, p. 3.

48 'Shipping', *The Mercury* (Hobart), 10 January 1883, p. 2; 'Shipping', *The Argus*, 11 January 1883, p. 6.

49 *The Examiner* (Launceston), 23 January 1883, p. 3.

50   Ibid., 24 January 1883, p. 2.

51   Georgiana McCrae, *Georgiana's Journal: edited by High McCrae, Grandson of the Diarist*, Sydney, Angus & Robertson, 1992, p. 54.

52   Positions as wet nurses were more commonly advertised in country newspapers than in Melbourne, but see *The Argus*, 14 December 1882, p. 3; in Melbourne they were usually obtained through agencies or doctors, see *The Argus*, 19 December 1882, p. 12.

53   'Brussells [*sic*] in Melbourne', *Truth* (Melbourne), 31 October 1903, p. 5.

54   *The Bulletin*, 8 June 1889, p. 12.

55   'Brussells [*sic*] in Melbourne', *Truth* (Melbourne), 31 October 1903, p. 5.

56   The two children mentioned were Elizabeth, age eleven, and Augustus, eighteen months: *The Herald*, 9 June 1884, p. 2.

57   Personal communication, Michael Reason, curator at Museum Victoria, 6 April 2022.

58   Aaron Watson, *The Savage Club: a Medley of History, Anecdote, and Reminiscence*, London: T. Fisher Unwin, p. 19.

59   Ibid., p. 26.

60   'Good night and Good morning', words by Lord Houghton, music by Alfred Plumpton, *The Standard* (London), 3 May 1872, Issue 14901.

61   Melbourne's Savage Club was founded in 1894; Thomas Carrington, *The Yorick Club: Its Origin and Development, May 1868 to December 1910*, Melbourne: Atlas Press, 1911, p. 37; Joseph Johnson, *Laughter and the Love of Friends: a Centenary History of the Melbourne Savage Club 1894–1994 and a History of the Yorick Club 1868-1966*, Melbourne: Melbourne Savage Club, 1994, p.48.

CHAPTER 17: RETIREMENT PLANS

1   The 'Greenaway dress' is a reference to the children's illustrator Kate Greenaway whose pictures of children in Regency-style clothing sparked a like fashion in the 1880s and 1890s.

2   *An Act to Amend the Law Relating to Neglected Children* 1887, 51 VICTORIAE No. 941 s21.

3   39 Beaconsfield Parade, Victoria Certificate of Title. Volume 2240, Folio 447911, purchased 3 March 1890.

4   Robert King died 1 October 1883, Births, Deaths and Marriages Victoria, registration No. 12752/1883, and Agnes Girvan [sometimes 'Girvin'] King took over as landlord until her death on 13 December 1891, Births, Deaths and

Marriages Victoria, registration No. 18133/1891, both died at 'Girvinvilla', Beaconsfield Parade, St Kilda.

5   51 Park St, Victoria Certificate of Title, Volume 2265, Folio 452990, purchased 31 May 1890.

6   'The Second Advent', *Christian Colonist*, 1 August 1890, p. 6, reprinted in Varley, *The War Between Heaven and Hell in Melbourne*, p. 9.

7   'Prostitutes in Lonsdale St', 19 November 1883, PROV VPRS 937/P0, unit 310; 'List of brothels in Lonsdale St', 27 January 1898, PROV VPRS 807/P0, unit 305; 'Re conduct of brothels in Lonsdale St', 17 December 1906, PROV VPRS 807/P0, unit 305.

8   Varley, *The War Between Heaven and Hell in Melbourne*, p. 9; quoted without comment in Robinson, *Madame Brussels*, p. 7.

9   McCalman, *Vandemonians: The Repressed History of Colonial Victoria*, p. 127.

10   See Minchinton, *The Women of Little Lon*, pp. 222–25; what follows is paraphrased from that material.

11   *Lilydale Express*, 18 June 1890, p. 4; *Sportsman* (Melbourne), 27 August 1890, p. 2; see also *Horsham Times* 22 April 1890, p. 1, 'An Irishman, testifying in a police court, was asked to explain why he had "shown the white feather" on a certain occasion. "'Tis better to be a coward for five minutes than dead all your life," he replied.'

12   *The Australasian*, 23 March 1889, p. 9.

13   'Wedding at All Saints', *The Herald* (Melbourne), 6 March 1888, p. 4.

14   *The Australasian Sketcher with Pen and Pencil*, 12 July 1888, p. 107.

15   Princess Alexandra of Denmark married Albert Edward the Prince of Wales on 10 March 1863.

16   *The Gippsland Farmers' Journal and Traralgon, Heyfield and Rosedale News*, 5 September 1890, p. 3.

17   'Immoral Houses in Melbourne', *The Age*, 9 May 1889, p. 5.

18   'Brothels in Lonsdale Street: Prosecution of "Madame Brussells"', 10 May 1889, 'Brief of Case for Hearing', L. Gleeson, PROV VPRS 937/P0, unit 327.

19   'John Gibbs Seeks Destruction of Letters he Handed Mr Varley', 16 December 1890, PROV VPRS 937/P0, unit 347; a copy of this letter was reproduced in Minchinton, *The Women of Little Lon*, p. 224.

20   'Gibbs Insane Letter re Nrothels', 19 January 1891, PROV VPRS 937/P0, unit 332; John Gibbs (1856–1934) was a glass-blower who possibly suffered from intellectual disability due to lead-poisoning.

21 Varley may have misappropriated an image from his time in England, when, during the W.T. Stead furore, there was a demonstration of thousands of people who used white flowers and white dresses to represent 'both purity and mourning', but the young girl whose purity was in question had a red feather in her hat that 'symbolized immodesty and peril', O'Donnell, *Inspector Minahan Makes a Stand*, pp. 7–8 and p. 223.

22 See Appendix 1 Summary of Property Transactions.

23 This and following material from 'Madam Brussells' [*sic*] House in Beaconsfield Parade', 1892, PROV VPRS 937/P0, unit 336.

CHAPTER 18: A POLICEMAN'S DEATH

1 Resignation from his extra-police duties ('as inspector of nuisances, etc.'): *The Kerang Times*, 5 February 1892, p. 2.

2 The will spells her name 'Chatworthy', but there is no person of that name in the records; the misspelling appears again in the codicil: will of Studholme George Hodgson, PROV VPRS 7591/P2, 51/683; report of his will in *The Kerang Times*, 11 April 1893, p. 2 quotes 'Agnes Clatworthy'.

3 Obituary of Agnes Clatworthy: *Kerang New Times*, 29 May 1917, p. 2.

4 Will of Studholme George Hodgson, PROV VPRS 7591/P2, 51/683.

5 Robinson, *Madame Brussels*, pp. 82–4; Probate Studholme George Hodgson PROV VPRS 28/P2, 51/683.

6 Victoria Police, Record of Conduct and Service, Studholm [*sic*] Hodgson, Register No. 2498.

7 Cruelty to animals: *The Age*, 22 October 1874, p. 3; 'Rape', *Kerang Times and Swan Hill Gazette*, 31 October 1879, p. 3.

8 Henrietta Clatworthy born 1882 St Arnaud, Births, Deaths and Marriages Victoria, registration No. 5607/1882, died 1884 age 2 St Arnaud, Births, Deaths and Marriages Victoria, registration No. 6259/1884.

9 In Victoria it was referred to as 'the abominable crime of buggery' in the criminal code, for example *The Criminal Law and Practice Statute* 1864, 27 VICTORIAE no 233 ss. 58–60.

10 John Studholme Hodgson, will 3 August 1891: living at '8 Dunluce St, County Rd, Walton, Liverpool', left all his property to his sister 'Louisa Mary Jones the wife of Lieutenant Colonel Lewis John Fillis Jones'; he appointed her his executrix, and died at sea on 28 March 1895. Information obtained from https://probatesearch.service.gov.uk.

11 'Memories of Brussels', *Truth*, 31 March 1906, p. 6.

12 Personal communication, Denis James, great-nephew of Charles Hodgson
1 May 2018; 'Anthony Hordern Sons', Sydney Living Museums,
sydneylivingmuseums.com.au/stories/sydneys-home-furnishing-stores-
1890-1960/anthony-hordern-sons, accessed 4 March 2022.

13 The letter is now held at State Library Victoria, Caroline Hodgson Collection,
MS Box 4985, but it was part of a larger family collection, more of which can
be found in Charles Studholme Hodgson papers, 1885–1945, MLMSS 10256,
Yj703N49, State Library New South Wales.

14 'Brussells [*sic*] in Melbourne', *Truth* (Melbourne), 31 October 1903, p. 5; for a
discussion on the use of 'Greek' in relation to homosexuality in Melbourne in
the 1890s, see Lucy Sussex, *Block Buster! Fergus Hume & the Mystery of a
Hansom Cab*, Melbourne: Text Publishing, pp. 211–25.

15 George Sawkins, 'Saint Sandy the Super', in *Vagrant Papers: A Facetious
Classic*, self-published, Melbourne, n.d. [1880–81].

16 Studholme George Hodgson died 7 February 1893, Births, Deaths and
Marriages Victoria, registration No. 3896/1893; Walter Balls-Headley was also
a Masonic Grand Master from 1905 to 1907, *The Australasian*, 7 January 1905,
p. 27.

17 Personal communication, Rosalie Savage, 3 March 2019 and 26 March 2021.

18 *The Argus*, 8 February 1893, p. 1.

19 *Lancaster Index and Transcription of Records of A.A. Sleight 1893*, Blackburn
Vic., Australian Institute of Genealogical Studies Inc., Vol. 15, pp. 11–12;
Roman Catholic Compartment A, Grave 452.

20 *The Age*, 8 February 1893, p. 8 [and *The Argus*, 8, 9, 10 February 1893, p. 1;
The Australasian, 11 February 1893, p. 46].

21 PROV VPRS 7591/P2, 51/683 Studholme George Hodgson

22 The following details are from PROV, VPRS 28/P0 and 28/P2, 51/683
Studholme George Hodgson.

23 Cannon, *The Land Boomers*, p. 17.

24 Mortgage to William John Butcher 24 March 1892; the mortgage with the
Australian Deposit and Mortgage Bank Ltd was eventually discharged on
23 May 1903, Victoria Certificates of Title Volume 1972 Folio 394211 and
Volume 1912 Folio 382230.

25 The verses are the first and last of seven from 'The Hour of Death', by Felicia
Dorothea Hemans (1793–1835), composed in 1823, good-death.english.cam.
ac.uk/thou-hast-all-seasons-for-thine-own-o-death/, accessed 4 March 2022.

26 *The Argus*, 7 February 1894, p. 1

27 Personal communication, Rosalie Savage, 3 March 2019.

28 *The Sydney Morning Herald*, 2 Mar 1894, p. 4.

29 *The Argus*, 12 Mar 1894, p. 4.

CHAPTER 19: A NEW HUSBAND

1 'Brussells [*sic*] in Melbourne', *Truth* (Melbourne), 31 October 1903, p. 5.

2 'Mrs. Studholme Hodgson child and maid' on RMS *Britannia*, *The Sydney Morning Herald*, 2 March 1894, p. 4.

3 Alfred Plumpton was musical director at the Palace Theatre in Manchester in 1894 and visited Paris late that year: *The Morning Post* (London), 16 July 1894, p. 3; *The Morning Post* (London), 3 September 1894, p. 6.

4 Personal communication, Rosalie Savage, 4 March 2019.

5 Caroline Hodgson, born Potsdam, Germany, father John Lohmar, married Jacob Pohl on 10 April 1895, Births, Deaths and Marriages Victoria, registration No. 2277/1895.

6 Caroline Pohl, 2 October 1906, PROV, VA 2549 Supreme Court of Victoria, VPRS 283/P0 Divorce Case Files, Melbourne 1906 No. 127.

7 Hubert Cooney had been the Sacristan of St Patrick's Cathedral for fifty-six years when he died, *Advocate*, 19 April 1951, p. 7.

8 Senior Constable Canty Report 20 February 1896, National Archives of Australia Item 1801522 Series A712 1896/C889 Caroline Pohl.

9 There was one incident reported as having taken place at 'Madame Brussels' house in Lonsdale-street' in August 1896 which suggests her brothel was still open, but a later report places the attack 'at the corner of Spring and Lonsdale streets': 'Brutal Assault on a Woman', *The Age*, 1 August p. 7 and *The Daily Telegraph*, 7 August 1896, p. 4, followed by *The Age*, 8 August 1896, p. 8.

10 Martha Burrell, occupant, Charlotte Adams owner, 218 Stephen [Exhibition] Street, PROV, VPRS 5708/P0000, 1896, p. 47 (https://prov.vic.gov.au/ archive/76405303-F4D1-11E9-AE98-9B60ED886762?image=47).

11 PROV, VPRS 5708/P0000, 1896, p. 24 (https://prov.vic.gov.au/ archive/76405303-F4D1-11E9-AE98-9B60ED886762?image=24.)

12 The following argument and quotes are derived from Memorial for Letters of Naturalization, National Archives of Australia Item 1801522 Series A712 1896/ C889 Caroline Pohl.

13 Ibid.

14 See Peter Gill, 'Topp, Charles Alfred (1847–1932)', *Australian Dictionary of Biography*, National Centre of Biography, Australian National University,

https://adb.anu.edu.au/biography/topp-charles-alfred-4735/text7861, published first in hardcopy 1976, accessed online 28 April 2022.

15 PROV, VPRS 948/P0001, Jan–Feb 1896, p. 572 (https://prov.vic.gov.au/archive/26A80CCA-F7F0-11E9-AE98-6538A9088815?image=572.)

16 e.g. his advertisement at 'No. 88 Lonsdale st., Near St. Francis' Church', *Advocate*, 26 February 1887, p. 1; *The Daily Telegraph*, 10 May 1889, p. 5.

17 PROV, VPRS 948/P0001, Jan–Feb 1896, p. 542 (https://prov.vic.gov.au/archive/26A80CCA-F7F0-11E9-AE98-6538A9088815?image=572).

18 *The Age*, 8 February 1896, p. 3.

19 For details of land purchases and mortgages, see Appendix 1 Summary of Property Transactions.

20 One of Maria's children died during the year that Caroline and Irene were there (Bertha, age thirteen, died 29 August 1894): Schumalski, 'Baum, Peter', p. 17.

21 Caroline Pohl, 2 October 1906, PROV VPRS 283/P0, 1906 no. 127.

22 Senior Constable P. Canty, report 20 February 1896, National Archives of Australia, Item 1801522, Series A712, 1896/C889 Caroline Pohl.

23 PROV, VPRS 947/P0000, Sep–Dec 1896, p. 245 (https://prov.vic.gov.au/archive/429361A1-F96C-11E9-AE98-C92B31760F95?image=245).

24 *The Advocate*, 6 February 1904, p. 21.

25 'Celebrating 150 years Presentation Sisters in Tasmania', presentationsociety.org.au/2016/10/26/150-years-presentation-sisters-in-tasmania/, accessed 13 October 2022.

26 *The Argus*, 8 February 1897, p. 1.

27 Information regarding Mrs Kemp's finances, for example, can be found in her will and probate papers, PROV, VPRS 7591/P2, 59/685; PROV, VPRS 28/P0, 59/685; PROV, VPRS 28/P2 59/685; for Caroline Hodgson's finances see Appendix 1 Summary of property transactions.

28 The timing of the reopening is uncertain, but probably in 1897 (there are no rate books for that year). According to 'Malodorous Melbourne', *The Tocsin*, 3 February 1898, p. 7, 'Annie Wilson's house, of stolen-mace fame, and Madame Brussell's establishment' had 'lately … disappeared', suggesting that 32–34 was not operating as a brothel at that time, but police records dated 27 January 1898 show 'Madam Brussells' at 32 & 34 Lonsdale St having 'four prostitutes often stand at the gate': PROV VPRS 807/P0, unit 305; when rates were collected in April 1898 Caroline Hodgson was occupying 26: PROV,

VPRS 5708/P0 1898 Melbourne City Council Rate Books (Gipps Ward) no. 808, previously known as 'Boccaccio House'.

CHAPTER 20: ON TRIAL AGAIN

1   Superintendent O'Callaghan of the Bourke District was promoted to Inspecting Superintendent of the metropolitan district in December 1897, *The Age*, 10 December 1897, p. 5; Victorian Parliament, 'Royal Commission on Police', 1883, Thomas Kidney question 5368 to 5371.

2   Unless otherwise indicated the quotes in the following discussion are drawn from the papers relating to the 1898 'crusade against disorderly houses' in PROV VPRS 807/P0, unit 305, 1906 File B225.

3   *The Age*, 7 February 1898, p. 1.

4   Caroline Hodgson was charged with being the keeper of a disorderly house 'at 32 and 34 Lonsdale-street', where the police claimed that 'four girls of immoral character had been residing there within the last few weeks': 'Gay Houses', *The Herald*, 5 August 1898, p. 1 ['Gay' in this period meant libidinous, often in a sexual services sense, rather than anything to do with homosexuality].

5   Presiding magistrate Mayor (Councillor M'Eacharn), Police Magistrate Mr Panton, and Messrs Lancashire, Power and Cherry, Justices of the Peace: 'Alleged Disorderly Houses', *The Argus*, 6 August 1898, p. 14.

6   Presumably this refers to the removal of the brothels from what was then Stephen Street in time for the International Exhibition of 1880 – the women largely moved into Lonsdale Street; this and following quotes from 'Crusade Against Disorderly Houses', *The Age*, 6 August 1898, p. 10 or 'Gay Houses', *The Herald*, 5 August 1898, p. 1.

7   *The Herald*, 3 September 1898, p. 4; *The Tocsin*, 6 October 1898, p. 5.

8   'The Crusade Against Disorderly Houses', *The Age*, 29 September 1898, p. 6.

9   The Mayor (Cr. M'Eacharn), Mr Panton. P.M., and Messrs R. Cherry, R. Power, H. Edwards, S. Lancashire, W. Bell, T. Bent, and Capt. Russell, J.'s P., 'Those Gay Houses', *The Herald*, 11 November 1898, p. 2.

10 'Those Gay Houses', *The Herald*, 11 November 1898, p. 2.

CHAPTER 21: INFLUENCE OR CORRUPTION?

1   *The Criminal Law and Practice Statute* 1864, 27 VICTORIAE No 233 Part I (6) s.48; *Crimes Act* 1891, 55 VICTORIAE No 1231 Part I ss.5–7.

2   'Brothels in Lonsdale Street Prosecution of "Madame Brussells"', 10 May 1889, Senior Constable L. Gleeson Brief of case 4 April 1889, PROV VPRS 937/P0, unit 327.

3   'A Sad Case of Depravity', *The Age*, 8 October 1892, p. 8.

4   'Brothels in Lonsdale Street Prosecution of "Madame Brussells"', 10 May 1889, Statement by Maggie O'Connor 1889, PROV VPRS 937/Po, unit 327; 'Immoral Houses in Melbourne', *The Age*, 9 May 1889, p. 5.

5   It has not been possible to trace many of the women or determine their age because so many used noms de plumes, and few appear in the prison registers (which include aliases).

6   A police report from 23 November 1885 noted that 'not a single authentic instance can be produced of any girl in Melbourne, 14 years of under, leading "a life of shame"': 'Mr Anderson Re. Young Prostitutes', PROV VPRS 937/Po, unit 316 Bundle 1.

7   'The Suppression of Disorderly Houses', *The Herald*, 8 May 1889, p. 3; 'Immoral Houses in Melbourne', *The Age*, 9 May 1889, p. 5.

8   'The Suppression of Disorderly Houses', *The Herald*, 8 May 1889, p. 3.

9   'Brothels in Lonsdale Street Prosecution of "Madame Brussells"', 10 May 1889, Memo John Sadlier to Chief Commissioner of Police, 5 April 1889, PROV VPRS 937/Po, unit 327; 'Immoral Houses in Melbourne', *The Age*, 9 May 1889, p. 5.

10   For example, 'Const Ryan 2122 Found in a Brothel', PROV VPRS 937/P, unit 289 Bundle 1; 'Sr Const Ahern Found Creating a Disturbance in a Brothel', PROV VPRS 937/Po, unit 296; 'Re. Alleged Misconduct of Certain Plain Clothes Patrols Re. Brothel Keepers', PROV, VPRS 937/Po, unit 302 Bundle 1; 'Consts Matear, Spillane, O'Brien & Keily Misconduct', PROV VPRS 937/Po, unit 313; '"Girl McDonald" Statement', PROV, VPRS 937/Po, unit 321; 'Police Said to Frequent Lily Walker's House', PROV, VPRS 937/Po, unit 332; 'Constable Campbell Compelled to Resign for Misconduct', PROV, VPRS 937/Po, unit 333; 'Constable Galvin Consorts with Prostitutes', PROV, VPRS 937/Po, unit 335.

11   For example, 'Prostitutes in Lonsdale St', PROV, VPRS 937/Po, unit 306 Bundle 6; 'Annie Holmes Brothel Keeper – Constables', PROV, VPRS 937/Po, unit 323 Bundle 2.

12   'The Police Commission', *The Bendigo Advertiser*, 28 September 1882, p. 2; 'Report of the Police Commission', *The Argus*, 16 October 1882, p. 9.

13   Victorian Parliament, 'Royal Commission on Police', 1883, Patrick Weldon questions 6803 to 6927 and 7376 to 7493; James Cash question 6977.

14   'Report of the Police Commission', *The Argus*, 16 October 1882, p. 9; Superintendent Winch was not sacked, he was 'called on to retire', 'The Police Commission', *The Argus*, 13 October 1882, p. 10.

15   'The Case of Madame Brussels', 11 May 1889, *Weekly Times*, p. 12.

16 'Immoral Houses in Melbourne', *The Age*, 9 May 1889, p. 5.

17 Quoted by *The Inquirer and Commercial News* (Perth), 24 May 1889, p. 5.

18 'Brussells [*sic*] in Melbourne', *Truth* (Melbourne) 31 October 1903, p. 5.

19 'Insulting Behaviour', *The Age*, 9 August 1887, p. 6.

20 'The Suppression of Disorderly Houses', *The Herald*, 8 May 1889, p. 3.

21 '"Madame Brussels" Again', *The Daily Telegraph*, 23 May 1889, p. 4.

22 'Immoral Houses in Melbourne', *The Age*, 9 May 1889, p. 5; 'The Case of Madame Brussels', *Weekly Times*, 11 May 1889, p. 12.

23 'Immoral Houses in Melbourne', *The Age*, 9 May 1889, p. 5; 'The Raid on Disorderly Houses', *The Argus*, 9 May 1889, p. 9; 'The Case of Madame Brussels', *Weekly Times*, 11 May 1889, p. 12; *The Ballarat Star*, 9 May 1889, p. 2; 'The Suppression of Disorderly Houses', *The Herald*, 8 May 1889, p. 3; *The Daily Telegraph*, 13 July 1889, p. 4.

24 *The Daily Telegraph*, 15 July 1889, p. 4.

25 *The Daily Telegraph*, 15 July 1889, p. 5.

26 *Table Talk*, 6 September 1889, p. 1.

27 *The Argus*, 28 July 1890, p. 1; *The Herald*, 31 July 1890, p. 4.

28 Barry Collett, 'Mason, Francis Conway (1843–1915), *Australian Dictionary of Biography*, National Centre of Biography, Australian National University, adb.anu.edu.au/biography/mason-francis-conway-4164/text6685, published first in hardcopy 1974, accessed online 31 May 2022.

29 'Death of Mr James Garton', *Weekly Times*, 20 October 1900, p. 14.

30 *The Daily Telegraph*, 10 May 1889, p. 5.

31 'The Clifton Hill Mutual Improvement Society', *Mercury and Weekly Courier*, 5 July 1884, p. 3; 'South Melbourne', *Table Talk*, 8 August 1890, p. 17; *The Age*, 11 January 1871, p. 2.

32 'Immoral Houses in Melbourne', *The Age*, 9 May 1889, p. 5; 'The Case of Madame Brussels', *Weekly Times*, 11 May 1889, p. 12.

33 'Despatch in the Courts', *The Herald*, 11 January 1889, p. 3.

34 Police regularly complained about taking women to court only to have the magistrates either dismiss the charges, caution the women or impose minimal fines. For example, Constable Holland's report 11 September 1882, 'Dr Rowan Re. Prostitutes in Collins St', PROV VPRS 937/P0, unit 307.

35 'Death of an Old Colonist', *The Ballarat Star*, 15 Jan 1898, p. 4.

36 Mr Justice Williams (Supreme Court), Captain [Mr. A.] Currie (chairman

of the Marine Board), Professor Kernot (University of Melbourne), 'The Alleged Bench-Packing: A Board Appointed', *The Argus*, 25 November 1895, p. 5.

37   This and following quotes from 'Honorary Magistrates', *The Argus*, 30 March 1896, p. 5.

38   'The Charges Against Magistrates', *The Argus*, 12 February 1896, p. 5; 'The Charges Against Magistrates', *The Argus*, 3 March 1896, p. 6.

39   'Honorary Magistrates', *The Argus*, 30 March 1896, p. 5.

40   'The Charges Against Magistrates', *The Argus*, 13 February 1896, p. 6.

41   'Honorary Magistrates', *The Argus*, 30 March 1896, p. 5; 'Gay Houses in a Main Street', *The Herald*, 5 August 1898, p. 1.

42   'Alleged Disorderly Houses', *The Argus*, 6 August 1898, p. 14; 'The Police Court and Madame Brussels', *The Tocsin*, 17 November 1898, p. 5.

43   'Those Gay Houses', *The Herald*, 11 November 1898, p. 2.

44   'Immoral houses in Melbourne', *The Age*, 9 May 1889, p. 5; 'The Case of Madame Brussels', *Weekly Times*, 11 May 1889, p. 12.

45   Cherry travelled from Hawthorn to sit on the bench at Werribee: 'Honorary Justices', *The Williamstown Chronicle*, 20 July 1895, p. 3; Lancashire was also magistrate on the North Melbourne Bench: *Sands & McDougall's Melbourne and Suburban Directory for 1900*, Melbourne: Sands & McDougall Limited, 1900, p. 1538; *The Herald*, 23 April 1898, p. 1.

46   For example, 'Attempt to Reform a Girl Vagrant', *The Age*, 1 February 1894, p. 3.

47   *The Age*, 5 Nov 1914, p. 11.

48   'The Police Court and Madame Brussels', *The Tocsin*, 17 November 1898, p. 5.

49   Weston Bate, 'Bent, Sir Thomas (1838–1909)', *Australian Dictionary of Biography*, National Centre of Biography, Australian National University, adb.anu.edu.au/biography/bent-sir-thomas-2978/text4343, published first in hardcopy 1969, accessed online 31 May 2022.

50   David Dunstan, 'McEacharn, Sir Malcolm Donald (1852–1910)', *Australian Dictionary of Biography*, National Centre of Biography, Australian National University, adb.anu.edu.au/biography/mceacharn-sir-malcolm-donald-7350/text12765, published first in hardcopy 1986, accessed online 31 May 2022.

51   'Disputed Elections', *The Herald*, 11 March 1904, p. 6; 'The Melbourne Election', *The Herald*, 27 April 1904, p. 1.

CHAPTER 22: A MADAME'S ENTERTAINMENT PRECINCT

1   Report of Senior Constable Canty, 27 January 1898, 'Pursuit of Lonsdale & Exhibition St brothels', PROV, VPRS 807/Po, unit 305.

2   Pearl, *Wild Men of Sydney*, p. 202, paraphrasing from 'Memories of Brussels', *Truth* (Melbourne), 31 March 1906, p. 6.

3   'Household Furniture and Effects', *The Argus*, 22 August 1908, p. 2.

4   Pearl, *Wild Men of Sydney*, p. 202 and 'Memories of Brussels', *Truth* (Melbourne), 31 March 1906, p. 6.

5   'A Broken-Up brothel', *Truth* (Sydney), 5 October 1902, p. 6.

6   Maggie O'Connor's evidence in 'Brothels in Lonsdale Street prosecution of "Madame Brussells"', 10 May 1889, PROV, VPRS 937, Po, unit 327.

7   'A Doctor in the Divorce Court', *Geelong Advertiser*, 19 December 1900, p. 1.

8   Caroline Hodgson, Births, Deaths and Marriages Victoria, registration No. 10481/1908; 'Disbursements: Dr Stirling £46 4s', PROV, VPRS 28/Po, 108/351, Caroline Pohl.

CHAPTER 23: AN ERRANT HUSBAND AND THE RISE OF *TRUTH*

1   *The Argus*, 7 February 1899, p. 1.

2   'Bag Snatching in Collins Street', *The Age*, 3 March 1899, p. 9.

3   'Charge of Bag Snatching', *The Age*, 17 March 1899, p. 3.

4   This and following information from Caroline Pohl divorce PROV, VPRS 283/Po, 1906 no 127.

5   'Presentation Convent', *Advocate*, 25 December 1897, p. 7.

6   Flyleaf of Irene's German textbook, personal communication, Rosalie Savage, 4 March 2019; 'Melbourne Deutsche Turn Verein', *The Argus*, 12 October 1889, p. 16.

7   *The Argus*, 7 February 1900, p. 1.

8   *The Argus*, 7 February 1901, p. 1.

9   *The Australasian*, 18 April 1903, p. 44.

10 Personal communication, Denis James, 23 May 2018; Madame Melba travelled from Melbourne to Sydney on 2 April 1903 and returned on 8 April, *Geelong Advertiser*, 8 April 1903, p. 1, and *The Herald*, 8 April 1903, p. 4.

11 Pearl, *Wild Men of Sydney*, p. 21.

12 Michael Cannon, *That Damned Democrat: John Norton, an Australian Populist, 1858–1916*, Melbourne: Melbourne University Press, 1981, p. 10.

13 Pearl, *Wild Men of Sydney*, p. 201; 'Chows v Courtesans', *Truth* (Brisbane),

9 February 1902, p. 5 and *Truth* (Sydney), 9 February 1902, p. 5.

14 The following quotes are taken from 'Brussells [*sic*] in Melbourne', *Truth* (Melbourne), 31 October 1903, p. 5.

15 'The Suppression of Disorderly Houses', *The Herald*, 8 May 1889, p. 3.

16 PROV, VPRS 5708/P0 Melbourne City Council Rate Books (Gipps Ward) show Caroline Hodgson as 'occupant' from 1903 to 1907; *Sands & McDougall's Melbourne and Suburban Directory for [1903 to 1907]*, Melbourne, Sands and McDougall Limited, show 'Madam Brussels' as the tenant for the same period.

17 The words are probably Norton's rather than the policeman's, 'Madame Brussels' Notorious Bawdy House', *Truth* (Melbourne), 10 March 1906, p. 5.

18 'Olive Douglas' Impersonated "Fanny Montgomery No 8 Lonsdale Street"', 'The Melbourne Election', *The Herald*, 27 April 1904, p. 1.

19 Ibid.

20 Ibid.

21 'Alleged Impersonation', *The Herald*, 20 June 1904, p. 1; 'Question of Means', *The Herald*, 6 May 1904, p. 1.

22 'Has No Means', *The Herald*, 11 May 1904, p. 6.

23 'Alleged Impersonation', *The Herald*, 20 June 1904, p. 4.

24 This and following quotes from *The Age*, 7 March 1906, p. 8.

CHAPTER 24: COTTAGES AND COACH HOUSES

1 'Chows v. Courtesans', *Truth* (Brisbane), 9 February 1902, p. 5 and *Truth* (Sydney), 9 February 1902, p. 5.

2 'Brussells [*sic*] in Melbourne', *Truth* (Melbourne), 31 October 1903, p. 5.

3 Ibid.

4 Pearl, *Wild Men of Sydney*, p. 201; 'Madame Brussels' Notorious Bawdy house', *Truth* (Melbourne), 10 March 1906, p. 5.

5 PROV, VA 2549 Supreme Court of Victoria, VPRS 19093/C1 Application Examiner's Notes, Application No. AP037699, 11 November 1908.

6 'Brussells [*sic*] in Melbourne', *Truth* (Melbourne), 31 October 1903, p. 5.

7 PROV, VPRS 9288/P1, No. 2462/1886.

8 'Lechery and Lucre', *Truth* (Melbourne), 1 December 1906, p. 4.

9 Ibid.

10 Pearl, *Wild Men of Sydney*, p. 202.

11   Descriptions drawn from the sale of her furnishings by Arthur Tuckett and Co. on 28 August 1908: *The Argus*, 22 August 1908, p. 2.

12   *The Herald*, 28 February 1903, p. 4.

13   'Brothels in Lonsdale Street Prosecution of "Madame Brussells"', 10 May 1889, Report of Constable Stokes re 'Mary Lawrence & Nellie Golding arrested in a brothel in Lonsdale Street east kept by Madam Brussell', 17 March 1889, PROV VPRS 937/P0, unit 327.

14   'The Infamous Madame Brussels', *Truth* (Melbourne), 13 April 1907, p. 5.

15   Anne Cunningham, PROV, VPRS 28/P0002, 91/906 (https://prov.vic.gov.au/archive/BE2086DB-F1E8-11E9-AE98-8398A77567E9?image=7) – land 'about 48 feet frontage to Casselden Street by a depth of about 27 feet with WB house thereon', valued at £200, '7/- per week rent'.

16   Anne Cunningham died 25 July 1904, Births, Deaths and Marriages Victoria, registration No. 7787/1904; notice of application for probate was advertised *The Herald*, 9 August 1904, p. 2; sold to Caroline Pohl on 27 September 1905 for £150: PROV, VA 2549 Supreme Court of Victoria, VPRS 18870/C1 Application Search Notes, box 126 AP035625 (Victoria Certificate of Title Volume 3099 Folio 619720 issued 14 March 1906).

17   'Motorman Davidson's Doings, A Wild, Whirling Career', *Truth* (Melbourne), 24 March 1906, p. 5 and *Truth* (Perth), 7 April 1906, p. 2.

18   Pearl, *Wild Men of Sydney*, p. 201; sale of furniture and goods from 32–34 Lonsdale St, 'new linoleums recently purchased at Buckley and Nunn's', *The Argus*, 22 August 1908, p. 2.

19   'Hard Earnings Lost', *The Herald*, 21 April 1906, p. 3.

20   Victoria Certificate of Title, Volume 3099, Folio 619720, issued 14 March 1906 to Caroline Pohl.

21   'A Wild, Whirling Career', *Truth* (Perth), 7 April 1906, p. 2.

CHAPTER 25: ANOTHER TRIAL AND A DIVORCE

1   'Squatter's City Adventures', *The Age*, 9 March 1906, p. 6; 'Grazier's Adventures', *The Herald*, 9 March 1906, p. 6; 'Madame Brussels' Notorious Bawdy House', *Truth* (Melbourne), 10 March 1906, p. 5.

2   *Table Talk*, 8 March 1906, p. 4.

3   'Detaining a Watch', *The Age*, 20 March 1906, p. 7.

4   Quotes from 'A Disorderly House', *The Herald*, 29 March 1906, p. 1; 'A Disorderly House', *The Age*, 30 March 1906, p. 6.

5   Cannon, *That Damned Democrat*, p. 11.

6   Pearl, *Wild Men of Sydney*, p. 214; 'because he was a drunkard [he] denounced drunkards with pathological fury', pp. 221–22; '"Age of Consent!"', *Truth* (Sydney), 27 September 1896, p. 1; Pearl, *Wild Men of Sydney*, p. 111.

7   These and following quotes are from 'Madame Brussels' Notorious Bawdy House', *Truth* (Melbourne), 10 March 1906, p. 5.

8   'Brussells [*sic*] in Melbourne', *Truth* (Melbourne), 31 October 1903, p. 5.

9   See Appendix 3 Summary of Property Transactions, Caroline Pohl, 2 October 1906, PROV, VPRS 283/P0, 1906 no 127.

CHAPTER 26: A POLITICAL STORM AND THREE MORE TRIALS

1   This and following quotes from 'Lechery and Lucre: An Open Letter to the Honorable Sir Samuel Gillott, K.C.M.G., M.L.A., Chief Secretary and Minister for Labor, Alderman of the City Council and Ex-Lord Mayor of Melbourne', *Truth* (Melbourne), 1 December 1906, p. 4 and an edited version in Michael Cannon, *That Damned Democrat*, pp. 136–38; for more on Samuel Gillott, see (1) David Dunstan, 'Gillott, Sir Samuel (1838–1913)', *Australian Dictionary of Biography*, National Centre of Biography, Australian National University, adb.anu.edu.au/biography/gillott-sir-samuel-6390/text10921, first published in hardcopy 1983, accessed online 15 May 2022, and (2) Barbara Minchinton, 'The Rise and Fall of Lady Gillott in Melbourne's Turn-of-the-Century Society', *Victorian Historical Journal*, Vol. 91 No. 2, 2020, pp. 291–318.

2   Cannon, *That Damned Democrat*, p. 11.

3   Pearl, *Wild Men of Sydney*, p. 221.

4   Pearl, *Wild Men of Sydney*, p. 125; Cannon, *That Damned Democrat*, p. 3.

5   'Judkins on the Warpath', *The Register* (Adelaide), 3 December 1906, p. 5; *The Argus*, 3 December 1906, p. 7.

6   The story of the Gillotts' social rise and fall is told in Minchinton, 'The Rise and Fall of Lady Gillott', pp. 291–318.

7   This quote and following information drawn from Graeme Davison and Keith Dunstan, 'Judkins, William Henry (1869–1912)', *Australian Dictionary of Biography*, National Centre of Biography, Australian National University, adb.anu.edu.au/biography/judkins-william-henry-6889/text11943, published first in hardcopy 1983, accessed online 15 May 2022.

8   This and following quotes from 'Judkins the Jackal', *Truth* (Melbourne), 8 December 1906, p. 1; see also 'Judkins's Plagiarised Jaw', *Truth* (Melbourne), 8 December 1906, p. 3.

9   '"Madame Brussels" in the Divorce Court', *Truth* (Melbourne), 8 December 1906, p. 5.

10 'Divorce Court', *The Age*, 17 November 1906, p. 15; 'Divorce Court', *The Argus*, 20 November 1906, p. 1; 'A Benevolent Old Lady Obtains a Divorce: Madame Brussels', *The Daily News* (Perth), 5 December 1906, p. 3.

11 This quote and the following are from '"Madame Brussels" in the Divorce Court', *Truth* (Melbourne), 8 December 1906, p. 5.

12 'Gillott's Resignation', *Truth* (Melbourne), 8 December 1906, p. 4 and 'Sir Samuel Gillott's Resignation due to an Open Letter by John Norton', *Truth* (Perth), 22 December 1906, p. 1.

13 Information drawn from 'A Grazier's Little Spree', *The Age*, 9 April 1907, p. 8; 'Prodigal Expenditure', *The Argus*, 9 April 1907, p. 8; 'The Infamous Madame Brussels', *Truth* (Melbourne) 13 April 1907, p. 5.

14 'A Grazier's Little Spree', *The Age*, 9 April 1907, p. 8.

15 *The Australasian*, 27 April 1907, p. 39; Pallenberg returned to Melbourne and lived at the Yarra Family Hotel and then at the house of the hotel's owner until his death in 1914 at the age of fifty. Heinrich Pallenberg, Births, Deaths and Marriages Victoria, registration No. 7112/1914.

16 Notes about this case drawn from 'Social Problem', *The Argus*, 10 April 1907, p. 4.

17 In 1898 the bench consisted of the Mayor (Cr. M'Eacharn), Mr Panton. P.M., and Messrs R. Cherry. R. Power, H. Edwards, S. Lancashire, W. Bell, T. Bent, and Capt. Russell, J's P., 'Those Gay Houses', *The Herald*, 11 November 1898, p. 2; in 1907 Sarah Russell's case was heard by Messrs Panton, P.M., R. Power, S. Lancashire, W. Bell, and C. Pleasance, J.P.'s, 'Social Problem', *The Argus*, 10 April 1907, p. 4.

18 This and following quotes from 'Social Problem', *The Argus*, 10 April 1907, p. 4.

19 *The Argus*, 17 April 1907, p. 5.

20 'Lonsdale-Street Nuisance', *The Argus*, 19 April 1907, p. 3.

21 This and following quote from 'The Passing of Brussels', *Truth* (Melbourne), 20 April 1907, p. 3.

22 The quote comes from 'Lechery and Lucre', *Truth* (Melbourne), 1 December 1906, p. 4.

23 *The Bendigo Advertiser*, 7 May 1907, p. 8.

24 'Disorderly Houses in the City', *The Age*, 17 May 1907, p. 6.

CHAPTER 27: CORRUPTION AGAIN

1 *Table Talk*, 8 March 1906, p. 4.

2 'Judkins the Jackal', *Truth* (Melbourne), 8 December 1906, p. 1.

3   For a thorough historian's assessment of the theft of the mace, see Wright, 'Who Stole the Mace?'.

4   'Social Problem', *The Argus*, 10 April 1907, p. 4.

5   'Disorderly Houses in the City', *The Age*, 17 May 1907, p. 6.

6   Ibid.

7   'Mr Panton's Retirement', *The Australasian*, 6 July 1907, p. 42; Caroline Hodgson, Births, Deaths and Marriages Victoria, registration No. 10481/1908.

8   'A Squatter's Troubles', *The Age*, 7 March 1906, p. 8.

9   Victorian Parliament, 'Royal Commission on the Victorian Police Force: Report on I. The efficiency of the police force in connexion with the repression of crime; II. The present condition, organization, and administration of the said force; with Appendix and minutes of Evidence', Parliamentary Paper, no. 10, 1906.

10   'Brussells [*sic*] in Melbourne', *Truth* (Melbourne), 31 October 1903, p. 5.

CHAPTER 28: WORKERS AND CLIENTS

1   'class of women': John Norton, 'Brussells [*sic*] in Melbourne', *Truth* (Melbourne), 31 October 1903, p. 5; the young women who gave evidence in 1889 named two registry offices, 'Mrs Brooks' and 'Mr Copeland', and one said she went there 'to see her cousin': 'Brothels in Lonsdale Street Prosecution of "Madame Brussells" [*sic*] 10 May 1889', PROV, VPRS 937/0, unit 327.

2   For example, 'Lottie Temple' mentioned by Ellen Golding, 'Immoral Houses in Melbourne', *The Age*, 9 May 1889, p. 5, and 'Miss George' named by Maggie O'Connor, 'Brothels in Lonsdale Street Prosecution of "Madame Brussells" [*sic*] 10 May 1889', PROV VPRS 937/P0, unit 327.

3   Ellen Golding, 'Immoral Houses in Melbourne', *The Age*, 9 May 1889, p. 5.

4   'The Case of Madame Brussels', *Weekly Times*, 11 May 1889, p. 12.

5   Mary Lawrence and Nellie Golding undated statements, 'Brothels in Lonsdale Street Prosecution of "Madame Brussells" [*sic*] 10 May 1889', PROV, VPRS 937/P0, unit 327.

6   Lizzie Emmanual undated statement, 'Brothels in Lonsdale Street Prosecution of 'Madame Brussells [*sic*]' 10 May 1889', PROV VPRS 937/P0, unit 327.

7   Ibid.

8   'The Melbourne Election', *The Herald*, 27 April 1904, p. 1.

9   This and following quote from 'Lechery and Lucre', *Truth* (Melbourne), 1 December 1906, p. 4.

10   Mary Lawrence undated statement, 'Brothels in Lonsdale Street Prosecution of "Madame Brussels" [*sic*] 10 May 1889', PROV VPRS 937/P0, unit 327.

11   Mechant, 'Selling Sex in a Provincial Town', p. 81.

12   'Madame Brussels' Notorious Bawdy House', *Truth* (Melbourne), 10 March 1906, p. 5.

13   Lizzie Emmanuel, 'Brothels in Lonsdale Street Prosecution of "Madame Brussells" [*sic*] 10 May 1889', PROV VPRS 937/P0, unit 327.

14   Davidson: 'A Wild, Whirling Career', *Truth* (Perth), 7 April 1906, p. 2; Pallenberg: 'The Infamous Madame Brussels', *Truth* (Melbourne), 13 April 1907, p. 5; 'Sandridge', *The Argus*, 16 August 1870, p. 6.

15   'Pianiste Wanted at Charlotte Kane's Brothel', Report Senior Constable L. Gleeson 6 August 1888, PROV, VPRS 937/P0, unit 325.

16   Mary Lawrence statement, 'Brothels in Lonsdale Street Prosecution of "Madame Brussells" [*sic*] 10 May 1889', PROV, VPRS 937/P0, unit 327.

17   *Newcastle Morning Herald and Miners' Advocate*, 13 May 1889, p. 7.

18   'The Melbourne Election', *The Herald*, 27 April 1904, p. 1.

19   Tim Evans, 'Compulsory Voting in Australia', Australian Electoral Commission, 2006, aec.gov.au/About_AEC/Publications/voting/files/compulsory-voting.pdf, accessed 9 May 2022.

20   The Commonwealth of Australia, Electoral Roll, State of Victoria, Division of Melbourne, Gipps Polling Place 1903.

21   The Commonwealth of Australia, Electoral Roll, State of Victoria, Division of Melbourne, Gipps Polling Place 1905.

22   Olive Douglas described herself as a woman 'of Lonsdale Street', 'Question of Means', *The Herald*, 6 May 1904, p. 1.

23   'The Melbourne Election', *The Herald*, 27 April 1904, p. 1; evidence given by Maggie O'Connor that she and Lizzie Emanuel 'left Madame's [and] went to Fitzroy to live with two "gentlemen"', 'The Suppression of Disorderly Houses', *The Herald*, 8 May 1889, p. 3.

24   Cannon, *The Land Boomers*, pp. 55–60.

25   'Sir Malcolm M'Eacharn', *The Australasian*, 21 November 1903, p. 38; unfortunately for Sir Malcolm, when his opponent (Dr William Maloney of the Labor Party, a staunch supporter of women's suffrage) protested about the numerous irregularities in the forms filled in by voters in favour of McEacharn, a byelection was called to resolve the matter and Maloney won convincingly. David Dunstan, 'McEacharn, Sir Malcolm Donald (1852–1910)', *Australian Dictionary of Biography*, National Centre of Biography, Australian

National University, adb.anu.edu.au/biography/mceacharn-sir-malcolm-donald-7350/text12765, published first in hardcopy 1986, accessed online 11 May 2022; Geoffrey Serle, 'Maloney, William Robert (Nuttall) (1854–1940)', *Australian Dictionary of Biography*, National Centre of Biography, Australian National University, adb.anu.edu.au/biography/maloney-william-robert-nuttall-7470/text13015, published first in hardcopy 1986, accessed online 11 May 2022.

26   Pearl, *Wild Men of Sydney*, p. 201.

27   This and following two quotes from 'Memories of Brussels', *Truth* (Melbourne), 31 March 1906, p. 6.

28   'Judkins the Jackal', *Truth* (Melbourne), 8 December 1906, p. 1.

29   These and the following details from Mary J. Kemp's probate papers, PROV, VPRS 28/P0000, 59/685.

30   F.K. Terry, Australian Club 102 William St., *Sands & McDougall's Melbourne and Suburban Directory for 1895*, Melbourne, Sands and McDougall, 1895, p. 1101.

31   John Rickard, 'Walch, Garnet (1843–1913)', *Australian Dictionary of Biography*, National Centre of Biography, Australian National University, adb.anu.edu.au/biography/walch-garnet-1095/text7963, published first in hardcopy 1976, accessed online 3 June 2022.

32   Mary Jane Kemp death, *The Argus*, 21 December 1895, p. 14; Francis King Terry death, *The Age*, 31 August 1905, p. 1; Garnet Walch death, *The Australasian*, 11 January 1913, p. 4.

CHAPTER 29: DEATH OF A WOMAN

1   'Brussells [*sic*] in Melbourne', *Truth* (Melbourne), 31 October 1903, p. 5.

2   '"Madame Brussels" in the Divorce Court', *Truth* (Melbourne), 8 December 1906, p. 5.

3   For example, 'a stylishly dressed woman' *The Age*, 9 August 1887, p. 6; 'Well-Dressed', *The Herald* (Melbourne), 14 May 1889, p. 4; 'in a fashionable costume', 'The Passing of Brussels', *Truth* (Melbourne), 20 April 1907, p. 3.

4   'The Infamous Madame Brussels', *Truth* (Melbourne), 13 April 1907, p. 5.

5   'Madame Brussels' Notorious Bawdy House', *Truth* (Melbourne), 10 March 1906, p. 5; 'The Passing of Brussels', *Truth* (Melbourne), 20 April 1907, p. 3.

6   Evidence from Mary Lawrence, 'Immoral Houses in Melbourne', *The Age*, 9 May 1889, p. 5.

7   These and following details from Caroline Pohl probate papers, PROV, VPRS 28/P0, 108/351, and PROV, VPRS 28/P2, 108/351.

8   Saunders Benjamin provided a loan of £272 10s on the jewellery at £4 15s per month interest; it was redeemed on 25 September 1908 with a payment of £57 10s interest, suggesting that it was pledged in about July 1907. He then charged the estate £1 1s to value her jewellery, which he put at £374 13s 6d.

9   Dr Stirling's fee amounted to £46 4s; 'A Doctor in the Divorce Court', *Geelong Advertiser*, 19 December 1900, p. 1.

10   *The Argus*, 8 February 1910, p. 9.

11   *The Argus*, 22 August 1908, p. 2.

12   This and following details from Caroline Pohl, Will, PROV, VPRS 7591/P2, 108/351.

13   *The Age,* 22 August 1908, p. 2.

14   Lily Grelcke [Irene Maria Yvonne Hodgson] married Arthur Herbert Bolger, 20 April 1909, Births, Deaths and Marriages Victoria, registration No. 1108/1909; Raymond Lawrence Bolger, born 3 November 1909, Births, Deaths and Marriages Victoria, registration No. 26968/1909.

15   Senior Constable Canty Report 20 February 1896, National Archives of Australia Item 1801522 Series A712 1896/C889 Caroline Pohl.

16   'The Melbourne Baby Show', *The South Australian Chronicle* (Adelaide), 19 October 1889, p. 16.

17   Personal communication, Rosalie Savage, 26 March 2021.

18   'Madame "Brussels" Dead', *Truth* (Melbourne), 18 July 1908, p. 5.

19   Personal communication, Rosalie Savage, 26 March 2021.

20   'A Squatter's Troubles', *The Age*, 7 March 1906, p. 8.

21   Stud Hodgson was also a smoker: *Ballarat Star*, 17 November 1887, p. 2.

22   Personal communication, Rosalie Savage, 26 January 2023.

23   'Lost, Meerschaum Cigarette Holder', *The Argus,* 16 October 1885, p. 1.

24   *The Argus*, 18 May 1886, p. 1.

CHAPTER 30: END OF AN ERA

1   See, for example, Caroline Pohl, PROV, VPRS 28/P0, 108/351; Sarah Fraser, PROV, VPRS 28/0, 21/453; Mary J. Kemp, PROV, VPRS 28/P0, 59/685 and 28/P2, 59/685.

2   'Mrs Sarah Reynolds – Complaints Against the Police', Report C.H. Nicolson, 14 January 1873, PROV, VPRS 937/P0, unit 296.

3   *Police Offences Act* 1907, 7 EDWARD VII No. 2093.

4   'Scarlet Sirens of Suburbia: Review of the Past and the Present', *Truth* (Melbourne), 26 October 1912, p. 5.

5   See, for example, Samuel Gillott's story, Minchinton, 'The Rise and Fall of Lady Gillott', pp. 291–318.

6   Caroline Pohl, PROV, VPRS 7591/P2, 108/351.

7   *The Age*, 13 July 1909, p. 1.

8   Personal communication, Rosalie Savage, 4 March 2019.

9   For example, Dick Meudell, *The Pleasant Career of a Spendthrift*; Montague Grover, 'Big Lon and Little Lon', *The Bulletin*, 7 June 1933, Vol. 54, No. 2782, p. 36; Pearl, *Wild Men of Sydney*; Keith Dunstan, *Wowsers*, Cassell, Sydney, 1968; Dunstan also periodically mentioned her in articles for *The Bulletin*, for example vol. 93, No. 4754 (8 May 1971) p. 9, vol. 104, No. 5412 (17 April 1984) p. 47, and vol. 106, No. 5432 (4 September 1984) p. 120.

10   Correspondence with Carly Peters, Records & Archives Officer, Southern Metropolitan Cemeteries Trust, between 22 March 2022 and 16 January 2023.

11   Mechant, 'The Social Profile of Prostitutes' and Conner, 'The Paradoxes and Contradictions of Prostitution in Paris', pp. 841–57.

12   Caroline Pohl, Will PROV, VPRS 7591/P2, 108/351.

13   Rebecca Yamin, 'Wealthy, Free and Female: Prostitution in Nineteenth-Century New York', *Historical Archaeology*, Vol. 39, No. 1, 2005, pp. 4–18; for the Australian context and references, see Ramona Lola Angelico, '"A Disorderly Brothel at the Rear of Wesley Church": Identifying Sex Work in the Archaeological Record of Jones Lane', MA thesis, La Trobe University, 2021, p. 73.

14   'Statement of Assets', VPRS 28/P0002, 108/351, https://prov.vic.gov.au/archive/D451F4BE-F1EB-11E9-AE98-F354BA74AE94?image=11.

15   'Lost', *The Argus*, 18 May 1886, p. 1.

APPENDIX: 1

1   Unreadable on title, but 'Lechery and Lucre' in *Truth* (Melbourne), 1 December 1906, p. 4, says 1881.

INDEX

Page numbers in **bold** refer to images.